ABHANDLUNGEN DES GEOGRAPHISCHEN INSTITUTS
ANTHROPOGEOGRAPHIE

BAND 35

HERAUSGEBER:

F. BADER, G. BRAUN, U. FREITAG, G. KLUCZKA,
A. KÜHN, K. LENZ, G. MIELITZ, F. SCHOLZ

SCHRIFTLEITUNG:

H. LEONHARDY

VERANTWORTLICH FÜR DIESEN BAND:
F. BADER

ABHANDLUNGEN DES GEOGRAPHISCHEN INSTITUTS
ANTHROPOGEOGRAPHIE

BAND 35

HASSAN A. EL MANGOURI

The Mechanization of Agriculture as a Factor Influencing Population Mobility in the Developing Countries: Experiences in The Democratic Republic of the Sudan

(Auswirkungen der Mechanisierung der Landwirtschaft
auf die Bevölkerungsmobilität in Entwicklungsländern:
Fallbeispiel - die Republik Sudan)

BERLIN 1983

DIETRICH REIMER VERLAG BERLIN

V

CIP-Kurztitelaufnahme der Deutschen Bibliothek

Mangouri, Hassan A. el:

The mechanization of agriculture as a factor
influencing population mobility in the developing
countries: experiences in the Democratic
Republic of the Sudan = (Auswirkungen der Mechanisierung der Landwirtschaft auf die Bevölkerungsmobilität in Entwicklungsländern: Fallbeispiel -
die Republik Sudan) / Hassan A. El Mangouri.
- Berlin : Reimer, 1983.
  (Abhandlungen des Geographischen Instituts
  Anthropogeographie ; Bd. 35)
  ISBN 3-496-00312-X

NE: Institut für Anthropogeographie, Angewandte
Geographie und Kartographie ⟨Berlin, West⟩ :
Abhandlungen des Geographischen ...

ISSN 0721-9687

        Gedruckt mit Unterstützung
        des Präsidenten der Freien Universität Berlin
        und des Deutschen Akademischen Austauschdienstes DAAD

D 188

CONTENTS

page

page

PREFACE

Apart from the traditional contribution of geographers
to the study of population, this particular thesis
attempts to divert the emphasis of geographical enquiry
towards the examination of how particular innovations
affect the population distribution and the organization
of human society. It deals specifically with questions
concerning the demographic, social and economic impact
of population mobility on both sending an receiving
areas. It attempts to shed light on the different variables that work to produce a selective type of population
mobility within a particular socio-economic set-up. Although various aspects of population mobility have been
studied in some detail during the present decade, no
attempt has been made, however, towards a concrete pre-
sentation of its multiple causes and its socio-economic
impact on the areas and people that are left behind. Far
from assuming complete coverage of all interrelated fields
of study we attempt here to draw attention to the expected socio-economic repercussions of population mobility
as induced by a particular factor, namely agricultural
mechanization. Certain limitations, however, have made
it difficult to deal with every aspect of population
mobility in the Sudan.

The first chapter provides a general discussion of the
foundations of mobility study, to be utilized as a theoretical background along the course of study. The second
chapter deals with the historical explanation for population mobility in the African countries. This is meant
to reflect the most important causes which induced the
African people to join the process of migration in the

colonial and post-colonial times.

The third chapter attempts to shed light on the effect
of rural development measures, including the adoption
and expansion of agricultural mechanization, on the
population mobility in the developing countries, with
particular emphasis on the African countries.

The fourth chapter presents a general background to the
adoption and expansion of the mechanized agriculture
- both irrigated and rainfed - in the Sudan. This particular chapter is meant to reflect the scope and magnitude of the mechanized agriculture, to be related later
on to the phenomenon of population mobility in the
country.

Chapters five, six and seven contain three cases of study.
The first one deals with the circulation of the skilled
workers (tractor drivers) between the different agricultural schemes within the rural areas (rural-rural
population movement); the second case of study deals with
the movement of the skilled workers into the urban centres, particularly Greater Khartoum (rural-urban); the
third case study deals with the impact of the technical
locations of agricultural mechanization (workshops) on
the rural population. By all these cases of study it is
 intended to provide some illustrations of the substantive
contribution that a social geographer can make to the
understanding of how the organization of human society
in a particular region is governed by the development
in the different economic sectors. By relating the mobility process of a particular population segment, the
skilled labour, to the factor of mechanization, it is
 intended to support the view that population mobility, at

least in the developing countries, is an automatic
consequence of spatial economic disparities, and not
merely a behavioural process.

Chapter eight touches more briefly the different types of
unskilled labour movements as caused by agricultural mecha-
nization.With this chapter it is intended to reveal the overall impact of this particular tool of development on
the spatial distribution of different groups of people.

In the last chapter it is intended to present the main findings of the study as a basis for some concluding remarks.
It is hoped that the proposals raised at the end of this
thesis will stimulate further researches in the field
of social geography.

Finally, the author would like to register his thanks
to the large number of friends and colleagues who assisted
in one way or another at the various stages of preparing
this thesis. He is particularly indebted to his super-
visor, Prof. Dr. F. Bader, and co-superviser, Prof. Dr.
G. Heinritz, for their good-natured support and encourage-
ment through all the years of his studies in Germany.
Thanks are also due to the DAAD (Deutsche Akademischer
Austauschdienst) and the Hamboldt-Ritter-Stiftung for
their generous financial assistance. Thanks must also
go to colleagues in the Department of Geography of the
University of Khartoum and to the students who kindly
assisted in conducting the field surveys needed for
this study.

INTRODUCTION

The study deals with socio-geographic problems within the
framework of the mechanization of agriculture and, specially, possible effects of mechanization on population mobility. In previous investigations into mechanization in
agriculture these socio-geographical questions were dealt
with more incidentally and if at all at a macro-level,
i.e. related to a country as a whole or to several countries. An important reason why, for example, decision processes in labour behaviour of agricultural employees have
not been examined in more detail is that, generally, in
just those areas in which mechanization has a long tradition or a continual development, the social aspects represent well-developed adjustment to the respective framework
conditions and are therefore considered to be a matter of
course rather than suitable material for research.

Such a reason does not apply to newly created agricultural
areas where, in some cases, as a result of extensive political and economic actions entire population groups were
mobilized, especially when they had no previous experience
with mechanized agriculture.

Through the discussion of suitable measures to promote
rural development in developing countries the question of
the use of technical means has become topical again in
the last few years with special emphasis on the social
and economic aspects of the mechanization problem. Special
attention was also given to the effects of mechanization
on the population situation.

The study is limited to two main problems which are closely interrelated and particularly important in newly

created and mechanized areas: firstly, the creation of new
jobs within the agricultural sector through mechanization,
and the extent to which mechanization attracts the various
population groups and the possible socio-economic effects
of such population movements; secondly, the qualifying effect of mechanization which stimulates both rural-rural and
rural-urban movements of skilled manpower, with the possible effect of increasing the pressure in the towns and
creating a deficit in areas with relatively lower socio-
economic incentives. However, there is no exact imaginat-
ion on the extent of this particular type of mobility at
the present time. Thus the purpose of this study is to
disclose the relationship between the expansion of the modern agricultural sub-sector centered around mechanization
and the circulation of some groups of the population in the
Sudan.

Of course many factors bear upon the manpower and employment situation, but mechanization of agriculture is known
to have both direct and indirect effects on the manpower
needs and employment opportunities. By definition mechanization is a replacement of human labour by machines. Hence
the introduction of new agricultural techniques in connection with new crops and livestock varieties as well as new
cultural practices such as intensification, diversification,
specialization and increasing dependency on a market-oriented production system is considered to be a factor affecting agricultural employment and consequently inducing population circulation. But the effect of agricultural mechanization on population mobility, however, could not be
treated in isolation from external factors such as rapid
urbanization, industrial development and infrastructure.
They are also considered to be a cause and effect of the
present intra- and interregional population mobility.

The republic of the Sudan with its extensive agricultural projects provides an extremely valuable situation and a somewhat rare opportunity to study the effects of mechanization on population mobility at this stage.

The traditional interest in unskilled wage-labour movements presents a somewhat restricted view of the total mobility process; thus it must be supplemented by analysis of some other short-term circulatory movements of skilled labour. It is worth mentioning here that these types of population movements remain undifferentiated even in the two census of 1956 and 1973, though it has become, particularly in recent times, a feature of the Sudanese population mobility. Thus the study that attempts to reflect its magnitude, analyze and explain its demographic and socio-economic repercussions becomes more vital than ever before.

This type of study is only possible at the so-called micro-level, i.e. at the level of the individual and small groups, since the available data offer no or only limited information about the individuals, their characteristics and behaviour. Hence this study aims to complement the aggregate studies which focus essentially on the structural characteristics of movement, i.e. the volume, distance, direction and timing. It aims to bring together the closely related elements of mechanization through agricultural development and population mobility by considering the implications of mechanization for the manpower as reflected in the pattern of movement generated. Focus is therefore placed upon a single category of migrants - the skilled labour minority within the circulating sector of the population. The fact that this minority is not randomly selected from the rest of the people and that it is characterized by a relatively higher education level and qualification imply that this group should have a pronounced effect on both areas of origin and areas of destination. To present this effect is one of the aims of this study.

The relationship between agricultural mechanization and the mobility of skilled labour could be explained in terms of the qualifying role of mechanization. Acquiring qualification through mechanization acts as a major catalyst to the rise aspirations by offering a contact possibility with the surrounding world. Hence mechanization as a training institution resembles education as the route to socio-economic status. Although the movement associated with higher qualification represents only a small segment within the context of the Sudanese population movements, yet it is regarded as the most important one in terms of the socio-economic and political weight it possesses. The role played by this group becomes increasingly important as agricultural mechanization is continuing to dominate the Sudanese modern agricultural sub-sector, and as this sector continues to expand at the expense of the other economic sub-sectors, particularly the traditional sub-sector. Thus this study attempts to identify and explain the movement patterns resulting from adopting the present development strategies which emphasise the expansion of agricultural mechanization.

The study follows an inductive approach which begins the sequence of analysis by formulating logical and internally consistent hypotheses which are to be tested empirically against data drawn from actual observations. We sum up our main hypotheses in the following points:

- Measures to develop rural areas do not stabilize the population situation there but, on the contrary, cause a mobilization of the rural population, thus intensifying in-migration pressure in the towns and increasing the tendency to polarization. In this way

regional and sectoral disparities increase sooner
than it was thought from the beginning.

- The more a place is affected by mechanization, i.e.
  the nearer it is situated to the functional location
  of mechanization (workshop) or the longer such locations already exist, the greater is the probability
  of increased out-migration. This migration is selective in that above all, young active males migrate.
  This form of migration influences not only population
  structure but also socio-economic conditions in both
  the place of origin and destination.

- The better the qualifications of a person trained as
  a result of the mechanization of agriculture, the
  better are his chances of finding a job quickly when
  he moves away. The low risk of unemployment at the
  place he moves to increases the readiness to out-
  migrate.

- Qualified workers have little or no job opportunities
  at their place of origin. To make use of the qualifications gained through the mechanization of agriculture they are compelled to migrate.

- At their destinations they act as contacts for relatives and friends still living at the home village,
  whom this exchange of information motivates to migrate.

- The mechanization of agriculture also causes a deterioration of the living conditions of some families
  (few opportunities of employment, less leasehold land,
  inflationary phenomena). In such families the sons
  can expect nothing more from their fathers. They have
  to look after themselves, the authority of the father
  declines. Such disintegrating families are more ready
  to migrate.

I.   FOUNDATIONS OF MOBILITY STUDY

1.   GENERAL NOTE

Population mobility is a subject of concern to many academic disciplines, which has recently become a rapidly developing branch. It is now studied by several groups including historians, economists, psychologists, sociologists, demographers and geographers, each one of which approaches the subject from a different point of view relative to its respective subject.

Of all types of population mobility, however, the residential movement of the human population is universally recognized as the most important and essential movement, which is both a multi-disciplinary and also, in its widest sense, an inter-disciplinary field of study. Awareness of the importance of population movement in creating and sustaining a wide range of patterns of human activity is continually increasing. To examine the various changes that accrue to human activity, a limited range of related studies is to be conducted by the different academic disciplines. Most important of these is the study of the motives of population movement, the identification of those who move, the evaluation of the structural context of places of origin and points of destination as well as the flows between them, and finally tracing out the impact of such mobility on both sending and receiving areas.

To carry out such studies, each different discipline is required to concentrate on particular fields of enquiry to the exclusion of others. For an economist, for example, the movement of labour is more important than the other types of population mobility, since he considers labour as an important form of resource redistribution. Hence he has to discover the motives behind any labour movement and to try to show the impacts of such movement on both areas of origin and areas of destination. The major concern of a sociologist is the inter-relationships between the migrant and his own or other social groups. He is therefore inclined to study the effects of migration on the areas, communities or societies of both sending and receiving areas. The role of the migrant in the general evolution of population is the main concern of a demographer. To the traditional geographer the spatial flows, the interaction between different places and the areal differentiation between sending and receiving areas is the most important field of enquiry with regard to population mobility. Recently the field of concern of a geographer has broadened, since it has been recognized that the residential movements of the human population have spatial manifestations and that redistribution of population through horizontal mobility can have a profound impact on the whole spatial patterning of human activities, the repercussions of which may be felt long after the movement activity has stabilized. Maps of world population distribution, worked out by geographers, are nothing but a reflection of population mobility that occurred in the past with relation to patterns of natural population growth both past and present. Population mobility in the past century was, to a large extent, responsible for the present picture of population distribution in the New World. Moreover, the present suburban expansion and rural depopulation particularly in the Third World is a result of past and present population movements. But population movements are considered not only because of their impact on distributing human beings spatially but also because of their impact on redistributing and restructuring certain social and cultural attributes such as educational achievement, intelligence, occupation, age, sex, family status, social and cultural attitudes, language and religious affiliation.

Such attributes are of crucial importance in bringing
about structural changes both in areas of origin and areas
of destination. The scale of these structural changes depends to a considerable extent on the volume of population
mobility. Accordingly, the geographer dealing with population mobility has to find out who participates in that
mobility and what attributes he possesses if he is to evaluate the effect of any population mobility.It should be
remembered, however, that mobility may lead to change in
an individual's attributes, though this may not always be
the case: it has been shown by GALTUNG (1971, p. 194) in
his study of Western Sicily that immigrants undergo atti-
tudinal changes prior to emigration and are socially lost
to their Communities of origin before actual movement
occurs.

Of significant importance to a geographer, apart from individual attributes, are the factors which induce people to
move. He has to investigate the reasons behind the movement of certain groups of population and what aspirations
they have.

2.   DEFINITIONS OF POPULATION MOBILITY

The term "mobility", in the sense that will be used in this
study, is generally defined as the circulation of workers
between two or more places. In this study the term mobility
will be used in connection with population movement which
involves a change in the place of residence at a scale
varying from a transfer between dwellings within the same
district to intercontinental movement. Residential movement, a type of population mobility which involves migration, must centre on the migrant's place of origin as a

permanent point of reference. HAEGERSTRAND (1957, pp. 27-8), in his major study on Swedish migration fields, defines this type of migration as the change in the centre of gravity of an individual's mobility pattern. This change in the centre of gravity does not necessarily involve a change in the destinations of the mobility flows. He illustrated his arguments by the following examples:

An individual who undertakes a local intra-regional move does not necessarily need to change the termini of the journey to work, recreational and shopping movements (Fig. I.1.A), while in an inter-regional move they are required to change (Fig. I.1.B and C).

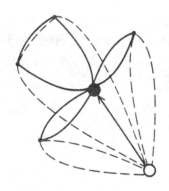

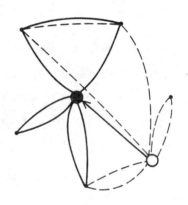

Fig. I.1.A (retaining the same termini)

Fig. I.1.B
(partial change of previous termini)

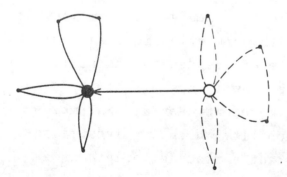

a = previous residence
a^1 = recent residence
b,c,e,... = previous termini
b^1, c^1, e^1 = new termini

Fig. I.1.C (total change of previous termini)   SOURCE : W. KULS (1980, P. 169)

C.C. ROSEMAN (1971) calls these two types of migration 'partial displacement' and 'total displacement', respectively.

While these definitional suggestions are very useful, there are some problematic cases to which such concepts do not apply, i.e. in the case of some nomads who have no fixed residential base and who are hence without a definite centre of gravity. Similarly, it is difficult to apply this concept to cases in which an individual has more than one residence.

This concept, however, is highly relevant to our case study. We use the term migration as a sub-set of mobility to mean any residential movement between administration units over a given period of time. More concretely, we confine ourselves to the movement of certain groups of people for the sake of work or betterment of their living standard. For practical reasons, we exclude other forms of population circulation which are to be touched briefly along the course of this study in their respective context.

3. DATA SOURCES OF POPULATION MOBILITY

The first of the sources for population mobility is population census, which is a source of the most important quantitative data on population movement, using the administrative units as a base for birth place migration data. This type of population mobility data is given in the form of tables showing the present residence of individuals as against their places of birth. This data, however, brings information neither about the intensity of mobility of an individual nor about the time spent at the different stages of mobility flows. For this reason it is not advisable to depend on birth place data sources derived from the population census only.

The second source of data is so-called "Continuous-data",
whereby all residential moves are recorded. This type of
data collection is being practised in some European countries like West Germany, Switzerland and the Netherlands. In
this case only the change of residence from one "Gemeinde"
to the other is registered without referring to the sets of
flows between the different "Gemeinden". By calculating the
period between the date of arrival and the date of departure
it is possible to determine the time spent in a "Gemeinde"
by an individual. As in the case of population census, the
continuous data is presented in the form of tables and only
in rare cases, like that of Switzerland, summary tables of
population movement to and from each "Gemeinde" or "Parish"
are published. In the developing countries, including our
case study, such sources of migration data are lacking.

The third source, which is more commonly available than the
Continuous-data, is the survey data. It is regarded as the
most important source of data which provides detailed information about the characteristics of each individual migrant.
Behaviour and attitudes of an individual were able to be
assessed by using questionnaire-based surveys. This source
of data collection is used not only as source complementary
to the data acquired from the other two sources but also as
the only source in cases where all other information about
population flows is completely lacking. It is by far the
most imporatnt source of data in studies of most developing
countries. The bulk of data for this study has been acquired
by this means although reference is sometimes made to population census as a complementary source. Generally speaking,
quantitative data were obtainable from population census
and continuous registration, wherever they were readily available for consultation (LAWTON 1978). On the other hand,
qualitative data was obtainable through an extended questionnaire - based survey. The quality and coverage of national

population censuses varies considerably but most of them
deal with the collection of information on how many people
migrate, whence and to where over a specified period of
time and within a defined framework of administrative areas.
Information of certain characteristics of individuals is
now commonplace only in the census of the statistically advanced countries. Hence, complete disaggregation of individuals according to their demographic, social and economic
attributes are rare, or only available at unsuitable spatial
scales. Such a detailed picture of the migrant participants
is often obtained by resorting to survey methods.

For the purpose of evaluating the impact of population movement on a particular region, the gross flows between the
regions is a vital consideration. In some places,where such
gross flows are difficult to obtain, an attempt to calculate the net flows may be advisable. If data on the popula-
lation totals at two different time periods (p^t and p^{t+n})
are available, and if the numbers of birth ($B^{t,t+n}$) and
death ($D^t + D^{t+n}$) between t and t+n are also known, the net
migration ($NM^{t,\ t+n}$) can be calculated from the formula for
the basic demographic equation (Woods, R.I.,1979):

$$NM^{t,t+n} = p^{t+n} - p^t - B^{t,t+n} + D^{t,t+n}$$

Woods, in his population analysis in Geography (1979) attempted to calculate net migration for smaller demograohic
groups. This was found to be possible only where p^t and
p^{t+n} are available disaggregated by sex and age, and where
the deaths are similarly known for this disaggregation.
But even at this level such data are said to be inferior to
information on gross flows in the analysis of population
mobility impact.

From the discussion so far, it can be argued that the question of the definition of population mobility data are so

closely linked that the types of data available often dic-
tate the kind of migration problems which can be examined.

4.   CAUSES OF POPULATION MOBILITY

Studies on population mobility show generally that the migrants believe themselves to be more satisfied in the places
of destination than in their origins. It is the perception
of an individual of his surrounding world that induces him
to draw a comparison between the various alternatives. But
this perception does not always lead to positive results,
since an erroneous perception may lead an individual to decide to change his situation and to move to other places.
Thus it is hard to believe the normative explanation of population mobility which stresses particular factors and ne-
glects consideration of perceptions prevalent at the time
of starting the move. Although one or two factors may be
most decisive in inducing a person to migrate, the summation
of all working factors is of considerable importance in
evaluating the process of migration. Only recently have
attempts been made to incorporate the subject appraisals of
migrants in costs-benefits models of population movements
(BOGUE, 1977).

The most decisive factor that induces an individual to start
migration is his perception of the different opportunities
offered in spatially differentiated regions. Thus it is not
only the prevalence of regional differences that induces
population mobility, but also the ability of an individual
to perceive such differences. In the pre-industrial period
the agrarian society was almost undifferentiated in comparison to the post-industrial period, where spatial differentiation has become more manifest and has increased in

intensity particularly in the developing countries with dis-
proportional economic development in which regional development is unevenly undertaken. RAVENSTEIN (1885) recognized
the importance of economic development in stimulating population mobility, and this realisation is a basis of
ZELINSKY'S (1971) work on changes in population mobility over
time.

Considering the process of decision-making of potential migrants, J. WOLPERT (1965, 1966) has introduced certain behavioural concepts, among which is the notion of 'place
utility which can be defined as an individual's degree of
satisfaction or dissatisfaction with a place. Of course,
place utility would differ markedly between different individuals because each individual would consider different
attributes of a place in his scale of satisfaction or dissatisfaction. Moreover, each individual evaluates the surrounding world differently according to his limits and the
quality of information he receives about other places. Information flows through letters, personal visits, conver-
sations with others who visited other places, mass-media,
etc., are very important for a potential migrant to develop
an idea of place utility for a range of competing places.
Thus mobility may occur either because the delineation of
place variables has changed or because a new flow of information about other places becomes available. Some scholars
stressed the importance of information flow between the
pre-migrants and the potential migrants (TANNOUS 1942).
They believed that new migrants are convinced to follow the
original migrants, thus setting up the familiar pattern of
a chain mobility flow; where each migration event leads to
another after a time-lapse in which information is sent
back by the previous migrants. Once an individual feels
pressured by the insufficiency of his place utility, he
starts looking for an alternative (BROWN & MOORE, 1970,p.1).

The decision to move is preceded by a period of inquiry and information flow (MICHELSON, 1977). It is quite debateable whether it is the merits of a place which is the good of a move that brings about population mobility as WOLPERT (1965) suggested. This behaviouristic approach to an explanation of the causes of population mobility, though it provides a satisfactory background to undersatnding the selectivity of migration or what is sometimes called "mobility differen-tials"still fails to provide a reasonable set of predictive models. The reason for this is the fact that behaviourist ideas are only fully applicable at the level of the indi-vidual decision-maker, while prediction is only possible in the social sciences at the level of aggregates.

As regards the selectivity nature of population mobility, it has been noted that age, sex, education and socio-economic status are of particular importance in explaining the likelihood of mobility among the people of a particular region.

Generally, the readiness to migrate is found to be greatest in the young adult age-groups, particularly between school-leaving and the age of thirty. Such mobility is generally associated with the search for a job, and with job changes occurring at the lower ranges of the career ladder.

The sex differences in population mobility have been treated by RAVENSTEIN (1885), who concluded that females are more mobile than males, particularly in short distance displace-ment. This was later considered by GRIGG (1977), who re-viewed the work on nineteenth century population mobility in England, and came to different conclusions from RAVEN-STEIN. In societies other than England, sex differentiation in population mobility shows that males are more mobile than the female sector of the society, particularly in the

developing countries with seasonal labour mobility, as will
be seen in this study. PETERS (1976) suggested that sex
may be the basis for selectivity in population mobility,
but it does not operate in all cases, nor need it always
operate in the same way.

Educational background had been suggested by several studies
to be an important factor in migration selectivity (HANNAN,
1969; GALTUNG, 1971). It has generally been found that
those who acquire a higher level of education are more mobile than those with a lower education level. The role of
education in promoting the readiness to move may be attributed to the fact that education may change the attitude of
the individual towards a particular place and also it may
make the appraisal of available information more efficient
as will be seen from the movement of school-leavers into
the towns in chapter six of this study.

The socio-economic status also plays a role, as it is believed that in the developed countries selectivity operates
in favour of the professional or white-collar element in
the employed population, hence they are found to be overrepresented among migrants, while in the developing countries
internal population mobility is more common among those of
low socio-economic status (PRYOR, 1969, p. 74).

It has been suggested that some apparent occupational differentiation in population mobility may be caused by the
response of the different socio-economic groups to different stimuli, manual and unskilled labourers moving for
higher wages and the professional classes moving in antici-
pation of future promotional opportunities (HART, 1973).
"With low economic standard staying becomes difficult because the necessities of life are not met. With low social
standard moving becomes difficult because of the decrease

in perspective, the lack of initiative and connections."
(GALTUNG, 1971, p. 205).

The movement of the poor in the developing countries stated
previously by PRYOR may be explained in terms of the difficulty of life in the areas of origin and the hope of betterment in areas of destination, even where that aspiration
has little chance of being fulfilled.

It may be generally said that population mobility is selective of potential movers according to a wide range of economic and social attributes of the popualtion, and that
such attributes are found to differ from place to place and
from one migration flow to another. Both occupational and
social status of potential movers are significant in deter-
mining the type and amount of information available on which
the decision to move can be based. It is for this reason
that movers are not randomly selected from all population
strata.

5.   CLASSIFICATION OF POPULATION MOBILITY

It is important to consider a number of approaches to the
problem of classifying population mobility, since such an
approach provides insight into the fact that population
mobility is a multi-dimensional phenomenon and that each
decision may be important in its relative context.

As previously stated, the operational definition of population mobility varies from study to study according to the
type of data available (see chapter I.3). "The classification of modern population appears to derive from statistics
that are collected, whether or not these have any relevance
to theoretical questions....." (PETERSEN, 1958, p. 264).

It is possible to classify population mobility according to
the geographical distance covered by an individual. This
distance is found to be extremely variable from one case to
another ranging from mobility within a particular administrative unit to a crossing of international boundaries.
The geographical distance is believed to be important in relation to the cultural and social distance crossed by a migrant. But this assumption should not be taken as valid for
all cases, since it is possible to move long distances and
even cross international boundaries without being met with
differentiated cultural and social patterns as is the case
in Northern Belgium in relation to the southern part of the
Netherlands. On the other hand, internal movements may cross
different cultural and social boundaries as in the case of
India. Therefore, in considering the geographical impact of
population mobility, it is not always correct to stress the
geographical distance.

Another way of classifying population mobility is by the
time period over which the movement is effective, whereby
temporary and permanent population movements are differentiated. The former involves the seasonal movements of people
over periods varying from a few months to a number of years,
while the latter involves moves from which the mover never
returns. This time factor is significant particularly for
a returning mover, since it provides him with new attitudes
and aspirations to be communicated to his community members.
This sort of communication is important in two ways: in
that it brings about a change in that community and in that
it paves the way for other temporary or permanent moves.

It is extremely difficult, however, to identify return movers in any mobility flow, since movemeent process may continue by any particular mover till the end of his life. In
some cases migrants were not able to return home though

this had been their intention at the beginning (PORTER, R. 1956). In other cases potentially permanent migrants who intend to settle down in a place of destination may prefer, by retirement, to move back to the place of origin (CRIBIER, 1975).

A third and most common means of classifying population mobility may be based on the environmental context of the sending and the receiving areas. Accordingly, it is common to differentiate between rural-rural, rural-urban, inter-urban and frontierward movement (ZELINSKY, 1971). The only drawback of this classification is its ignorance of the counterflow in the direction opposite to the mobility stream.

A fourth classification is based on the ecological attributes of the sending and receiving areas as causes behind any particular move. The term economic movement is most relevant in this context as opposed to educational and retirement movements.

These last two classifications will be followed in the course of this study in an attempt to identify the types of population movements, their characteristics, directions and intensity among a particular group of people in a particular area, with the aim of shedding light on the probable repercussions related to population mobility as induced by a particular factor, namely, agricultural mechanization.

6.   DIFFERENT PATTERNS OF POPULATION MOBILITY

In the preceding discussions, some aspects of population mobility have been presented. The following sub-chapter will be devoted mainly to volume, shape, length and directions of mobility flows. These patterns are believed to be of particular importance in understanding the impact of mobility. They are considered to be indicators of the mobility process and functional links within the mobility system between sending and receiving areas. In this sense analysis of mobility flows complements an understanding of the process of selectivity mentioned previously and provides the needed background for a comprehensive view of the multiple effects of any mobility process.

Some scholars have distinguished between two approaches that may be adopted in analyzing mobility flows (WHITE & WOOD, 1980). The deductive approach which recognizes, identifies and describes actual population mobility based on available information, and then attempts to correlate the data to discover patterns and processes which may explain population mobility. The second approach is an inductive one which begins the sequence of analysis by formulating logical and internally consistent theories which may then be tested empirically against data drawn from actual observations.

It is obvious that these two approaches are not mutually exclusive and are considered as vital ingredients of social scientific enquiries. For this reason, the present study employs a more dialectic approach, which allows for more flexibility where the actual data requires modification of the theories. However, the fact that actual data on population mobility is not adequately available requires that we depend more upon the inductive approach, formulating hypotheses and testing them empirically by means of personal findings.

7.   SHAPE, DIRECTION, LENGTH AND VOLUME OF POPULATION
       MOBILITY FLOW

To represent mobility flows it is conventionally agreed to

link the sending and receiving areas by a straight line
which can provide the length and direction of the flow. The
volume of mobility flow may be represented proportionally
as the width of that straight line. To provide the exact
length and direction of the flow it is important to identify the exact points of origin and destination. Such identification is only possible through a field survey which is
essential for drawing the mobility flows. Three possibilities of presenting such flows are shown by Fig. I.2 in
which A represents the mobility flow from different places
of origin to different places of destination; B deals with
a case in which movements proceed from a single place of
origin towards a number of places of destination, and C reflects a case in which people from different origins are
heading towards a single place of destination.

Fig. I.2

(A)   (B)   (C)

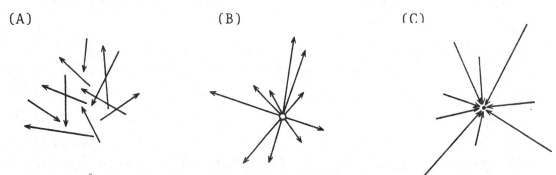

However, it is extremely rare to find only one place of origin and only one place of destination for any particular
flow. Our case study shows different places of origin and
different places of destination as in Fig. I.2.A. Moreover,
mobility flows in this study are considered as moves between
areas rather than between points of origin and destination,
since it is found difficult - even by census organizations -
to submit such actual points. Thus the analysis of population
flows in this particular study are largely concerned with
skilled labour movements between administrative units, i.e.
provinces or geographical regions.

Regarding the direction of population mobility, it is possible to recognize a number of scales varying between the intra-regional and international movements. In some cases it is found to be relevant to relate the directional bias in population mobility and the type of population distribution as in the case of the United States of America, where the direction of the move is from the densely populated North-East to the less populated South-West and South-East (SCHWIND, 1971). In the developing countries including our case study, the direction of the flow is in the reverse direction, i.e. from the relatively less populated provinces to the densely populated ones. As stated by GETIS & BOOTS (1978, pp. 86-120) the direction of the migration flows is constrained by the geometry of population distribution within a fixed area. The distance covered by a particular mover is another important characteristic of a mobility flow. The principle of least effort associated with the friction of distance effort has often been observed in geographical studies. It has been stated that the potential mover in his application to the place utility matrix stated earlier will choose the place of destination most near to him assuming that all other factors remain the same. The reason for this option is readily given in terms of decreased cost of movement compared with long distances. Short distances are not only important in reducing the cost of a journey but also in providing the potential mover with the needed information about other places since he is likely to know less about distant than nearby places (MILLER, 1972, p. 475). In this study a combination of short-distance and long-distance moves is followed.

In considering the volume of a mobility flow, it is important to review some of the ideas stated by some scholars. ZELINSKY (1971) argues that population mobility is a function of time, i.e. the rate of population movement increases

over time and that it is higher in the economically advanced
than in the developing countries. But this argument should
not be taken as valid throughout, since even the pre-industrial societies are said to have been mobile (P. CLARK,
1972). A number of studies in Africa have come to the conclusion that both short-distance population movement and
age- and sex- selective long-distance movements occur
(CALDWELL, 1968; RIDDELL, 1970; CLAESON, 1974; MASSER &
GOULD,1975). Contrary to the findings of ZELINSKY (1971) in
England, these scholars argued that high rates of mobility
are fundamental characteristics of these poor societies and
that these movements are both a cause and effect of the
modernization and urbanization processes. Our case study
makes no exceptions in this respect, since the trend is from
the less-developed towards the more advanced regions. But
despite this fact, ZELINSKY's view has some relevance, since
residential movement particularly in its long-distance form
did increase during the period of industrialization and now
stands at a high level in the countries with advanced econ-
omies. In Western Europe and North America about 10% and 20%
are said to be the annual average turnover rate, respectively (WHITE & WOODS, 1980, p. 31).

8.   DIFFERENT LAWS OF MOBILITY

A number of scholars have contributed to population mobility
theory and analysis. The most important of these are the
three students of population in the nineteenth century,
namely: T.R. MALTHUS (1766 - 1834); W. FARR (1807 - 1883)
and E.G. RAVENSTEIN (1834 - 1913). Although their work was
subject to criticism even in their lifetimes, their ideas
have proved stimulating to social scientists and demographers even in the twentieth century. The most important

contribution to our knowledge of population mobility were
the statements of RAVENSTEIN, which he called laws of migration. They are broad generalisations of the characteristics
of migrants and migration streams and have been treated recently by a number of scholars like PORTER (1956), LEE
(1966) and GRIGG (1977). It is necessary to list the statements and try to test their validity by consulting our own
findings along the course of this study.

RAVENSTEIN gave ten statements which he considered to be
the laws of any population mobility:

- Most migrants move only a short distance.

- The volume of migration increases with the development of industry and agriculture.

- The direction of migration is mainly from agricultural to industrial areas.

- Most long-distance migration is to the major industrial and commercial centres.

- Migration proceeds step by step.

- Each migration stream or flow has a counter-stream.

- Migrants are only adults - families rarely migrate
  over long distances.

- A majority of migrants are females, but males comprise a majority of industrial migrants.

- Migrants are more likely to have rural than urban
  origin.

- The major causes of migration are economic.

The universality of Ravenstein's statements varies from one
law to another. Evidence of most of these laws has already
been mentioned in the foregoing discussion. It is clear
that the statements were the product of his time, hence

they are not necessarily all valid for recent times.

It is true that the migrant prefers to move short-distance
to reduce the physical and financial effort, but this statement does not hold true for technologically advanced areas
with modern means of transportation and communications or
in cases where migration takes place in spite of the high
cost of transportation, as shown by the movement of seasonal labour in the developing countries.

The volume of migration does increase with the development
of industry and commerce but the correlation should not be
taken as a simple linear one (ZELINSKY, 1971). Such increase
in volume could also be partially attributed to the increased importance and general awareness of spatial differentiation of opportunities as a result of economic development.

In a period and place of rapid urbanization such as Ravenstein's, it is expected to find population movements directed from agricultural to urban centres. This situation is -
at least at a mature stage of population mobility - still
prevalent in the less developed countries, including our
case study. In some of the developed countries, where
nearly two-thirds of the countries' population are classified as urban, the direction of the flow may be urban-
urban or even urban-rural.

Ravenstein's statement 'that movement of females are dominant may be relevant only for times when many young women
were in service as in the European late nineteenth century.
By contrast, the present social and economic conditions in
many of the less developed countries, including our case
study, reveal this statement to be particular rather than
universal. This could also be said of the statement 'that
most long-distance movement is to the major industrial and

commercial centres'. In contrast to Ravenstein's time, most
of such movement today is directed - particularly in its
initial stages - towards other rural areas, where agricultural schemes have been implemented, as will be seen from
this particular study. Furthermore, this movement involves
not only single adults, as stated by Ravenstein, but also
children and whole families.

The statement which is most valid for the developing countries is that dealing with the causes of population movements.
The reason for this may be sought in the similarity of the
economic conditions in the late nineteenth century in Western Europe and in the less developed countries at present.
This explanation of population mobility as a factor of economic development has been discussed by political economists
since the eighteenth century. ADAM SMITH (1723 - 1790) in
his Wealth of Nations (1776) maintained that 'the demand for
men, like that for any other commodity, necessarily regu-
lates the production of men', and ARTHUR YOUNG (1741 - 1820)
in his Political Arithmetic (1774) claimed that "employment
is the soul of population" (WHITE and WOODS, 1980, p.35).
But in spite of the importance of the economic factors, it
should not be taken as the only factor inducing population
movements even at the present time. The whole series of potential variables, particularly those suggested by the beha-
viourists, should be incorporated in explaining the reasons
behind population mobility. For practical reasons, particularly the lack of needed data, it is not possible to assess
all the variables that induce population mobility in our
case study. But nevertheless, as we shall see from the results of the field surveys carried out among a particular
group of people, the economic factor is the dominant one.

Generally speaking, Ravenstein's statements have broad
applicability only in the context in which they were made,

since they were inductive in origin; they stem from an analysis of particular population data derived from one particular area in a particular time-period. Recent empirical studies continue to demonstrate the applicability of these laws for societies as different as the Soviet Union and Malaysia (GRANDSTAFF, 1975; PRYOR, 1969).

Of particular relevance to our case study is the statement dealing with the process of population movement. Ravenstein stressed the step-like mobility whereby the places of those who migrate to urban centres are taken by other migrants coming from less developed regions. He showed a chain of movement comprising rural-rural, rural to small towns, small town to large city to metropolis. Although such chain movement is dominant at present in the developing countries, including our case study, it is quite difficult to assess, since population statistics are confined only to places of origin and places of destination but are completely lacking for the places in between. The only possible way is to consult a certain group of people in a particular area in a definite time-period as in the case of our empirical data collection to be presented in chapters 5, 6 and 7 of this study. For this reason it is not justified to consider such a statement as a 'law' capable of universal application.

The explanation for this type of population mobility is readily found in the individual migrant's increased access to information sources. It is clear that the migrant who moves from a backward area to the nearest small urban or industrial centre will be able to increase his information about distant relatively large centres, thus being stimulated to take a further step until he reaches the end of the spectrum where he prefers either to settle down permanently or to join the counter-stream movement.

Apart from the increase in information access, an individual may gain a new socio-economic status by his first or
second step by being exposed to new opportunities of increasing his educational achievements or qualifications.
Thus by acquiring a new skill, he will be stimulated to take
a new step in the movement chain. Such stimulated movements
have been dealt with by a number of scholars among whom is
TAEUBER (1961; 1966) who has investigated the mobility patterns of rural farms, rural non-farms, small town, large
town and large city populations using survey data of individuals. He concluded that different stages of movements may
involve more than one generation of movers, and admitting
that his survey data are not capable of testing the validity of the statement that deals with step-like population
mobility. Even the data reviewed by SHYROCK & LARMON (1965)
and the analysis of ELDRIDGE (1965) of the American census
statistics of 1960 proved inadequate to substantiate this
statement. Nevertheless, these studies stressed the importance of such chain movement in increasing the flow of information about other places or destinations. They argued
that population movements comprise pioneer or primary movers and followers or secondary movers. The former group is
said to be dominated by young adult males in search of a
better standard of living, while the latter group consists
of dependants, relatives and friends, who have received information about other places from the primary group. As will
be shown later in this study, it appears that knowledge of
a relative or friend already living in a place of destination can establish a crucial link in the process of population mobility. The presence of such a relative or friend is
important both as a source of information to the potential
mover and as assurance of accomodation at least in the first
days after his arrival at the new destination. DESAI (1963),
in his study amongst the Indian immigrants in Britain,

showed that the majority of the immigrants from a particular region of Western India were helped to migrate by a
primary group of migrants who found them employment and accommodation and generally assisted them in making the transition to an alien culture and environment. It was the continuous communication between the origin and destination
that sustained the type of chain movement. This view was
supported by the findings of more recent studies such as
that of E. WEBER (1977), who examined the social modernization process of nineteenth century France. GREENWOOD (1970)
stressed the importance of a chain population movement as
the most natural means by which mobility streams develop for
the potential or secondary groups of movers.

II.   POPULATION MOBILITY IN AFRICAN COUNTRIES

1.   SOME HISTORICAL EXPLANATIONS

The economic history of the integration of some African
peoples into production for the world market economy and the
history of the consequent population mobility begins as
early as the seventeenth century with the Europeans' voya-
ges of discovery which facilitated the capture and transport of slaves to the other side of the Atlantic, where they
were destined to serve in areas where the indigenous population was insufficient to carry out the needed work in the
newly emerging agricultural farms of the new world. The
consequence of this early population transference was an
economic ruin and a near end to the further development of
indigenous African culture. The prosperous capital cities
of West African Kingdoms, for example, as centres of crafts
and trans-Saharan trade declined abruptly (BROOKS, 1971).
For European traders and plantation owners in the new world
the slavery meant profit and economic development. Profits
gained in the slave trade are argued to be the cause of the
initial success of some of today's most reputable commercial enterprises in America and in Europe (W. RODNEY, 1972,
p. 398). Thus West African regions served as a source of
young adult male and female slave labourers for commodity
production in the American colonies before it was turned -
at the end of the nineteenth century - into a source of natural resources for European industrial expansion. In fact
the transference of African labourers was stopped due to
the abolition of the slave trade by the end of the nineteenth century, and accordingly population movements were
directed to serve the European interests inside the Continent. This continued integration of the African people into
the system of a market-oriented production began with the

establishment of a free-labour cultivation by the Colonial
Governments to provide wholesome and profitable occupation
(C.W. NEWBURY, 1965). The century-long depletion of the African population by the slave trade meant that there was
more than enough land for the African people to continue to
produce their basic necessities for themselves without further participation in the market economy had it not been for
the interference of the European settlers, who siezed the
best, most fertile land and took special measures to meet
the problem of labour shortage. It had been reported that
even in the older and more developed areas of European agriculture and mining of South Africa the transition from rural
communal employment to rural or urban wage contracts was no-
where made easily or without considerable displacement of
African peoples (H. HOUGHTON, 1971). It became evident that
the mere political slogan of admitting a free-labour market
was not enough to create expansion of exportable staples
which was expected to occur automatically. To meet the increasing demand for public works, railways, the construction
of the farms and mining some rural areas of South Africa had
been destined to serve as labour reservoirs. To ensure a
continuous flow of labourers the Native Recruiting Corporation was established by the Colonial administration in South
Africa in 1912 to substitute the Witwatersrand Native Labour
Association (C.W. NEWBURY, 1975). In the less endowed regions of Colonial expansion and settlement in West,Central
and East Africa other methods had been adopted. Among the
measures taken to mobilize the rural population to take part
in the transformation of the subsistence agriculture into
export-oriented agriculture both in the British-protected
areas and German and French West Africa was the adoption of
what was called domestic slavery - a phrase attributed to
W.F. WARD (1952) - as a substitution for the external slave
trade. Recruitment of liberated slaves through military or
civil administrators as well as through indigenous rulers

was reported by C.W. NEWBURY (1961) to be adopted in the
1890's in West Africa. It has been argued by A.G. HOPKINS
(1968) that the rise of legitimate commerce, far from
bringing about the abolition of internal slavery, actually
increased the demand for cheap labour within the continent,
and slave raiding continued in order to meet growing domestic needs. This viewpoint could be taken as a more realis-
tic starting point for a general study of the formation of
an African wage-labour force than the rural-urban emphasis
on works which concentrate on the late Colonial economic
and social aspects of African manpower (C.W. NEWBURY, 1969).
The recruitment of the necessary labour for the expanding
market-oriented agriculture brought about the decomposition
and destruction of the pre-colonial societies due to the
prolonged displacement of populations, high mortality rates
and the decline of the home regions.

In East Africa forced labour went hand in hand with the expropriation of all or part of the peasants' land. This was
especially the case in Kenya as early as 1904 where the
majority of the good quality lands were alienated to non-
Africans resulting in the restriction of some tribes on
inferior soils. By depriving the indigenous population of
all or part of their means of subsistence they were forced
to work as agricultural labourers on land that had only a
few years before belonged to them. In principle, such
methods of mobilizing labour for the production of commodities were not very different from the measures which
had accompanied the early colonizing adventures in the Am-
ericas. But in practice they were different. In order to
avoid a demographic decline which would leave the colonized lands without an adequate labour force, it appeared
that some colonizers had learned that - in their own self-
interest - it was necessary to exercise restraint in the
disruption of indigenous production. Thus in many parts of

East Africa, the majority of the peasants were allowed to
keep at least some of their land, on which they continued
to meet their own subsistence (B. STOCKEY & M.A. FAY, 1980).
In some of the East African countries, particularly in
Kenya (East African Protectorate) there was a tendency to
realize a quick transition from a system of forced labour
to one of free employment by introducing wage measures for
a limited time. The colonial governments were interested
in implementing their economic plans by using the cheapest
and, if possible most legitimate measures, since they believed that a system of slave labour and wage labour are
mutually incompatible. But even the system of wage labour
failed to attract African people from their traditional
rural societies to regions where they were most needed.
The reason for their reluctance was argued to be the mere
fact that the idea of organized labour was utterly foreign
to most of the tribesmen. But this assumption should not
be overemphasised, since the African people had already
come into contact with the European people and had become
well acquainted with the system of organized labour through
the adoption of domestic slavery. The most convincing explanation could be given in terms of the low wages offered
by the Colonial governments as reported by W.J.MONSON (1903)
in his report on slavery and free labour in the British
East African Protectorate. The pull factors were not enough
to detach a native worker from his secure life within his
traditional social arrangement. Even the introduction of
some push measures such as the adoption of head tax payments reported by P. GIROUARD (1913) proved to be insufficient to produce a continuous labour supply.

The levying of taxes was officially justified on the grounds
that the colonized population should contribute to the
cost of maintaining the colonial administriation which was
bringing them so many benefits. But in reality the imposi-
tion of such taxes meant that the people now had need for

money to pay the newly levied taxes. There were two ways
in which the indigenous population could get money:

1) by working as wage labourers in the mines or in the
   lands that had been expropriated by the colonists
   (A. KRAUTER, 1979);

2) by raising cash crops for market sales on the plots
   of lands that had remained in their own possession.

Thus taxation monetarized the participation of the colonized peoples in providing commodities for world market,
and thereby made such participation appear 'voluntary' and
a normal part of international trade. It followed that,
particularly in areas where land was scarce, the production
of food for local consumption fell (F. BREMER, 1977; K.
HABERMEIER, 1977). The prices the peasants received for
their cash crop commodities were just high enough to enable
the payment of taxes and nothing could be saved to allow
for the purchase of agricultural inputs which might improve
the level of productivity in peasant farming. Even the
wages earned were not enough to feed the workers and their
families over the payment of taxes. They had to depend on
the rural activities of their families for their subsistence needs (M. CAUFIELD, 1974; D. METZGER, 1976; B. ROGERS,
1978). For the wage workers themselves, employment in the
European enterprises was only a temporary activity for most
of them, migration became a way of life (J. FRIEDMANN,
E. McLYNN, B. STUCKEY, C. WU, 1973). They practised a sort
of seasonal migration whereby workers spent part of the
year on the plantations and the rest at home working on
their own land with their families. Only those who went to
work in the cities or mines stayed away for several years
at a time (R.L. SKLAR, 1975). Such temporary migrant labour
offered colonial enterprises producing for the world market
significant advantages over the permanent labour force.
Migrant labourers provided the employer with continuous

supply of labour power without his being responsible politically or accountable financially for the long-term sur-
vival of that supply. There was no provision for illness,
injury, unemployment, families or old age. All these "social
needs" were provided by the rural subsistence economy provided by tha African villages. Thus the existence of the
rural subsistence sector and the development of complex
patterns of migration allowed capitalist enterprises operating in many areas of the Third World to externalize the
costs of reproducing their labour force. To a much greater
extent than in the nineteenth and twentieth centuries in
Europe, the employers of wage-labourers were exempted from
bearing the full costs of maintaining their labourers (B.
STUCKEY and M.A. FAY, 1980).

So far it could be argued that the explanation of the swift
incorporation and massive participation of Africans in employment in the modern economic sub-sector over the past
half-century cannot be attributed to economic incentives
alone. Part of the historical explanation may be seen in
the various measures by which foreign or local administrations have sought to exert the needed 'push' to induce
labourers to leave their lands and way of life. This viewpoint has been supported by the International African Institute and UNESCO (1956, p. 34) in an article dealing with
the social implications of industrialization and urbanization in Africa south of the Sahara.

2.   SOME EXPLANATIONS TO THE RECENT POPULATION MOVEMENTS
     IN AFRICA

It is only recently that sufficient demographic and economic data have been collected to show the scope and intensity of the African population movement, particularly of

African wage-labour. It has been suggested that the number
of wage-earners in the African countries expanded most
rapidly between 1930 and 1955 and that 'the population of
Africa, although small, is still too large in proportion
to the means of subsistence obtained from the soil' (ILO,
1958, p. 107).

This imbalance between subsistence production and the availability of temporary employment - rural or urban - is
essential to an understanding of the pattern and persis-
tence of population mobility in the African countries including our case study.

The dynamics of African wage-labour mobility, however, has
been treated by a number of workers devoted to socio-
economic problems related to population movements. Emphasis
has been placed particularly on motivation and effect
within the traditional societies and on the assimilation
of migrants into an urban environment. The broader aspects
of environmental, capital and government intervention into
the labour market have only recently been synthesized in
order to construct models of population mobility. One of
the most important models relevant to any explanation of
the development and perpetuation of mobility streams and
counter-streams is that by CLYDE MITCHELL modified by WIL-
SON (J. GUGLER, 1968). This model includes the following
variables:

Rural Push	Urban Pull
Need for money to pay for food, school fees, taxes, etc.. These push factors are supplemented by social needs e. g. 'bright lights', desire to escape from a situation of stagnation that offers only heavy, unrewarding jobs with little hope of improvement.	Need for labour in the growing urban centres as pull factor for rural population, 'bright lights' of the town: social, cultural and educational facilities.
Rural Pull	Urban Push
Need to maintain agricultural production, land rights and social connection for purpose of security in old age, supplemented by desire to live in family surroundings (both social an geographical).	Necessity for employees to be originated in rural areas to keep their wages low and so that employers need not be responsible for housing families of workers.

The model is based on the possible exchange of labour between the traditional and the modern sectors of the economy. It demonstrates the reason for continuous flow of people to and from the relatively developed regions. It stresses the pull of wages in the modern sector and the push to supplement socio-economic needs in the traditional sector as the most important variables resulting in traditional-modern sector movement. The need to preserve socio-economic connections for the purpose of security in areas of origin as pull forces and the low wages and the lack of socio-economic security in areas of destination as other variables resulting in the counter-flow of population movements. Thus the continuity of such population movements depends on a balance of push and pull factors within a social set-up that tends to act centripetally. It has been attempted to maintain this balance even in the post colonial time to ensure the flow of cheap labour force as will be seen in this case study.

The variables of this model, however, should not be taken
as applicable in all cases. In some African countries including our case study, population movements were caused
not only by the wage factor and aspirations of the natives,
but also by the influence of trade routes, indigenous
markets, occupational specialization by different tribal
groups and the intention of the administrative bodies
(M. PIAAULT, 1962, pp. 323-338).

It is to be stressed, however, that recent trends in public
and private investments in most of the African countries
bring about a fundamental demand for wage-labour. This demand has been met with an abundant supply of labour from
the relatively underdeveloped areas. To secure a continuous
flow of cheap labour from areas of origin and to avoid
stabilization of migrant labour in areas of destination, it
has become necessary to formulate an administrative low-
wage policy whereby urban wages must be kept more or less
at parity with agricultural wages and no differential to
defray the rural labourer's cost in displacing himself from
the land to the town (A.G. HOPKINS, 1966, p. 146). This
policy is thought to be essential, since it is believed
that raising wages for target workers would satisfy their
wants more quickly, leading to a decrease in the labour
supply (E. BERG, 1961, pp. 473-489).

A number of new forms of population mobility in Africa
have been reported in the last decade (RIDDELL, 1970 b;
SOUTHALL, 1971). It was generally argued that the knowledge of population movements, representing as it does a
cause and effect of societal process, remains fundamentally
important to a complete understanding of social change, economic development and political organization (CLAESON &
EGERO, 1972 a, p.1). In this sense population mobility must
be regarded as a two-way process which is not only a

product of new socio-economic development and political circumstances but also a cause of change in both sending and receiving areas. This fact has been stressed by CLARKE (1965), OMINDE (1968) and CLAESON & EGERO (1972, b).

It is essential to distinguish between three significant features of recent African population mobility. The first of these is the increasing importance of the individual, i.e. recent movements involve individuals rather than the previous large-scale, long-term corporate migration as the result of the new types of labour needs in areas of destination (J.C. MITCHELL, 1961). The second feature is the change towards economically motivated movements due to the appearance of the modern economic sector as opposed to the traditional tribal moves caused by famine and/or warfare (PROTHERO, 1968).[1] The third feature is the change in the direction of the flow away from rural areas to the growing

---

1) Recent movements should be seen in the context of the 'push' factors that cause people to leave home and the 'pull' factors that attract them to a particular destination. Broad distinctions can be made between areas of low emigration and primitive subsistence economy, areas of heavy emigration which lack cash crops or in which land is short, areas of low emigration and highly developed cash economy had finally areas of high economic and education advancement with emigration at the professional level. These combinations often overlap. (For more details about these combinations reference is made to A.W. SOUTHALL, 1961).

urban centres of economic activity (CALDWELL, 1969).[2]

As is the case in other parts of the globe, these features are the results of diverse processes operating to influence the modern population movements in Africa. Such a complexity of processes has stimulated a considerable number of studies dealing with the patterns involved at a variety of scales over varying time periods. In almost all cases it has been observed that male-dominated labour movement is a cause and effect of regional disparities in income levels, social welfare and opportunities for economic advances. These motivated moves, started since the turn of the century, are well documented as part of the population studies in Africa (RICHARDS, 1954; MIDDLETON,1960). Individual studies of the major labour supplying tribes have been supplemented by more comprehensive national surveys of labour movements within Africa (SOUTHALL, 1961; DAK, 1968; OMINDE, 1968; CLAESON, 1974).

The findings of these studies reflect a spatial pattern characterized by long-distance highly directional movements mainly from the backward areas described as underdeveloped

---

2) With rising economic awareness and with diminished working opportunities in one's own stagnating territory, there was an overwhelming tendency to move elsewhere. The move becomes a socio-economic necessity. Ecological factors push people, especially young males who have not yet acquired land but desperately need money for marriage. Ecologically favourable locations for economic practices attract people with the result of overpopulation, as is the case in almost all the river deltas, fertile plains and oases. The result of this, in some places, is the phenomenon of desertification which compels people to remigrate to other ecologically suitable places, as is the case of the shifting cultivation in the traditional agricultural sub-sector in most of the African countries south of the Sahara in general and the rain-fed mechanized cultivation in the modern agricultural sub-sector in the Sudan in particular.

periphery to the economically advanced cores. Causes for
such movements have been sought in the prevailing ecological, cultural and economic conditions at areas of origin
and areas of destination within a push-pull framework.

RICHARDS (1954) studied the fertile South-Central Zone in
Uganda and discussed the social and economic consequences
of large-scale migration to this region as reflected in the
relationships formed between relatively poor labourers from
peripheral districts and the wealthy South-Central region.
In their destinations the immigrants show a multi-nucleated
residential pattern which emerged distinguished from the
bases of the geographical origin (HIRST, 1975).

The impact of population mobility is a theme also considered
by CLAESON and EGERO (1972 b), who illustrate the effects of
selective migration on the demographic structure of Tanzania's
major towns emphasizing the dominance of adult males and
the marked sex imbalance within the different age groups.
Analysis of the geographical impact represents an important field of inquiry in the developing societies of Africa.
The impact of sex imbalance at places of origin and places
of destination resulting from labour movements has been
discussed in Ghana by HUNTER (1965), in Zambia by KAY (1967)
and in Kenya by OMINDE (1968).

As a result of multiplicity and complexity of population
mobility in tropical Africa and due to the increasing
interest in the subject, several attempts have been made to
summarize and review the various findings for the whole
continent (PROTHERO, 1964; GUGLER, 1968, 1969). In addition
to these attempts some effort has been made to classify the
various types of mobility within a quantitative frame-work
(PROTHERO, 1968; HANCE, 1970). More recent comprehensive

studies, based on improved quality and quantity of population mobility information derived from improved population
censuses, reflect the application of more spohisticated
models and techniques in order to improve levels of explanation GODDARD, A.D., et al, 1975; HIRST, 1976).

III. RURAL DEVELOPMENT MEASURES AND POPULATION MOBILITY

1. AGRICULTURAL DEVELOPMENTS AS A CAUSE OF POPULATION MOBILITY

The critical state of the world food supply has placed agricultural production in the forefront of public attention.
Food supplies must be increased to meet the requirements of
a growing rural and urban population and to improve nutri-
tional standards particularly in the less developed countries. For this purpose all available resources, particularly
land, manpower, capital and technology have to be mobilized.
This policy has been followed to a considerable extent in
the developed countries, where the use of mobile steam engines to augment human and animal power in the late nineteenth century and the introduction of the internal combus-
tion engine to provide light-weight, highly mobile and efficient sources of power in the beginning of the twentieth
century have contributed to increasing productivity and reducing the drudgery of work for the farmer. The development
of industries in particular centres has induced the mobilization of resources, particularly the rural populations,
who have been displaced by the introduction of new production systems. The continuous use of a high-level technology
meant that a declining number of labourers was needed to
work a growing number of acres. For many millions of people
this has meant a new phase of forced migration from rural
homelands. Such development is significant for our assessment of the effect of agricultural mechanization on population mobility in the less developed countries. Its significance lies in the fact that the increase in output and productivity achieved through mechanization of agriculture are
not being used to augment the food intake of rural populations. Rather as in the colonial past, production is

directed to the much more lucrative world market.

This process of the late nineteenth and early twentieth centuries is now going on in almost all the developing countries, including our case study. For economic factors, limited technical knowledge and social conditions the speed is relatively slow.

In the developing countries today there is a wide spectrum of development methods, since each country has its own unique set of conditions (natural resources, social, economic and political factors). Without question every country hopes to develop and improve the standards of living of its people, and specialists from many disciplines cooperate to formulate national plans and national policies to speed up the rate of development. Of crucial importance to the developing countries are measures to develop rural areas with the aim of reducing the regional disparity, particularly between rural and urban areas. They have to devise strategies especially designed to achieve the welfare of the majority of their populations.

Mainly because of their rapid population growth, the developing countries have to increase their agricultural production much faster than ever before, and at the same time do so in ways that also increase employment opportunities within the rural areas as fast as possible to reduce rural-urban population movements which are cause and effect of development disparity. But these two basic aims are not always completely compatible since the strategy that will increase the production will not necessarily solve employment problems at the same speed. Mechanization and the introduction of new cereal varieties are particularly components of such a strategy. Unfortunately, these two components have been used unwisely, with the result of undesirable displacement of labour. In most of the developing countries an implementation of development policies is not carried out by a group of specialists, who are aware of the interconnection of the productivity and employment problems. In most cases agricultural engineers and to some extent economists have to form national policies, which give no consideration to regional development. Interdisciplinary cooperation between agricultural engineers and social scientists is not yet available to a substantial degree due to lack of adequate data base.

Generally, agriculture is such a dominant feature of the developing countries, that the strategies chosen to implement rural development will determine to a great extent the nature of the entire socio-economic development that will emerge. Agriculture will remain for decades to come the main livelihood for most of the people in the developing countries. Since the main objective of agricultural policies has been to increase the total amount of food produced, there has been relatively little concern with the wider aspects of rural development, particularly with how to bring rural population into modern life. Only recently are national governments becoming more sensitive to the broader range of issues closely related to the creation of more rural jobs and a more equal distribution of income with the aim of reducing regional disparity.

One of the most arguable attempts adopted by most of the developing countries is what is called "The Green Revolution", which is intended to play a very important part in implementing policies releated to rural development by raising productivity and incomes of many millions of peasant farmers (GRIFFIN, K., 1974). The most important

element of the Green Revolution is new high-yielding varieties of wheat, rice, maize and other coarse grains which
have been spreading in the Asian countries since the mid-
sixties and in the African countries only recently (D.G.
DALRYMPLE, 1969).

It is not our intention to present all the repercussions of
the adoption of the Green Revolution in the developing
countries, but it is worth mentioning that discussions on
how countries can sustain the new agricultural policy have
tended to neglect the relationships between land and capital, on the one hand, and the employment of manpower on the
other hand. Advocates of this new policy argued that the
new varieties were to be the potential seeds of the rural
regeneration that is essential to the development of the
poor nations. It was expected to help provide productive
jobs in the agricultural sector as well as to initiate the
necessary increase in productivity in order to raise the
living standards of millions of peasants in rural areas.
But this new development policy could also contain danger
such as the widening of socio-economic inequalities within
the rural areas and the creation of unrest which may threa-
ten any rural development. It is argued that the increased
yields result only under certain conditions - the purchase
of the new hybrid seeds, regular irrigation and the use of
expensive high-quality inputs like pesticides and fertilizers (G. WILKES, 1977). Such inputs, of course, demand a
far higher capital outlay than the average peasant in the
developing countries could afford. It is further argued that
'in spite of the credit systems which are set up in some
countries to allow for the participation of the smallholders
in the programme, the major beneficiaries of the new agricultural policy are the large commercial farmers and the
producers of the necessary agricultural inputs' (K. GOUGH,
1978, pp. 12-13).

The expansions of the Green Revolution have left their marks
on the economic situation in the developing countries. Land
previously used as a means of production in the rural subsistence sector has been transformed into a resource for
world market production. The peasants and their families -
being faced with increasing hunger in the villages - were
forced to migrate. The migration patterns of the disposses-
sed rural population today have received far more attention
in the academic literature than the expropriation of land
which forced their migration. Scholars are concentrating on
the complexity of migration or on searching for psychologi-
cal explanations for it, rather than examining the economic
situation that induces it.

The question of agricultural mechanization in relation to the
Green Revolution is of particular importance in this context
which will be dealt with separately and elaborately in the
following discussions, since this is considered to be the
most influential factor in population mobility.

2. THE PARADOX OF AGRICULTURAL MECHANIZATION IN THE DEVELOPING COUNTRIES

Mechanization of agriculture in the developing countries,
including our case study, has been taking place slowly but
steadily over the past few decades. Its introduction is
causing cocern among governments and labour leaders with
growing disagreement as to its benefits and costs. It has
attracted the attention of technocrats and policy makers at
national and international levels. There is a strong belief
that the trend towards mechanizing agriculture is historical in nature and is brought about by economic and social
processes. The rapid increase in the use of tractorization
has been recently recognized as one of the most important

strategic measures relevant to rural development in the less developed countries along with the spread of the Green Revolution.

Paradoxically, the accelerating trend towards mechanization is occurring at a time of growth in the rural labour force, the result being the displacement of peasants and agricultural labour. As part of the new agricultural policy, mechanization is expected by its advocates to define the future of the whole agricultural sector, to raise productivity and income levels for many producers, to reduce the gross inequality of earnings between urban and rural areas as well as between various economic sectors, to utilize the labour force more efficiently and equitably and to lessen the frustration of job seekers, mainly the young, by enabling them to obtain the type of work or the remuneration which they consider adequate (ILO, 1972).

It is clear that even in those countries which have achieved a high level of economic development, the employment problems have remained in most cases. Indeed, successful growth, as conventionally measured has frequently exacerbated the employment situation, particularly from the standpoint of income distribution. This has been well documented in the case of the Green Revolution in countries like India, Pakistan and Latin America, where, as elsewhere in the developing countries, it has been recognized that resolving the purely economic problems, difficult though it is, is inadequate, and that this has led to a re-ordering of development priorities. Thus some countries are now giving priority to development strategies that attempt to deal with one or more aspects of the social problems associated with economic development, particularly employment problems. In this context the criteria for mechanization at the farm level can no longer relate exclusively to the objectives

of increasing farm output and incomes; nor can the effects
of the innovations on rural income distribution and employment be disregarded. One of the multiple objectives on
the long-term basis is the substitution of mechanical power
for human and animal effort. Although this objective would
appear to be essential for the achievement of a sustained
increase in rural incomes per capita, it is the immediate
and short-term consequences of farm mechanization which has
the greatest impact on the welfare of the developing countries. It is not only the economics of mechanization at the
farm level which must be considered, but also its impact on
the social and political framework and the distribution of
economic power and population. Thus it is not enough to
argue that "since by definition, technological change means
an increase in resource productivity, no such change can be
intrinsically bad" (G.F. DONALDSON & J.P. MELNERNEY, 1973).

Thus the key issue to be considered in regard to agricultural mechanization in the developing countries, however, is
"its paradoxity", a phrase attributed to BELL (1971) and relating to the replacement of an increasingly abundant labour force by increasingly costly machines. In the absence
of specially designed policies, small farmers are deprived
of the benefits of the new policy. Moreover there is the
"dilemma of mechanization": the need to reduce the physiacal
toil and drudgery of agricultural work, the main feature of
peasant agriculture in the developing countries, without ex-
acerbating the existing problem of unemployment, which is
argued to be the main cause of the drift from rural areas to
the urban centres, particularly among young people.

Although in the past decades mechanization of agriculture has proceeded at a rapid pace in some countries,
implying private net benefits, few studies have attempted
to measure the externalities that mechanization has created,

particularly in regard to employment and population mobility in response to the increasing regional and sectoral income
disparities.

ABERCROMBIE (1972) has clearly shown that mechanization has
created substantial rural unemployment and increased rural
income inequality in Latin America. He estimated that three
workers are displaced by each tractor in Chile and about
four workers in Colombia and Guatemala. Overall he estimates that "a total of approximately 2.5 million jobs have
been displaced by tractors in Latin America up to 1972". He
also points out that labour displacement by mechanization
increases with the size of the farm and that continued mechanization will have similar destructive effects on employment. Evidence from rice fields in Sri Lanka and the
Philippines also reveals an adverse effect on employment
per acre when mechanized techniques are used instead of the
traditional ones (IFTIKHAR, A. 1976; B. DUFF, 1975).

The consequences of rapid mechanization in Asia have been
well documented by GOTSCH (1973) with Pakistan as an example. He emphasised inequality induced by mechanization,
particularly where unequal land distribution prevails. He
indicated that mechanization could lead to 30% decline in
labour input. Miss KUSUM (1972) conducted a study of 130
farms in 13 villages in India and stated that mechanization
displaces human labour by 2,19%. These findings were confirmed by BILLINGS, M and ARJAN SINGH (1971) who examined
the changes in the demand for human labour with the introduction of modern technology to agriculture in the Punjab.
They stated that the aggregate of agricultural technologies
resulted in a displacement of human labour by 11.5%. Similar results were reached by BOSE & CLARK (1969) in West
PAkistan, who concluded that the direct social benefits of
tractor mechanization appear to be less than the direct

social costs. There is no straightforward method of taking
all the individual costs and benefits into account in such
an analysis, but it is apparent that if they were included,
the net benefit of mechanization to society would be signi-
ficantly negative.

In addition to the previously mentioned negative impact of
mechanization on employment, there are other potential social and economic effects. There seems to be little doubt
that the pattern of tractor ownership which has emerged during the past few decades has had adverse social consequences (A. IFTIKHAR, 1976). In Pakistan 92% of the farms
(accounting for 65% of the total farm area) own only 12% of
the tractors. Of the total area cultivated by the private
sector in 1969, 69% was on farms possessing their own tractors and 31% on custom farms, i.e. those hiring tractors
(IFTIKHAR, A, 1976, p. 90). Studies in Sri Lanka show
that tractors are not equally distributed among the different districts and that where they exist, they are owned by
a few affluent farmers, merchants and middlemen (K. IZUMI
& A.S. RANATHUNGA(1974);BILLINGS & SINGH(1970) suggested that
the distribution of tractors is likely to be skewed in favour of the larger farmers, many of whom own several machines
and at the same time are fairly well established in industry
and trade. These findings are backed up by another study
which proved that nearly half of the tractor owners are business men or planters and 14% of the rest obtained a substantial proportion of their income from non-agricultural
sources (CARR, 1973). Evidence from a survey of **tractor**
farms in the Pakistan Punjab clearly shows that following
the acquisition of tractors, the farm size increased through
land purchase. As many as 82% of tenants on farms whose owners purchased tractors were directly evicted and several
more on other farms were evicted indirectly when the tractor

farms rented more land (AHMED, B., 1972, p. 123).

Apart from the inequalities arising directly from distribution of land, income and wealth in favour of the tractor owners, the recent shortage of spare parts to foreign exchange difficulties has resulted in a squeeze on those who rent tractor service, particularly the small farmers (HARRIS, B., 1974).

The above mentioned negative results of agricultural mechanization were found to be in sharp contrast to the conclusions reached by some respected institutions and scientists. In India, for example, the National Council for Applied Research in New Delhi conducted a study in 1971 regarding the impact of agricultural mechanization, and came to the conclusion that mechanization was accompanied by more intensive and diversified farming which helped to find additional employment opportunities. The study stated that the net effect was 25% more labour input per hectare. Moreover, the introduction of machines to agriculture created more non-farm employment such as machinery production, distribution, financing, insurance, repairs and maintenance, etc., though it was not established quantitively, the significant possible effect of mechanization on output showed that it gave rise to further employment of labour directly or through a multiplier effect. The study further concluded that small farms increase family and hired labour input per hectare with mechanization. On the large farms there was a tendency to employ more permanent hired labour and less casual hired labour and family labour. These findings confirmed the conclusions of LAWERENCE, R.(1970) that the costs per unit of output decreased continuously as mechanical devices were added with an overall reduction of 50% as compared to traditional methods, and that the human labour employment per hectare on the mechanized farm remained nearly equal to the bullock operated farm.

By studying the changes in employment of farm labour under the impact of increasing use of tractors in India, Japan, North Korea, South Korea and Taiwan, HARRINGTON (1972) showed that the latter four Asian countries - more mechanized than India - use at least twice as many workers per hectare as in India. He further concluded that under-employment in rural India is a serious problem which could not be solved even by a restraint on the rate of farm mechanization. His argument was that high-yielding varieties and increased technical inputs demand more labour per hectare for land preparation, weed control, water management, insect and pest control as well as harvesting and threshing. For this reason he suggested that labour surplus countries can profitably use more farm labour with new agricultural techniques, but this desirable social goal should not be confused with unprofitable use of farm labour.

So far, conflicting conclusions have been reached regarding the effect of mechanization in displacing human labour, particularly in the densely populated countries. Such findings, however, are difficult to generalize, since they show results of studies in particular areas and in a particular time period, tracing the effects of mechanization on a defined production unit under certain socio-economic conditions. It is not mechanization as such which affects employment and productivity positively or negatively but the natural, social, economic and political context of that defined production unit.

3. HOW AGRICULTURAL MECHANIZATION CAME TO BE ADOPTED IN THE AFRICAN COUNTRIES

Before the advent of colonization and precisely up to the nineteenth century, most of the inhabitants of Subsaharan Africa were living outside the money economy. An exception to this were the cities and towns of the Savannah belt and the maritime entrepots along the East Coast. It was an agricultural economy of the household type with very limited specialization of production. Methods of production were directed by the prevailing environmental conditions and there was rarely any population pressure to force an intensification of land use. The limited volume of trade limited the output to the immediate needs of the tribe or family.

This situation was changing gradually through the impact of colonialism which created conditions conducive to raising agricultural output and commerce. The introduction of money obligations, the development of transport systems facilitated a rapid expansion of external trade that depended on a marketable surplus beyond subsistence requirements. This surplus was large enough to meet the demands of the expanding African Urban centres inhabited by the colonial administration as well as to provide for major exports such as raw materials for the expanding industries in the European countries. The return from these exports, little as it was, was necessary to finance imports needed to meet expanding demands, mostly for consumer goods, for the colonial, and some African elite classes.

To achieve an increase in agricultural production, there was a tendency to expand the cultivated area to new lands, to introduce new higher value crops and to allow for technological changes in the agricultural sector. This policy had been followed since the middle of the nineteenth century

and most notably since the first decade of the twentieth
century (YUDELMAN, 1975).

Technological changes in African agriculture, defined as
the introduction of new inputs in the production process,
are changes that took place at the farm level. The adoption
of these inputs was meant not to increase the productivity
of the African farmer but to increase profitability for the
colonizers.

Because a minimum requirement of scientists and technicians
needed for the development of a high-technology agriculture
was not locally available in the mid-nineteenth century,
nearly all the science-based technology and the needed
skilled persons were imported to Subsaharan Africa from the
European countries. Indigenous Institutions were developed
to play only a complementary role.

The first new inputs brought into Africa were introduced
spontaneously by travellers and traders coming from other
regions of the world. These first changes in agriculture
were not so much changes in techniques of production as in
the introduction of new crops (MARVIN, P.M., 1966; DE GREG-
ORI, 1969).

Initially, in the absence of direct government intervention
in agriculture, it was the missionaries and the private cor-
porations or individuals who assumed important roles in developing agriculture (OLIVER, 1972, TOTHILL, 1940). They
were responsible for the introduction and dissemination of
many important export crops in Africa such as cotton, toba-
cco and coffee to mention only a few (YUDELMAN, 1975). Moreover, they helped to spread the improved techniques of production and created some of the conditions necessary for
technological change in agriculture.

These initial contributions were later deliberately expanded by the colonial administrations which determined the
pattern of agricultural development in their respective colonized countries. They adopted a policy which placed increasing emphasis on the application of the new scientific
technology being followed in the European countries.

Although the principles of technological change and international transfer of technology tend to apply to all sectors of an economy, several aspects of this process are
peculiar to agriculture, especially with relation to trans-
fers from Europe to Africa. Transferred inputs included
what are called the reproducible and non-reproducible agricultural inputs. The former, such as seeds and animal breed-
ing stocks, are those which have inherent qualities of their
own, influenced by the physical environment and reproducing
themselves. The non-reproducible ones involve manufactured
goods associated with the level of the agricultural economy.
The transfer of the reproducible input underwent three
stages, namely: non-systematic introduction of new crops by
sailors and travellers, establishment of colonial hegemony
with the desire to develop export goods and finally, creation
of adequate research facilities within Africa to develop
local varieties, a stage which continues today. Such research
is of considerable importance since the transfer of reproducible input is faced with a number of physical constraints.

Contrary to the reproducible inputs, the non-reproducible
goods must be manufactured externally and applied mostly
without modifications to the African countries, irrespective of the physical constraints. A reason for this could be
found in the increase in trade between the agricultural and
non-agricultural regions, i.e. between the underdeveloped
and the developed countries. Such a division of labour is
vital to ensuring an open market for the articles

manufactured by extremely large-scale,capital-intensive,
high-technology industries located in the developed countries. An increasing proportion of the inputs purchased
with revenue from agricultural products must be imported.
Purely economic considerations have a bearing on the appro-
priateness of these transferred inputs.

In the high-income countries the relative scarcity of labour and the abundance of capital necessitated application of
the new technology in agriculture. By contrast, in the low-
income countries, including African countries, there was a
relative abundance of labour and scarcity of capital. Thus
the transfer of technology that is capital-absorbing and
labour-displacing was undesirable from the point of view of
increasing returns to society. In fact the colonial administration did not care much about the welfare of the African
countries. Their ultimate goal was the exploitation of available resources as quickly as possible. They forced the
African countries to fall back on capital-intensive technologies, since they had no interest in developing less sophisticated systems because of the low value of return.

The least successful attempts to foster technological change
in colonial Africa were made in the post- World War II years
by encouraging the use of machine technology, particularly
tractors, in the newly implemented agricultural schemes. The
costs of operation and maintenance of these machines rendered these schemes impracticable. Part of a reason for these
high costs was a shortage of trained and skilled domestic
personnel which had to be compensated by European immigrants
to Africa. Thus the transfer of agricultural technology was
accompanied by a transfer of skills. It was recognized that
technological change in agriculture is not a phenomenon isolated from events outside the agricultural sector. The inter-
dependence of agriculture and the other sectors, particularly

the industrial sector in Europe, and the subsequent inter-
sectoral linkages influence both costs and prices in agriculture, and thus, the adoption and spread of new inputs.
Indeed, because agricultural progress in tropical Africa
was closely linked to the development of world markets, the
major impulses for introducing technological changes in African agriculture came in response to development outside
Africa. In the metropolitan powers there were commercial
interests eager to exploit the resources of the colonies.
For example the British Cotton Growing Association (BCGA),
financed by the cotton manufacturers of Liverpool, was formed in 1902 to encourage cotton production in the hope of
finding an alternative source of supply to the southern
states of the United States. There is no doubt that this
Association assisted substantially in the founding and expanding of the cotton industry in Africa (YUDELMAN, 1975).

The trading companies were another element in the private
sector which fostered investment in agriculture and hence
technological changes in the African countries. They tried
to provide a means of resolving the dilemma of expanding
colonial hegemony while at the same time limiting governments' enterprise and extending government administrative
expenses. For this purpose what was called the chartered
company became an important vehicle which was employed in
the British, Portuguese and German colonies. From the three
British charterd companies founded in 1886, 1888, and 1889
for West, East and South Africa respectively, only one was
a financial success, namely the Royal Niger Company of West
Africa (YUDELMAN, 1975). The German chartered companies,
called the German 'Kolonialgesellschaften' were reported to
have undertaken the major task of agricultural development
between 1870 and 1915 and came to play an important role in
promoting technological changes in the German territories
in Africa (K. HAUSSEN, 1970). The first steam ploughing

engines and fertilizers were used by the German chartered companies in irrigated cotton plantations in East Africa.

By the turn of the century, the idea that the administration of the colonies was a public responsibility was gaining acceptance. In this connection there was much disagreement as to how great a role private interests should play in agricultural development, and especially over the question of large-scale European plantations versus African smallholdings.

As the notion of the Imperial responsibility developed, the public sector of the various colonial governments assumed an increasing interest in encouraging agricultural development and technical change.

But whatever the success of the colonial administrators in executing their economic plans, there was at least one great weakness in their approach, namely their failure to give adequate regard to local conditions and particularly to the African farmer. They failed to develop institutions which could produce the indigenous manpower needed to participate effectively in the management and direction of agricultural development in their respective countries. This weakness was one of the main causes of the failure and collapse of many agricultural undertakings (BALDWIN, 1957; McKELVEY, 1965).

Colonial administration policy, insofar as it relied on large-scale capital inputs, appears to have been followed by most agricultural projects initiated towards the end of the colonial era and even in the subsequent period of independence.

Although research and investigations were emphasised by most of the African governments in the post-colonial period, no attempt was made to develop African agriculture along its own lines to give more consideration to the socio-economic and agro-ecological factors involved in particular region.

Unlike the case in Latin-America and Asia, agricultural development based on mechanization has proceeded relatively slowly in Africa with little marked effect on income distribution and employment. CLAYTON (1972) suggested the dominance of communal land ownership and the small owner-occupiers as the reason, but did not touch the real cause of the negative results of agricultural production, namely the dilemma of mechanization. Like other developing countries African countries have to foster development, particularly in the agricultural sector if they are to approach the standard of living of their developed counterparts. But to achieve this they have to formulate development policies which give priority to mechanization irrespective of its negative consequences. This seems to be a rather strange situation particularly in countries where capital and foreign exchange are very scarce and where labour is plentiful and cheap, two features of most of the African countries, including our case study. The explanation of this anomaly is very complex, but obviously the scarcity of capital is not reflected in the prices that farmers are charged for agricultural inputs since these are substantially exempted from tariffs and taxes. As a result, agricultural equipment can be obtained at the official exchange rate for the price prevailing in the world market. Such subsidization of capital inputs not only distorts the price system in the economy but also tends to make labour-displacing machinery profitable even when wages are very low, and where there is a growing number of under-employed workers. But capital subsidization is not the only factor encouraging the use of modern agricultural inputs, particularly tractors, in the African countries. The sharp increase in agricultural machinery over the past few decades is closely related to the expansion of credit systems. Moreover, purchase of a machine appears to be initiated by social rather than economic factors, since there is a prestige factor in owning such a machine.

In the preceding discussions an attempt is made to show the negative results of agricultural mechanization with regard to population and income distribution.

In our case study, we attempt to reflect the repercussions of adopting agricultural mechanization in one of the African countries, the Republic of the Sudan, where agricultural mechanization determines, to a great extent, the scope and intensity of agricultural development.

IV. THE CASE STUDY: THE DEMOCRATIC REPUBLIC OF THE SUDAN

1. GENERAL NOTE

Sudan, the largest country in Africa, with a land area of about one million square miles (2.5 million km², STATIS-TISCHES BUNDESAMT, p. 16), ten times West Germany, and with population presently estimated at about 18 million, growing at a rate of 2.8% per year (STATISTISCHES BUNDESAMT, 1978, s.9)[1], is dependent very much on its agriculture. The per Capita GNP for 1978 averaged about US 290.[2] For most of the country there is no population pressure on presently develo-ped land. The density is calculated at less than 10 persons/ km² (STATISTISCHES BUNDESAMT, 1976 p. 18).

Although a large part of the country is desert or semi-desert, the Sudan nevertheless possesses great untapped po-tential for agricultural development. According to conser-vative estimates, about 120 million feddan (50 million ha) is suitable for crop production, and a further 150 million feddans (some 65 million ha) for range and forests (MINIS-TRY OF FINANCE & NATIONAL ECONOMY, 1977 p. 18). Presently, a total of about 13 million feddans (5.5 million ha) is under crop production in both the traditional and modern sectors (Table 1).

---

1) The most recent census in the Sudan was carried out in 1973. While many of the results are considered as pre-liminary, they represent the most reliable information currently available, which will be used in this study, particularly in relation to population characteristics and distribution (STATISTISCHES BUNDESAMT,1976 s.17, 1978 s.9).

2) No data are available on variations of the per Capita GNP. The country's overall estimated GNP is determined according to the per Capita GNP in the relatively deve-loped east-central part of the country where it is un-questionably higher than in the other parts of the cou-ntry (STATISTISCHES BUNDESAMT, 1978 s.26).

Table 4.1   Area under Different Crops in Both Traditional
            and Modern Agricultural Sub-sectors (1974/75 in
            Feddan)

Crops	Traditional sector	Modern sector	Total
Cotton	70,000	1,100,000	1,170,000
Rice	-	12,000	12,000
Maize	10,000	17,000	27,000
Sugar Cane	-	35,000	35,000
Sesame	2,040,000	830,000	2,870,000
Groundnuts	1,330,000	310,000	1,640,000
Rizinus	7,000	30,000	37,000
Wheat	34,000	427,000	461,000
Dukhun (Millet)	2,507,000	33,000	2,540,000
Pulses	35,000	-	35,000
Dura (Sorghum)	870,000	3,230,000	4,100,000
Vegetables	37,000	110,000	147,000
Total	6,940,000	6,134,000	13,074,000

Source: Yearbook of agriculture, Ministry of Agriculture,
        Food and Natural Resources, Kh. Sudan, 1977, p.19.

The country has been able to develop the largest irrigation
system in all tropical Africa, thanks to the availability
of surface water from the Nile and its tributaries. It is
argued that it is not so much the availability of land as
the availability of water that determines the extent and
intensity of agricultural development. The area under rainfed cultivation rose from about 6 million feddan in 1969/
70 to about 12 million feddan (100%) in 1974/75, whereas
the area under gravity and artificial irrigation from about

1.5 million to about 2.5 million feddan in the same period
(MINISTRY OF AGRICULTURE, FOOD & NATURAL RESOURCES, 1975,
p. 21).

The importance of the agricultural sector lies not only in
the sheer significance of its size in terms of its contribution to the GNP but also in its importance to the labour
force engaged in it. It contributes about 40% of the GNP,
90% of exports and 50% of Government revenues. It provides
the livelihood for about 85% of the population. From all
the arable lands only 13% are presently being utilized
(KISS, T. 1977, p.8). This means that the great potential
resources are not fully exploited. The amount and distribution of rainfall, the presence of underground water and
the possible increase in the Sudan's irrigation water from
the Nile and its tributaries all speak in favour of an extension of cultivated lands both in rainfed and irrigated
areas.[3] Apart from the availability of potential water reserves, the climatic conditions are favourable for a great
number of agricultural products for which a world demand is
continuously increasing. The agricultural sector is not only
capable of supplying crops for internal and external demand,
but also in contributing to the supply of animal products,
most needed by the majority of the developing countries. In
this respect the Sudan is regarded as the richest African
country in animal wealth.[4] The World Food conference 1974
stated that the Sudan alone is potentially capable of supplying about 40% of world food demand (AFRICAN DEVELOPMENT,

---

3) For the most part of the arable alnd, there is enough
   rainfall for rainfed agriculture, and huge reserves of
   underground water estimated to be about 12% of all the
   African water resources (KISS, 1977, s.24).

4) According to Fao estimates, there are about 16 million
   head of animals in the Sudan in 1977, and this amounts
   to 10% of the whole African animal wealth (FAO, 1977,
   p. 197).

1975, No.1, p. 12).

In view of the above discussion, development in the country is likely to be primarily dependent upon development in the agricultural sector. Deviation from the present export-oriented production policy in view of the planners and policy makers is not expected, at least in the foreseeable ˉ future, mainly because of the lower cost of production relative to prospective world prices and because of the present limitations of the domestic market.

An overall examination of Sudan's agricultural development reveals a marked dualism in the form of traditional sub-sector practising traditional crop production and livestock -raising characterized by low income and primitive production techniques on the one hand and a modern sub-sector practising crop production in irrigated and rain-fed mechanized agriculture characterized by relatively high income and modern production techniques on the other. About 30% of all culti-vated land is in the modern sub-sector (see Table 4.1).

The spatial distribution of these two sub-sectors turns on the question of agro-ecological and socio-economic constraints. Unequal distribution of rainfall, quality of soils, surface and underground water defines the limits of agricultural development in the different regions of the country. Accordingly, pastoral nomadism and shifting cultivation have been practised over much of the country as a sort of natural adjustment to the environmental conditions. In the Southern Sudan the main physical constraints lie in the quality of soil rather than in the amount of rainfall. A combination of all factors needed for agricultural developments are present only in limited areas. The central clay plain of the Sudan with its adequate surface and under ground water as well as good quality soil is argued to be the most favourable region for agricultural production. Thus it is not surprising to find that nearly all the major agricultural schemes are concentrated in this region, particularly in the present Gezira, Blue Nile (previously one province), Kassala and Southern Kordofan provinces.

Apart from these physical constraints, the regional development disparity is argued to be an effect of socio-cultural factors. The stagnation of agricultural development in the souhtern region is not only due to physical constraint but also the result of the Civil War started on the eve of independence which continued undisturbed for almost two decades. The causes of this war may be readily found in the ambition of the colonial administration to separate the southern from the northern part of the country with the argument that the two are culturally different.

The concentration of the modern economic sector (agricultural modern sub-sector, industrial sector and the most important infrastructure) in the North-East Sudan is a matter of both agro-ecological and socio-economic factors, an assessment of which would take the author beyond the scope of this study. All we need in this context is to trace back the development and expansion of the modern agricultural sub-sector as a field where agricultural mechanization has been used. Such a background is vital in shedding light on the scope and intensity of agricultural mechanization in the past and present whereby a prospect for future development may be assumed. By so doing it may be possible to reflect the probable effect of increased agricultural mechanization on the mobility of the Sudan's population with its expected repercussions.

2. ADOPTION AND DEVELOPMENT OF AGRICULTURAL MECHANIZATION
   IN THE SUDAN

2.1 Mechanization as a Means to Develop Irrigated Agricul-
    ture in the Sudan

Like many parts of Africa, it is thought that the supply of
irrigation water is the most important asset to the economic development of the Sudan. In climatic conditions such
as those prevailing in the Sudan with fluctuating rainfall -
particularly in the central clay plain, where other factors
are argued to be in favour of large agricultural schemes -
provision of irrigation water becomes an essential requis-
ite to better economic development. This statement has been
stressed by LEWIS as part of his consideration of a policy
of capital investment in African agriculture (LEWIS, 1964).
Hence the attempt to utilize the surface or underground
water for irrigation purposes in the Sudan seems to be justified.

In the Sudan, five main methods of irrigation can be distinguished: traditional water lifting devices using animal
and/or human power (Sagias and Shadufs), basin irrigation
and flush irrigation making use of the natural flow of
water; systematic irrigation by diesel pumps from river or
underground water, and finally systematic irrigation by gravity systems.

Although the traditional irrigation systems had been known
in the Sudan many centuries ago, it was only in the second
quarter of this century that modern irrigated agriculture
became possible on a commercial scale.[5] This modern

---

5) The possibility of a large-scale cotton cultivation had
   been realized as early as 1839 and the idea was toyed
   with throughout the nineteenth century (T. BARNETT,
   1977, p. 4)

irrigation system, centred around mechanization, is of more
relevance to our theme of study than the traditional irrigation system centred around animal and human power.

The first real move in the direction of developing large-
scale cultivation came in 1904 at Zeidab, when an American
company was granted a concession to experiment and grow
cotton (BARNETT, 1977, p. 4). The success of experimentation
in this area and parts of the Gezira particularly in 'Haj
Abdalla' motivated the British administration to plan for
irrigated agriculture in the Sudan with a primary intention
to raise revenue to meet the expenses incurred in the operation of the newly established government machinery including its services. The idea was not immediately realized
because the British government was unwilling to finance the
enormous irrigation works recommended by the British administration in the Sudan. It was only under pressure from the
Lancashire cotton industry, represented by the British
Cotton Growing Assoaciation that the idea of growing cotton
on a large scale was passed by the British government in
1913 BARNETT, 1977). This action coincided with the failure of the American and Egyptian crops of 1909, that brought
home to Lancashire spinners the peril of relying on only
two countries, especially for the longer and finer cotton
(GAITSKELL, 1959, p. 54).[6]

---

6) As early as 1904 there was considerable anxiety in Lancashire about overseas competition. This was only sympt-
omatic of a general trend. Whereas Lancashire had in the
past had a virtual monopoly of textile manufacture, in
the latter decades of the nineteenth century its position had been increasingly threatened from the United
States, Germany and even China. This competition resulted gradually in its being pushed into the finer end of
the market and in the process into greater dependence
on the fine long staple cotton produced in Egypt. But
the oppression of the 'Fellah' was so great that people
left the land and consequently cotton fields were drop-
ping. This coincided with the time when demand for fine
cotton was increasing, an incidence that made the position of the Lancashire cotton industry more precarious
(BARNETT, 1977, p. 5).

But this explanation should not obscure the fact that there was a strategic factor in the question of establishing large irrigation works in the Sudan. The fact that the British government required an imperial grand strategy was argued to be a reason that initially motivated the British government to control the Sudan and reconquer it in 1898.[7]

In all, it was a combination of this imperial strategy, the crisis in the British textile industry, the increasing world demand for good quality yarn and the favourable natural conditions that convinced the British parliament to allow for the construction of Sennar Dam some 350 km. south of Khartoum. Construction works were interrupted by the outbreak of World War I, and it was only in 1925 that dam construction and canalization were completed. Duly, the Gezira scheme, the largest and most significant agricultural undertaking got under way to start gravity irrigation on a large scale in the Sudan.[8] This gigantic irrigated scheme is regarded as the most remarkable example of development achieved by combining the entrepreneurial spirit of private enterprise with the paternalistic spirit of colonial government[9]. For the Sudan the scheme was regarded as a model of agricultural development to be followed in all the schemes.

---

7) The Sudan was of utmost importance to the strategy of the British Empire. It formed an important link in the vision of a stretch of red on the map from the Cape to Cairo. Most importantly, it was an area which was essential to safeguarding the Suez Canal and the route to India (BARNETT, 1977, p. 4).

8) The history of the Gezira scheme and its development has been described in some considerable detail elsewhere (GAITSKELL, 1959, ABDAL RAHIM, 1968 and BARNETT, 1977, to mention a few.)

By 1950, when the Sudan Plantation Syndicate was replaced
by the Sudan Gezira Board (a government corporation) the
total area under irrigation was already over one million
feddans (about 1/2 million ha), which reached nearly 2 million feddans by 1958 when the Managil Extension was completed (REPUBLIC OF THE SUDAN, SUDAN GEZIRA BOARD, 1963, p.14).[10]

It is to be mentioned at this juncture that the relative
success arising from this gigantic scheme at that time was
the main stimulus for applying the same experience in the
agricultural schemes that followed, particularly in the
privately-owned pump schemes.

This group of schemes was started parallel to the Gezira
schemes since the first decade of this century. They were
concentrated at first along the banks of the Nile in the
Northern province and later came to dot the banks of the
White Nile due to the erection of the Jebel Aulia Dam in
1937 (SUDAN COTTON GROWERS ASSOCIATION, 1964). The increase
in cotton production and proceeds in the Gezira scheme stimulated the private capital to venture into pump-irrigated

---

9) The creation of the Gezira scheme under the management
   of the British commercial companies (the Sudan Plantation Syndicate, SPS) and later also the Kassala Cotton
   Company (KCC) with the aid of a large loan guaranteed by
   the British Government, as having been a fortunate coincidence (GAITSKELL, 1959, p.53).

10) By this stadium the number of tenants rose to 96,000
    with an additional 1 million seasonal workers who parti-
    cipate yearly in the production of the cotton crop.
    Nearly half of the seasonal workers have to be recruited
    every season from other provinces, a feature of all other
    agricultural schemes (ILO, 1976, p. 256, NEUE ZÜRCHER
    ZEIT. 1977) This will be elaborated in relation to popu-
    lation mobility.

cotton production with great vigour, a 'white gold' rush.[11]
Accordingly their production rose from only 10% in the early
post World War II period to 30-40% of the whole cotton production of the Sudan by the mid-fifties. The number of pump
schemes increased fron 893 in 1952 to 2,468 in 1960, of which
a number of 1,227 (49.7%) were concentrated in only one province, Blue Nile (DAVIES, 1966, p. 199).[12] According to the
agricultural census of 1963 the area cultivated by some
2,283 pump schemes was 1.29 million feddans mainly concentrated in the Blue Nile and Northern provinces. They provided
a livelihood for some 97,000 tenants and their families.
Unlike the case in the Gezira the schemes were owned and operated by one or more investors whose main residence was in
Khartoum or other big town. He provided the mechanical equipment, land and water. This investment branch was the most
attractive field of private capital up to 1958 (WYNN, 1971,
p. 557). Cooperative schemes were extremely rare, only 9%
of the whole pump schemes up to the mid-sixties (BARDELEBEN,
1968, p. 33; THORNTON, 1964, p. 289).

By 1968, however, the Agricultural Reform Corporation was
formed to take over control and administration of the private pump schemes with the following objectives:

---

11) Between 1935 and 1955 cotton production in the Gezira
    scheme rose by 70% mainly because of mechanization and
    disease control. The proceeds increased 800 % because of the rise
    in the world price of cotton brought about by the Kor-
    ean War in 1950 (SHAKAK, K.I., 1977, p. 106).

12) HERZOG (1961, p. 54) stated that the total number of
    the pump schemes in the Sudan had already reached
    2,766 by 1959, (quoted after ÖSTERDIEKHOFF, 1980, p.302).

The second of these schemes is El Suki scheme executed in 1971/ 72 to commence an area of 90,000 feddans.[14] The third and the most recently implemented one is El Rahad scheme with a target area of 800.000 feddans. The first stage was expected to be completed by 1980/81 to cover an

---

13) (CONTD.) According to the investigation of the Hydrological Department in 1953, a narrow rocky gorge near Khashm el Girba was recommended as an excellent dam site. The first preliminary studies on the soil and configuration were carried out in 1954 which estimated the potentialities of the scheme area. But, according to political and economic reasons, the scheme execution was delayed till 1964, when it was thought necessary for the resettlement of the Halfaui people, being displaced by the construction of the King Dam, a coincidence which left its marks on the scheme development (EL MANGOURI, 1978; G. HEINRITZ, 1978).

14) The scheme was planned to make use of the Nile water gained due to the construction of the Roseires Dam (1966). The scheme was meant as a trial for a possible future improvement of the dominant land tenure system and water rates practised in the Gezira. New land tenure and water rates have to be tried in this to inject more incentives for increasing productivity and to be tested for further possible application in the prospective development schemes. It was also meant to test the use of electric pumps on a large scale and full mechanization of production. It produces cotton and ground nuts at 100% intensity and is supposed to offer a living for the semi-nomadic people of the area between the Blue Nile and the River Dinder. The trial to resettle part of Red Sea nomads in this scheme proved to be a failure (ABDEL SALAM, 1976, p. 47).

- to undertake necessary steps to improve management

- to try methods to reduce production costs

- to plan and supervise the execution of a production policy drawn on commercial bases

- to ensure flexibility. effectiveness and commercial soundness of these schemes

To fulfil these objectives an area of about 700,000 feddans of irrigated cotton and dura was put under its supervision and administration (OESTERDIECKHOFF, 1980, p. 302). Recently an attempt was made to reorganize the different schemes with the view of modernizing them, as part of the rehabilitation programme for all public schemes.

Apart from the development in the Gezira scheme and the privately owned pump schemes the area under irrigated agriculture has been extended by other relatively recent irrigated schemes.

The Sudan's socio-economic plans in the post-independence period emphasised the horizontal expansion of the irrigated areas as a means to increase the country's revenue by providing exportable crops, particularly cotton and oil, seeds, and substitute for imported foodstuffs particularly wheat and sugar. To achieve these objectives it was planned to implement new irrigated schemes the first of which was the Khashm el Girba scheme (presently New Halfa scheme) inaugurated in 1964 to cover an area of some 200,000 ha including a sugar plantation.[13]

---

13) This is a gravity irrigated scheme which makes use of the dam constructed on Atbara River at Khashm el Girba town. In fact the idea to construct a dam to utilize this most northerly tributary of the main Nile goes back to the 1940's (MINISTRY OF IRRIGATION,1955).
(CONTD.

area of some 300,000 feddans.[15]

So far, a brief review was made to show the historical development and the process of expansion in the irrigated
schemes of the modern agricultural sub-sector of the Sudan.
Due to the continuous expansion of the irrigated areas it
is hard to present accurate data on the actual area cultivated. Some authorities estimate the area under artificial
irrigation up to 1979 to be about 4 million feddan (ÖSTER-
DIEKELTOFF, 1980, p. 271). This reflects an enormous expansion of the irrigated sub-sector in a very limited time.[16]
Reasons for this expansion was the pos-
sibility of extending the gravity irrigation system which
allows for the irrigation of more land. The increase in
world demand for cotton and oil seeds was the main stimulus
to convert these lands to irrigated schemes to produce mainly for the external market, a policy which will be critically

---

15) The idea of utilizing the area East of El Rahad River
    goes back to 1963 when it was thought to make use of
    the river's flood for irrigation purposes. The inves-
    tigation of that year proved the possibility of having
    a perennial irrigation by means of a canal to be con-
    structed from the Blue Nile. According to the pre-
    investment study of 1964-65 the potential development
    area was estimated to one million feddans. The first
    proposal was to construct a canal commencing at the
    Roseires reservoir to permit gravity irrigation for the
    Rahad stage 1 of 410,000 feddans. After a further con-
    sideration a modified scheme was put forawrd with a re-
    duced area of 300,000 feddans and the idea of the grav-
    ity irrigation was replaced by a shorter supply canal
    which involved pumping from the Blue Nile (MINISTRY OF
    CULTURE AND INFORMATION, 1977). For more details see
    G. HEINRITZ, 1980.

16) In 1956, when the Sudan became an independent country,
    the area under artificial irrigation was 0.7 million
    feddan only (ÖSTERDIEKHOFF, 1980, p. 272).

discussed in the chapters to come. It is worth mentioning
here, that the area under irrigation will be further expanded, and at present there are a number of schemes under
implementation: the Rahad stage II with a planned area to
500,000 feddans, four public sugar plantations of 222,000
feddans, Settet/ Upper Atbara scheme with 600,000 feddans,
Kenana scheme with 300,000 feddans, Kenaf plantation with
30,000 feddans and an extension of the pump-irrigated
scheme of about 380,000 feddans. Thus by the completion of
these schemes in 1990, as projected, the total area under
irrigated agriculture will rise to about 5.5 million feddans
(ÖSTERDIECKHOFF,1980, p. 273). It remains to give a brief
review of the second part of the modern agricultural sub-
sector namely the rainfed mechanized agriculture.

2.2 Mechanization as a Means to Develop Rainfed Agriculture

In the foregoing discussions a brief historical background
is made to the development in irrigated agriculture which
produces mainly export commodities particularly cotton and
oil seeds. The increase in the production of the export-
oriented crops was accompanied by a considerable rise in
agricultural earnings, an incentive which stimulates people
to participate in agricultural production, particularly
food production. As the UN noted, methods of food production
though essentially stationary, have changed somewhat. The
expansion of irrigated and rainfed cultivation of food-
crops involves improvement in methods and labour productivity, with the result that mechanization of rainfed cultivation has reached a commercial stage (UN, 1958, p. 178).

Like the case in the mechanized irrigated agriculture, the
rainfed mechanized agriculture has been developed steadily
but faster. It is concentrated in the area named the 'Granary of the Sudan, lying roughly between isohytes 450-800mm

(AGABAWI, 1968, p. 71). According to conservative estimations with the suitable for mechanical cultivation is about 60 million feddan mostly to be developed to produce rainfed sorghum, dura, millet (dukhun), sesame and groundnuts. These potentialities have been developed in 3 stages (M.M. ABDEL SALEM, 1976,p.53)

The first stage: prior to 1953

The second stage: 1953 - 1968

The third stage: Mechanized Farming Corporation

The first stage:

Before the opening of the railway line Sennar via Gedarif in 1929, Durah production in rainfed areas was opposed on grounds that transporting the product was too difficult. But the real stimulus for the production of grains in rainfed areas was during and immediately after World War II, when the shortage of grain and the oil seeds had drawn attention to the Gedarif area. Production was started using manual labour with the objective of creating employment opportunities for the idle labour force concentrated in Khartoum. But this employment policy had to be modified by the year 1943 when the Sudan received a proposal from the Middle East Supply Corporation (MESC) to produce sesame on a large scale using mechanical methods to ease the world's shortage of oil seeds. This proposal was rejected on the ground that sesame production requires, by nature of its shattering varieties, speed to harvest for which the needed labour force was not available in the area and was not an easy task to recruit them from elsewhere under the prevailing transport conditions. As a compromise to this proposal the government decided to mechanize the durah production in the belief that the introduction of the mechanical equipment would not only increase the durah output but also free labour

for cultivation of high value products such as oil seeds.[17]
Accordingly, a preliminary work was carried out in 1945
with an area of 350,000 feddans at 'Gadmbalia' near 'Gedarif'
and the required machinery, mostly heavy wheeled tractors,
were imported prior to attesting as to its suitability to
the environment of the Sudan (HABASHI, 1968). The venture
proved to be a failure because the machinery chosen was not
that suitable one for the environmental conditions of the
Sudan. Moreover, the tenants lacked the experience in prop-
er husbandry and farm management techniques. Unlike the
case in the irrigated cotton production, research and experimentation in economic, engineering and agronomic aspects
were lacking. To achieve better results, the government took
a step in 1947 to raise the status of the farmer to full-
fledged partner on a crop-sharing system and to introduce
cotton as a cash crop in 1952. Both attempts failed to rectify the situation.[18]

The change of machinery in 1950 from the old inadequate
tracklaying and heavy-wheeled tractors to improved farm
tractors and wide level discs had special significance in
outlying a new phase in agricultural mechanization in the
Sudan. Administratively, the control of machinery was then
vested in the hands of the Agricultural Machinery Department (AMD) at Wad el Huri. This department hired machinery

---

17) In fact the need for agricultural mechanization has
long been recognized in view of the great abundance of
flat and fertile land in relation to the labour available for tilling the soil (R.G. LAING, 1953, p. 2).

18) It was intended to group the tenants and their families
in new villages connected with roads and supplied with
domestic water. But the big size of the plots to be
worked by the tenant and his family reduced their participation in carrying out the needed farm work and increased their dependence on hired labour, a typical behaviour of the semi-nomadic people (see AGABAWI, 1968).

to the Chief Engineer of the Ministry of Agriculture.[19]

By 1954 there was a need for a reappraisal of rainfed mechanized agricultural policy. Accordingly, a working party was set up which recommended that more suitable sites with more reliable rainfall should be investigated and that the role of the government should be limited to the provision of infrastructure (improved roads, more domestic water supplies, research, marketing, credit, etc.) leaving the scheme operation to private enterprise. This was the first step to encourage the private investors to participate in the mechanized rainfed agriculture. They were expected to purchase and maintain their own mechanical equipments. Thus land and capital were made available to individuals and cooperatives with the consequence of rising acreage as shown in Table 4.2.

---

19) Parallel to this was the establishment of 'Tozi' (later Abu-Naama) Research station, a landmark in the development of the mechanized rainfed agriculture in the Sudan. Part of this objective was to carry out the necessary investigation and experiments to promote production and to increase efficiency in machine works by means of training centre which offered a two month training course in tractor driving and maintenance.

Table 4.2: Acreage under Mechanized crop production in
           Kassala prov. for the period 1945/46 - 1959/60

Season	Surveyed and demarcated	Area cultivated in feddan
1945/46	---	12.000
46/47	---	21.000
47/48	---	3.000
48/49	---	8.000
49/50	---	6.000
50/51	---	31.000
51/52	---	20.000
52/53	---	19.000
53/54	---	12.000
54/55	---	5.000
55/56	412.000	56.000
56/57	412.000	200.000
57/58	712.000	500.000
58/59	712.000	700.000
59/60	1.212.000	1.200.000

Source: Ministry of Agriculture, Food & Natural resources,
        Khartoum in M. M. ABDELSALAM (1976, p. 54)

The second stage: 1953 - 1968

To put the recommendation of the working party into
effective use, many authorities were involved in selecting,
surveying, demarcating and registering land previously under traditional use. A Land Allotment Board was authorized
to allocate lands in areas suitable for rainfed mechanized
farming to individuals up to 1.000 feddans. National Cooperative Societies and registered companies were allowed
to be allotted up to 5.000 feddans and in specified areas
even more. Smaller units of 100 feddans were to be allotted

to small farmers. A nominal rate of 1 piaster (2.8 c. US, 1968) per feddan and year was charged to prevent users claiming ownership. The land was leased for 8 years renew-able. [20] To assist financing the equipment a gevernment-owned Agricultural Bank was created to grant credits at 6 % annual interest. [21] Consequently the private sector became enthusiastic for investing in this particular sub-sector of agriculture, despite the fact that the govern-ment Mechanized Farms of 1940's and 1950's were proved to be a failure (SHAZALI, 1966). Accordingly, the area under mechanized farming was expanded to include provinces other than Kassala, most notably Blue Nile and Kordofan provinces, where the agro-ecological conditions were in favour of such an investment (see map 1).

The trend of expansion in mechanized rainfed agriculture, started in the early fifties, was enhanced in the Ten year plan of Economic and Social Development (1961/62 - 1970/71) which laid much emphasis on producing more agricultural crops particularly American cotton for ex-port and durah for domestic use and export. [22]

---

20) Main criterion being Sudanese national, possessing the necessary capital, knowledge, experience, phy-sical ability and time. A tractor possession or the ability to possess it was a prerequisite to partici-pate in this enterprise. A bank guarantee of 2.000 (approx. US $ 6.000, 1968) should be obtained by those who did not posses agricultural equipments (AGABAWI, 1968).

21) This credit system was stopped because some of the farmers were unable to pay back the debt.

22) The plan aimed at opening up an additional new area of 0.5 million feddan in Gedarif area and 0.3 million feddans in Nuba mountains. After detailed soil study, the planned area was reduced to 0.6 feddan in the two areas to be cultivated on a three course rotat-ion, cotton, durah and sesame and fallow (The Ten Years Plan).

This policy was expected to increase the area under mechanized durah production from 998,000 feddans to 1,219,000 feddans and the productivity from 440,000 tons to 668,000 tons by the end of the plan period (The Ten Year Plan, p. 94). The table below presents the actual area under rainfed mechanized farming along the plan period.

Table 4.3.: <u>Acreage Under Rainfed Mechanized Farming (in 000 feddans) 1960/61 - 1968/69</u>

Season	Sorghum	Sesame	Cotton	Total
1960/61	625.7	50.6	20.4	696.7
61/62	874.3	137.3	28.3	1.039.9
62/63	700.0	75.3	33.0	808.3
63/64	765.6	151.8	18.6	939.0
64/65	941.7	90.0	18.4	1.051.1
65/66	892.7	71.9	21.8	986.4
66/67	1.146.7	218.7	30.2	1.395.4
67/68	1.634.4	321.5	36.6	1.992.5
68/69	676.3	298.5	34.6	1.009.4

Source: Mechanized Farming Corporation, Ministry od Agriculture, Food and Natural Resources, in M. M. ABDELSALAM (1976, p. 56)

The third stage: 1969/70 onwards.

By 1969 the mechanized farming corporation (MFC) was formed with the responsibility to prepare land for mechanical farming, survey and demarcate farms on a sound agricultural basis, direct tenants to adopt sound agricultural production techniques, grant necessary loans subject to certain prescribed terms and to market the crop produced. In the mechanized crop production schemes (MCPS), the corporation was authorized to allocate land to private investors and cooperatives who then clear the land and provide their own equipment, sometimes with credit from the Agricultural Bank. The total area under the MCPS was some 2.6 million feddans.

Another responsibility of the corporation was to represent the government by the supervision and the managment of the Mechanized Farming Projects (MFP), a private sector under the supervision of the state. For this group of farms which cover an area of about 400,000 feddans the corporation was responsible to provide some services (credit and machinery), clear the land and supervise farming. [23] Besides, the corporation undertakes the full operation of the state mechanized farm (SMF) which covers an area of 320,000 feddans. [24]
(see Table 4.4.)

Table 4.4.: Acreage under Rainfed Mechanized Farming (in 000 feddans) MCPS + MFCS, 1969/70 - 1974/75

Season	Sorghum	Sesame	Cotton	Total
1969/70	1.243.5	321.9	63.6	1.629.0
70/71	1.680.1	282.1	20.8	1.983.0
71/72	2.013.7	325.7	----	-------
72/73	1.746.1	513.6	22.6	2.282.2
73/74	2.421.8	730.4	34.2	3.186.4
74/75	1.488.8	571.1	28.6	2.098.4

Source: Mechanized Farming Corporation, Ministry of Agriculture, Food and Natural Resources, in M. M. ABDELSALAM (1976, p. 56).

23) The Corporation makes available the needed equipment through credits mainly from international organizations and institutions such as International Bank for Reconstruction and Development (IBRD), International Development Association (IDA) and Kuwait Development Funds (KDF).

24) The purposes of the SMF was to stabilize prices through equating supply and demand, demonstrate the use of modern technology in rainfed agriculture and to produce surplus for export.

As it could be seen from this table sorghum production
covers most of the cultivated area and the total area was
steadily increasing. Detailed data about the development of the rainfed mechanized agriculture in the last
five years was not available at the time of data collection for this study. But in the revised Five Years Plan
ending 1977, an area of some 2.8 million feddan was expected to be surveyed and demarcated (The Five Year Plan).

In the Six Year Plan 1977/78 - 1982/83 funds in the public
sector should be provided to strengthen the state mechanized farms as well as to assist in rehabilitation of some
private mechanized schemes that have deteriorated in productivity. Major development in this sector would, however,
come through the semi-private investment to be made in
the framework of the Arab Authority Programme in the Sudan.
The new projects include the development of about 6 million
feddans under mechanized farming in southern Kordofan,
Southern Darfur, and Blue Nile. An additional 0.5 million
feddan would be brought under mechanized farming in the
southern region. In the prospect of the Arab Authority
Programme, however, the area under mechanized rainfed
agriculture would be extendet to some 30 million feddans
by the year 2000 (The Six Year Plan, 1977 a). Thus, the
same as in the irrigated agriculture, mechanized rainfed
agriculture has been horizontally extended, a feature of
the whole modern agricultural sub-sector. The present availability of large potentials of cultivable lands divert
the attention from practising vertical expansion of
production. Paradoxically, this horizontal expansion is
taking place at a quick pace despite the fact that no
evidence of increase in productivity of the mechanized
durah cultivation is registered. On the contrary, the
tendency is even for a declining productivity per

feddan. It was registered that the average output in 1971/72
was 0.34 tons/feddan in the mechanized crop production
scheme, while for the whole country the average productivity was 0.46 tons/feddan in the same year. Extension in
marginal and semi-marginal lands together with rising
costs of production, would even make the situation more
difficult for a viable mechanized rainland agriculture
(M. M. ABDELSALAM, 1976, p. 58)

So far the different stages of the mechanized rainfed agriculture have been generally discussed as part of the development strategy of the whole agricultural modern sub-sector.
This review is relevant to our case study in the way that
it reflects extent and intensity of agricultural mechanization in the Sudan, since this sub-sector, unlike the
traditional sub-sector, is centred around mechanization.
Of crucial importance to our case study is the unequal spatial distribution of the mechanized rainfed schemes among
the different regions of the Sudan, a sign of polarization
to be considered in the last chapter. As shown in Table
4.5. the mechanized rainfed schemes are concentrated in
the provinces of central Sudan particularly Kassala, Blue
Nile, Kordofan and recently Southern Darfur.

Table 4.5.: Area under Mechanized Production in different
Provinces According to Official Information
(in 000 feddans) 1978

Prov.	Private Schemes	Companies	MFC Schemes	State Farm	Total
Kassala	1.352	.55	.770	.72	2.249
Blue Nile	1.411	.55	----	200	1.666
S. Kordofan	.286	---	.243	30	.559
Upper Nile	.500	---	----	30	.530
White Nile	.110	---	----	---	.110
S. Darfur	.40	---	----	70	.110
Total					5.224

Source: Mechanized Farming Corporation, Khartoum, in:
ØSTERDIECKHOFF, P. (1980, p. 330)

It is obvious that this agricultural sub-sector is un-
equally distributed among the different regions of the
Sudan. Some of the reasons were already given in terms
of the prevailing agro-ecological conditions. But the
policy of adopting mechanized farming in the Sudan, is
part of the whole economic development policy which
stresses modernization and increase in production in certain regions rather than others irrespective of the side
effects which may result.

In the following chapter we attempt to reflect the effect
of such a policy on population mobility and how this
works to intensify the prevailing regional and sectoral
disparity.

V. AGRICULTURAL MECHANIZATION AS A FACTOR OF POPULATION MOBILITY

1. GENERAL REMARKS

In this chapter an attempt is made to show the direct role played by agricultural mechanization in mobilizing some groups of people. Although many factors bear upon the manpower and employment situation in the Sudan, mechanization of agriculture is known to have both direct and indirect effects on manpower needs and employment opportunities. By definition, mechanization is the replacement of human labour by machines. The introduction of new agricultural techniques, new crops and livestock varieties as well as new cultural practices such as intensification, diversification, specialization and increasing dependency on a market-oriented production system are factors affecting employment in agriculture positively or negatively, and hence inducing population mobility. Nevertheless, the effect of agricultural mechanization on population mobility cannot be treated in isolation from other factors external to the agricultural sector. Rapid urbanization, industrial development, educational and national planning are related factors which stimulate intra- and interregional population circulation. We attempt in this particular chapter to disclose the relationship between these factors and agricultural mechanization as causes of population mobility in the Sudan.

The Sudan, as previously mentioned, has reached a substantial

degree of partial mechanization in agriculture.[1] This provides an extremely valuable situation and a somewhat rare
opportunity to study the effects of agricultural mechanization on population mobility at this stage of development.

The traditional interests in unskilled labour movements
present a somewhat restricted view of the whole mobility
process. Thus it must be supplemented by analysis of some
other short-term circulatory movements which are directly
caused by agricultural mechanization. The movement of skilled labour such as tractor drivers and mechanics is found
to be undifferentiated in the two census enumerations,
though they have become, particularly recently, a feature
of Sudanese population mobility. Accordingly, we attempt to
reflect its magnitude, analyse and explain its demographic
and socio-economic selectivity. This is only possible
through an empirical study at a micro-level, i.e. at the
level of the individual and the small group, since population censuses do not provide information concerning the
characteristics and behaviour of individuals. Hence we attempt to bring together the closely related elements of modernization through agricultural development by considering
the implication of mechanization for the manpower as reflected in the patterns of movement generated. Focus is therefore

---

1) Partial mechanization is a relative term to full mechanization both used to describe the level of machine involvement in various phases of farm production operations.
   In full mechanization a relatively large amount of the
   total work is carried out by machines. But full substitution of human and animal energy by the machine does not
   exist even in the highly developed countries. Thus the
   term partial mechanization is currently used to describe
   the stage of farm mechanization in the Sudan, where tractor performance is restricted to only a few operations,
   such as land preparation, seeding, weeding, pest control,
   and, recently, harvesting of some crops. Both scarcity of
   capital and abundance of labour force have reduced the
   use of fully equipped machines which perform all the
   needed agricultural operations.

placed upon a single category of migrants - the skilled
labour minority - who form a small group within the circulating sector of the population but which is considered to
carry significant socio-economic and political weight in
the development of the Sudan.

2. MECHANIZATION AS A QUALIFYING FACTOR

Although movements associated with qualification represent
only a numerically small segment within the context of the
Sudanese population movements, it is argued to be the most
important one. Its importance lies in the qualitative composition of this particular group of people.

Since the early years of independence the agricultural mechanization assumed a position of considerable importance as
a symbol of progress and institutional position of societal
advance. The central government adopted overall responsibility for the expansion and development of agricultural development (Chapter IV): In formulating national policy,
mechanization was regarded as an integral part of development planning (The Ten Year Plan, 1960; the Five Year Plan,
1970; and the Six Year Plan, 1977). The demand for skilled
manpower to operate and maintain the machines and mechanical equipment, made it necessary to establish training centres and workshops attached to each agricultural scheme. The
spatial distribution of the functional points to locations
of modern agricultural sub-sector formed an important element in creating qualification opportunities to satisfy
widespread popular demand and to fulfil the needs of hitherto under-provided areas. But despite the increase of qualification opportunities across the area under mechanized agriculture, it remains both a sex and a socio-economic selective process. Joining the functional location to mechanization

is a factor of a socio-economic status of an individual,
since the available vacancies fall far short of being able
to serve the potential number willing to be trained in
mechanical works, particularly among the school-leavers.[2]
Applicants from different locations with different characteristics and motivations have to compete for a limited
number of jobs as assistant driver or assistant mechanic in
a particular workshop. Generally, it may be suggested that
proximity to a functional location of mechanization stimulates young male people to apply for a job in it but the
selection is a question of economic and social constraints.
Social relations are highly decisive in the selection methods, thus those who had relatives or friends as references
in the same workshop have better chances than those without
relation. In this sense joining a functional location of
mechanization offers a continuation of the previous social
structure so that some social groups remain cohesive despite their spatial displacement. They set up the familiar
pattern of a chain mobility flow, where each participation
event leads to another after a time-lag in which information is sent back by a pre-migrant to a potential migrant
still living in the home area. Thus it is expected that
some groups are deprived of making use of the new opportunities - only because they have no relations in these
functional locations - and remain unrepresented among the
skilled labour of agricultural mechanization.

---

2) In a developing country like the Sudan, with an inbal-
anced formal education system which offers opportunities for only a limited number of persons to attain
higher education, mobility among the school-leavers has
become a necessity both for access to qualification and
employment opportunities. In this respect mechanization
of agriculture may be regarded as a sort of informal
education which offers opportunities for school-leavers
to acquire new qualifications.

3. MECHANIZATION AS A CAUSE OF A RISE IN ASPIRATIONS

The movement of young people, seeking qualification, to functional locations of mechanization outside the home area represents, for many, the first significant break with parental authority and may be regarded as the initial stage in their life-cycle migration. This separation from the home environment encourages a change in social relationships and cultural values, which stimulates further migration. Traditopnal codes of behaviour, customs, and tribal discipline are more easily modified or rejected (MOLOHAN, 1957).

Rise in aspiration is considered to be among the key factors that induce the circulation of this particular group of semi-skilled labourers and it is within this context that acquiring skills through mechanization plays a vital role. As HUTTON (1973, p. 97) suggests, movements come about not only because of absolute poverty, but because 'aspirations reach a level at which they cannot be satisfied by local opportunities'. In this sense acquiring qualification through mechanization acts as a major catalyst to the rise in aspiration by offering contact possibilities with the surrounding world. Hence mechanization as a training institution resembles formal education as the route to socio-economic status. 'This is evident not only in the desire of parents that their children should have a better chance in life, but in the ambitions of young people themselves who see in qualification the highway to material success' CASTLE, 1966, p. 18).

It is relevant to raise an important question, namely: what effect does acquiring new skills have upon the subsequent migration possibilities and preferences of young people in search of employment? New skills and additional experience

inevitably increase an individual's awareness of the range
of alternatives outside the area of origin and may act as
a catalyst to further mobility. Moreover, the influence of
parental discipline is generally weakened and the individual's role within the family alters in such a way as to
encourage freedom and independence. This suggestion is similar to that of CASTLE (1966) for the changing role of a
student within his family.

During the training period, which varies between one and
five years, an individual may earn some money necessary to
cover his limited needs, hence gradually becoming an independent family member. Consequently he becomes more stimulated to break away in order to fulfil other socio-economic
aspirations gained through the technical training. This is
the same as has been suggested by CALDWELL (1969, p. 60)
that 'the wide ranging impact of education is possibly the
most important matter to be considered in inducing rural-
urban migration'.

But unlike formal education, broadening experience through
technical training - as a form of non-formal education -
does not automatically lead young people to consider rural
life as inferior. By nature of their new experience and
qualification they have to search for employment - at least
in the early stages of their mobility process - within the
agricultural modern sector in rural areas. Thus the volume
of rural-urban movement is reduced at first by the number
of trainees and newly qualified workers who are still occupying jobs in rural areas before joining the stream of
rural-urban migration. It may thus be argued that if it
were not for the opportunities offered by agricultural mechanization, this segment of the population would also
have joined the stream of rural-urban migration to satisfy
their aspirations.

In the struggle to better his financial situation, a
trainee starts gathering information about other places
while he is still working as an assistant. This flow of
information is very essential in channeling the stream of
mobility even in this early stage, since a change in the
place of work will be ventured only if convincing stimula-
tions in other places are available. In this early stage
the traditional explanation in terms of the 'bright light'
theory in connection with rural-urban migration is inadequate. Of greater importance is the financial situation
created by the inability of some areas to provide young
people with the required living standard. While in most
cases the cause for joining a training technical centre is
the contempt for agriculture, the cause for changing the
place of work, as an assistant, is the new perception of
a better life to be expected in other destination.

After a training period of 1-5 years an assistant driver
or an assistant mechanic is upgraded to a driver or mechanic, who as such is differently classified from the assistant. In some cases they are awarded training certificates
which enable them to compete for more rewarding jobs. Thus,
acquiring a certificate or a driving licence is an additional stimulus to search for better employment opportunities
which are by no means equally distributed among the various
agricultural schemes. In some schemes, particularly the
newly implemented ones, there is a high and urgent demand
for skilled labour, while in others an over-supply is prevalent. It is expected that there will automatically be a
flow from areas with excess skilled labour to balance the
areas with a deficit, but the decision to move is a highly
complex process involving a variety of personal constraints
conditioned by cultural values and personal motivations.
Thus while manipulation of technical training may be

regarded as a possible way to encourage further mechanization by creating the needed skills, the ultimate success of
such a policy demands that due consideration be given to the
aspirations and preferences of the young people involved.
The spatial implications of occupational preferences are
therefore of considerable relevance within the framework of
development planning, given that at least the partial satisfaction of personal aspirations is a necessary pre-requisite
for social well-being and economic progress. Hence the traditional assumption that 'rural-urban movement is a natural
and inevitable consequence of the development in formal education alone' can no longer be seen as valid. Greater insight into the different factors influencing the volume,
distance and direction of population flows is required.

We attempt here to identify and analyse the spatial implications of occupational preferences from the individual's
viewpoint by examining the motives behind changing the
place of work.

Job availability in another place does not automatically
imply that an individual is motivated to move. The suggestion of WOLPERT (1965) that 'the movement of an individual is a function of three factors, namely: his characteristics, the information he has about other places and
the attractiveness of the place to which he may intend to
move' is not enough to explain the circulation of skilled
labour in our case study. More important are the 'push'-
factors, such as the overwhelming socio-economic conditions
in the place of origin that induce an individual to venture to change his place of work even if the other factors
are not present. Qualification is regarded in this context
as a catalyst which fosters mobility, since the better the
individual's qualifications and training, the better are
his chances of finding a job quickly when he moves away.

The low risk of unemployment at the place of destination increases his readiness to outmigrate. To prove this hypothesis a questionnaire-based study was carried out among a sample of tractor drivers in three selected agricultural schemes, the results of which will be presented in the following discussions.

4. A CASE STUDY TO SHOW THE RURAL-RURAL CIRCULATION OF SKILLED LABOUR FORCE (TRACTOR DRIVERS)

4.1 An approach to the case study

Since adequate and detailed information about circulation of skilled labourers was lacking in the Sudan, it was necessary to conduct field study on a micro-level. We have selected three agricultural schemes in North-East Sudan which we believed to offer some representation to other similar schemes in other parts of the country.[3] They have been purposely chosen due to certain technical and practical reasons:

a) Locational reasons:
They are located in central-east Sudan where irrigated and rainfed mechanized agriculture are concentrating (see map 2). Since the early fifties this region has received adequate attention of the development planners who have tried to make use of all available potential. As previously sketched (Chapter IV), this region is dotted with a number of important development projects which stimulate in-migration of a number of people, both skilled and unskilled, from other relatively underdeveloped regions. Thus it is expected to be a region with an increasing population and increasing socio-economic importance. As settlement schemes situated between the famous Sudan granary, where rainfed mechanized agriculture is practised and the old Gezira scheme, they

---

3) The three selected shemes are: the Khashm el Girba scheme, El Suki scheme and El Rahad scheme. A brief remark has been made on them in Chapter IV.

are expected to induce an interregional popualtion circulation particularly of skilled labour.

b) Time-lapse:

The three schemes were initiated in three consecutive decades (in the period between 1960 and 1980).[4] The fact that there is a period of almost two decades between the execution of the first (the Khashm el Girba scheme) and the third (El Rahad scheme) offers a good comparison of the effect of time-lapse on stimulating population mobility. This may help to prove our hypothesis that 'the longer a functional location of mechanization exists, the greater is the probability of increased population mobility'. Moreover, the time-lapse is important to demonstrate whether or not new schemes are really more attractive to skilled manpower than the relatively older ones, as has often been suggested.

c) The scope of acreage cultivated:

In terms of area cultivated in the three schemes, it is found to be the greatest acreage after the huge Gezira scheme (Chapter IV). This implies that a huge amount of mechanical equipment was necessary to work the cultivated area. Thus it is obvious that the probability of attracting more skilled labour to operate such machines is greater than in the smaller agricultural schemes. Of course the Gezira scheme, as the largest scheme in the country, might have been capable of attracting more skilled labour than the three schemes under study collectively but for

---

4) The Khashm el Girba scheme was initiated in the early sixties, El Suki scheme in the early seventies and El Rahed scheme in the late seventies and early eighties (see footnotes 13, 14, and 15 of Chapter IV).

practical reasons we have excluded it from the field survey.[5]

d) Subjective reasons:

In his capacity as an assistant inspector of the Department
of Rural Development and a research assistant to Professor
G. HEINRITZ of Munich University the writer is better

---

5) Financial situation and limited time for investigation
have rendered the inclusion of this largest and oldest
project a difficulty. Moreover, our intention was to
pick up some examples to reflect the mobilizing effect
of agricultural mechanization and not to cover all the
mechanized agricultural schemes in the country. For
practical reasons the rainfed mechanized schemes were
also excluded from the field-survey, since the time of
our investigations was outside the peak season for
high demand skilled labourers. In this particular sub-
sector the high demend for skilled workers is in the
period July - September when tractors are used for land
preparation, seeding and weeding. At the time of our
investigation in January and February there were only
a few tractor drivers still attached to this sector but
scattered over a wide area, thus difficult to be covered. We were informed that the majority of the tractor
drivers who had been participating in this sector had
joined the irrigated agricultural schemes, particularly
the sugar farm of the Khashm el Girba scheme which
prefers to employ temporary tractor drivers rather than
permanent due to the seasonality of production, and the
desire to reduce production costs.

acquainted to these particular schemes than others.[6] This
is very essential in reducing the constraints to gathering
information and furnishing him with the necessary perspective on the problem.

4.2 Limitations and Difficulties of Conducting the Field Survey

The writer was faced with the extremely limited information
about the scope and intensity of skilled labour circulation
in the Sudan, particularly in relation to agricultural mechanization. In fact only a few empirical studies have been
made in this country to present the different types of population mobility, in most cases as an effect of factors
other than agricultural mechanization. In this respect reference is made particularly to the studies carried out by
M.E. ABU SIN (1975), E. EL BUSHRA (1976), A. SWAR EL DAHAB (1978), M.E.
GALAL EL DIN (1979) and G. HEINRITZ (1977, 1980, 1982).

---

6) The writer worked as an assistant inspector in the Department of Rural Development in Kassala province for a period of two years within which time he got more acquainted with the socio-economic set-up of the region. The field
   surveys he conducted in this period and afterwards in his
   capacity as a teaching assistant in the department of
   geography, University of Khartoum have increased his
   awareness of the socio-economic problems of the region
   and stimulated him to do his M. Sc. in the same region.
   As a research assistant to Professor G. HEINRITZ of Munich University, who conducted three field surveys in the
   region in the years 1977, 1979 and 1980, the writer was
   able to increase his knowledge of data collecting methods
   with appropriate techniques.

Empirical studies on the micro-level on a group of skilled
labourers to test the broad hypothesis that the 'adoption
and diffusion of agricultural mechanization in terms of the
level or time of adoption as a factor of population mobility' is lacking. Similarly no work has been undertaken on
the macro-level to test the effect of agricultural mechanization on population redistribution and the subsequent
effects. Even the two national population censuses of 1956
and 1973 did not differentiate the circulation of the skilled labour force from other population segments nor did
they consider the role of agricultural mechanization as a
factor in population mobility. Furthermore, the lack of
registration methods such as those practised in some developed countries is a feature of all developing countries,
including the Sudan, which limits the information necessary
to present the population structure in each region.

As a consequence of all these limitations, we have had to
depend on our own investigations based on intensive field
surveys on a micro-level, i.e. covering a particular segment of the skilled labour force namely the tractor drivers
in a particular region. To undertake such surveys the
writer was confronted with some practical difficulties
which limited the desired representation: the fact that
mechanized agricultural schemes cover huge areas and are,
geographically, dispersed reduces the possibility of completely covering all skilled labourers working there. The
seasonality of mechanical operations as a function of cultivation practices in the Sudan, limits the field survey to
a limited time in the year, when the highest number of tractor drivers are present in the scheme. Furthermore, the al-
ternating high season in the irrigated mechanized schemes
with that of the rainfed mechanized schemes compelled the
writer to concentrate on the former group of schemes with

the exclusion of the latter.[7]

4.3   Methodology

Due to the practical difficulty of surveying all the irrigated mechanized agricultural schemes, we have had to sel-
ect a few examples, which we expect to be somewhat representative of the rest. It was not possible even in these
few examples to cover all the skilled workers, since they
were dispersed all over the area of each scheme. An attempt
to rely on a sampling framework such as employment lists,
registration cards and payroll of workers in each scheme
proved, by means of pre-tests and pilot surveys, to be insufficient for drawing a sample, because they are neither
complete nor conveniently ordered. Thus a number of randomly selected blocks were covered completely, questioning
all the tractor drivers present at the time of investigation.[8] In this respect our method resembles that of J.M.
BLAUT (1959, p.1) who gives great emphasis to an intensive
treatment with some representative coverage as a means of
achieving sufficient accuracy.

---

7) See footnote 5.

8) Each scheme is divided into a number of sections and each
   section is divided into a number of blocks and each block
   is provided with a number of tractors varying according
   to the variation in acreage between the different blocks.
   In El Rahad scheme we covered two blocks (block N.1 and
   N.3) with a total number of 150 tractor drivers; in El
   Suki two blocks (block 44 and block Salma) with 73 tractor drivers. In the Khashm el Girba scheme we covered
   all the tractor drivers participating in the sugar farm
   at the time of investigation whose number was 149. The
   confinement to the sugar farm as compared with the extended Khashm el Girba agricultural scheme (presently
   New Halfa scheme) has greatly reduced the time of investigation.

It was thought necessary to conduct face-to-face interviews
to answer a set of questions designed to cover most items
of the study. Group interviews were thought to be insufficient, since the aim of the study was to discover the real
motives and aspirations of an individual for joining agricultural mechanization and joining the process of migration.
Although the questionnaire was written in simple Arabic, it
was not possible for each respondant to answer independently, for the very simple reason that not all respondants
could read and understand the meaning of each question. A
pilot survey revealed that even those with elementary or
lower secondary school education were not all able to give
the study due consideration.[9] Thus the questionnaire had
to be carefully formulated and the interviewers had to be
adequately instructed to give more attention to the soundness of each answer.

The main survey - conducted in the period December 1979 to
March 1980 - was carried out with the help of some trained
interviewers selected from the students of geography, University of Khartoum. Apart from the task of supervising
and guiding the survey work of the students, the writer
participated personally in carrying out part of the questionnaire work. During the survey, the writer managed to
check and test the accuracy of the answers submitted by
each of the interviewers to avoid erroneous information.
Only in this way was it possible to minimize the errors
to a considerable degree and to call the attention of the
interviewers to particular issues.

The raw data collected was to be prepared for scientific
analysis. The first step was carried out manually by the
writer himself by doing the coding sheets and coding work.
The mechanical and electrical work, involving punching
and verification of the coded data was carried out by the

---

9) To test the practicability of a questionnaire-based field survey, a pilot
   survey was carried out by writer among selcted groups of tractor drivers in various agricultural schemes in the Spring of 1979.

'Leibniz-Rechenzentrum, Bayerische Akademie der Wissen-
schaften' according to the SPSS system, whereby the data
was prepared in form of tables and cross-tables for interpretation and analysis, the main task and responsibility of
the writer.

5. FINDINGS OF THE FIELD SURVEY AMONG THE TRACTOR DRIVERS

5.1 Demographic Structure

5.1.1 Age Composition

According to our field survey 73.6% of the respondants are
in the age-group of 20-30 years, which reflects the youth
element among the tractor drivers (Table 5.1).

Table 5.1   Age Composition of the Sample of Tractor Drivers
in the Three Selected Schemes

Age groups	Number of Respondants	Percentage of Total
17-19 yrs.	20	5.4
20-25 yrs.	140	37.6
26-29 yrs.	134	36.0
Over 30 yrs	78	21.0
Total	372	100.0

Source: Our own investigation (Tractor driver survey, 1980)

This age composition may be due to the high turnover among
this particular group of skilled workers. The older persons
were reported to be either promoted to the rank of mechanics

stationed at the functional locations of mechanization to
maintain the agricultural equipment and to instruct junior
tractor drivers and mechanics, or they gave up working in
this sector and joined other occupations. This suggests a
continuous replacement of older, qualified tractor drivers
with relatively younger, less qualified tractor drivers,
since the better the qualifications of a person trained as
the result of the mechanization of agriculture, the better
are his chances of finding a more rewarding job elsewhere.
In some cases qualified workers have little or no job opportunities   at their place of origin. To make use of the
qualifications gained they are compelled to change their
place of work with the result of creating a deficit.

By comparing the distribution of the age groups in the
three schemes, it could be seen that the tractor drivers
in the Khashm el Girba scheme are relatively younger than
those in the other two schemes (Table 5.2).

Table 5.2   Distribution of the Sample Tractor Drivers in
             Each of the Three Schemes According to Age
             Groups

Agric. schemes Age Groups	Khashm. el Girba N. of resp.	%	El Rahad N. of resp.	%	El Suki N. of resp.	%
17 - 25 yrs.	97	65.1	51	34.0	12	16.4
26 - 30 yrs.	42	28.2	67	44.7	34	46.6
over 31 yrs.	10	6.7	32	21.3	27	37.0
Total	149	100.0	150	100.0	73	100.0

Source: Our own investigation (Tractor driver survey, 1980)

This result confirms our hypothesis that 'the longer the functional location of mechanization exists, the greater is the probability of increased outmigration of older workers to the newly implemented schemes and immigration of younger tractor drivers to replace them'.

The higher percentage of the age group above 25 years (83.5 %) in El Suki scheme as compared with that in the more recently implemented El Rahad scheme (66 %) should not be regarded as contradictory to our previous assumption. [10] The reason for this unexpected result could be sought in the criterion used to appoint tractor drivers for the latter. To achieve the scheme objectives it was thought necessary to attract those skilled workers who had already acquired vocational technical training rather than others. Since acquiring vocational training is a recent trend among the tractor drivers in the relatively older Khashm el Girba and El Suki schemes, the majority of the newly employed tractor drivers in El Rahad scheme were directly recruited from training instititutions, such as Abu Naama and Tawzi training centres for mechanical operations connected with agricultural mechanization. [11] Such a selection method based on training certificates, motivated some tractor drivers to

10) It is expected that El Rahad scheme, by virtue of its recent execution and enormous incentives will attract the older tractor drivers with better qualification and more experience than the younger tractor drivers.

11) Our findings revealed that El Rahad scheme with 57.3 % has the highest number of trained tractor drivers over El Suki (30.7 %) and the Kashm el Girba scheme (4 %).

join a vocational training as a sort of upgrading presently attained at Khartoum, Wad Medani and Juba.

The importance of the age composition of this segment of
the labour force participating in agricultural mechanization may be seen in the context of the total economically
active population of the Sudan. According to the census
of 1973, 52 % of the total population is at the working
age of 15 years and over. Of these, that part of the labour force which is actually economically active is 55.2 %
of the total age-group (DEPT. OF LABOUR, 1973, p. 14).
This means that agricultural mechanization, in comparison
with other economic sub-sectors is not only sex-selective
(100 % as compared with 79 % adult male of the total national labour force), but also age selective. This could
be an important factor of population mobility, since most
migrants, particularly among skilled labour, are relatively young people. This age factor will be later connected
with other variables which are assumed to affect the movement of this group.

5.1.2   Marital status

A combination of marital status and the number of children
reveals that 52.2 % of all respondants, at the time of
investigation, are married and have children; 4.3 % are
married but have no children and 43.5 % are unmarried.
By comparing the three schemes with one another, it is evident that the proportion of unmarried tractor drivers in
the Khashm el Girba scheme is relatively higher (73.2 %)
than in El Rahad (26.0 %) and El Suki schemes (16.4 %).
Reasons for this variation could be sought in the composition of age in each of the three schemes. The high

proportion of the lower age-group 20 - 25 (54.4 %) in the
Khashm el Girba as compared with that in El Rahad (31.3 %)
and El Suki (14.3 %) may explain the unequal distribution
of the unmarried tractor drivers among them, since it is
expected that marriage occurs more often among higher age-
groups than among the lower age-groups.

This explanation, however, should not be taken as valid
in all cases, since marriage is not only a function of
age but also of socio-economic attributes of an individual.
Age as a factor of marriage in the Sudan may be relevant
only in relation to the ability to afford the costs of
marriage. The fact that the majority of the respondants
in the Khashm el Girba scheme have reported to be newly
employed as tractor drivers may be taken as evidence that
this group, unlike the case in the other two schemes,
could not afford the marriage expenses, which are presently enormously higher than a few years ago.

5.2   Social Structure

5.2.1   Regional composition (Province of birth) of the sample

Since all three schemes were implemented in an area which
had been hitherto occupied by mobile nomadic tribes, it
is justified to define the majority of skilled labour
force in each of them as in-migrants. Our survey indicates
that 58.7 % of all respondents are from the middle and
morthern Sudan (Blue Nile, Khartoum and Northern provinces), 33,3 % from western Sudan (Kordofan and Darfur)
and the rest from East and Southern Sudan (Table 5.3).

Table 5.3: Distribution of the Sample Tractor Drivers
           According to the Geographical Regions of Origin

Geographic origin	N. of resp.	perc. of total
Middle Sudan:	218	58.7
Blue Nile province	176	47.3
Northern province	35	9.4
Khartoum province	7	1.9
Western Sudan:	124	33.3
Darfur	85	22.8
Kordofan	39	10.5
Eastern Sudan:	26	7.0
Kassala	26	7.0
Southern Sudan:	4	1.1
Bahr el Gazal	2	0.5
Equatoria	1	0.3
Upper Nile	1	0.3

Source: Our own investigation (Tractor driver survey, 1980)

As to the volume and trend of migration from each province,
there are, hewever, considerable variations. The low percentage of the respondants born in the three southern
provinces is less surprising than the percentage of those
born in Kassale province. The southern provinces, with at
least 20 % of the total population of the country, is the

most economically underdeveloped region of the Sudan.
This fact should have induced a strong wave of out-
migration, particularly towards the relatively prosperous
regions of the north-eastern Sudan, had it not been for
the deliberate colonial policy of restricting movement
between the two regions. Out-migration was further
restricted by the civil war between the northern and
southern Sudan as a product of that colonial policy, which
created and intensified socio-economic differences. [12] If
the great distance which separates the two regions and
the poor communication systems are taken into account,
it will not be surprising to register such a low participation of the Southerners in the modern agricultural sub-
sector of the North-eastern Sudan. But a change in this
trend is gradually taking place and is expected to reach
a substantial degree in the near future if the present
favourable political conditions for the region prevail
and the economic development plans are realized.

More surprising, however, is the small contribution of
Kassala province in eastern Sudan to the skilled labour
in connection with agricultural mechanization. This province
is the second most mechanized after the Blue Nile province.
The reason for the low participation (7 %) could be
sought in the type of population dominant there, since it
is inhabited mainly by nomadic tribes who insist on continuing with their traditional way of life centred around

---

12) The Civil War which continued for almost two decades,
 was brought to an end in 1972 by means of an agree-
 ment (Adis Ababa-Agreement) between representatives
 of the Southern Provinces and the government whereby
 the Southern region attained semi-autonomy. However,
 this Civil War should not be exclusively attributed
 CONTD.

their livestock. Although mechanized agriculture has
been practised in this province since the early fifties,
it is still regarded by many nomadic tribes as the only
challenge to their inherited traditional life. They reserve their own conception of a better life and are reluctant to accept any change which disregards their inherited socio-economic set-up. [13] Perhaps, it was only
an illusion to expect that 'by superimposing modern agricultural techniques on to the traditional way of life,
the local population would automatically and effectively
participate', since they do not always perceive the benefits of the scheme in the same way as its initiators had
precalculated (The Ten Year Plan, 1960, p. 7). In fact
even the nomads who managed to participate in one of the
developing schemes were not convinced to adopt a settled
way of life or to make use of the benefits expected. Being
deprived of traditional grazing areas they were obliged to
strive for a plot in the new scheme to secure their living
conditions which is further aggravated by the deteriorating
environmental conditions particularly in the past decade.
But acquiring a plot does not automatically mean effective
participation and a complete integration in the new way

---

12) CONTD. to the influence of the colonial power in the
Sudan. Other factors such as differences in culture,
religion and language between the predominant Arab
elements of the northern Sudan and the Nidlotic tribes
of the southern Sudan should be regarded as well.

13) The writer (1978) treated critically the question of
integrating the nomads into the modern agricultural
sub-sector as part of his evaluation of the development of the Khashm el Girba scheme (see EL MANGOURI,
1978).

of life. The writer has pointed out, elsewhere, that this was one of the most effective factors which contributed to the failure of the second largest settlement scheme in the country, namely the Khashm el Girba scheme (EL MANGOURI, 1978).

The above mentioned attitudes of the nomads may explain the low participation of their young males in agricultural mechanization to acquire new skills. PAUL (1954, p. 132) suggested that the majority of the population of this province retain their own way of life and they are reluctant to move in large numbers to the urban areas. This is to be confirmed by our own findings in relation to the rural-urban movement of the nomads among the skilled labour force as will be seen in the second part of this chapter.

It should be stressed here that even this low participation is a sign of gradual change in the nomadic way of life and it is expected that in the long run there will be more contact and more diffusion of these innovations among the various nomadic groups. A glance at the data collected in the Khashm el Girba scheme, El Suki and El Rahad schemes, reveals that the first scheme, the oldest one, has a comparatively higher proportion of nomadic elements (15.4 %) as tractor drivers than the other two schemes with 2 % and 0 % respectively. Reasons for this difference may be sought in the length of time the functional location of mechanization attached to each of them has been in existence. Thus it is likely that within the next decade the number of participants in these schemes will increase as the nomads accept a settled way of life and as the technical skills are gradually transmitted by the present skilled persons to relatives and friends.

Apart from the Southern and Eastern Provinces, the Blue
Nile Province contributed almost half of all interviewed
tractor drivers. The fact that this province includes
the huge Gezira scheme and other important irrigated agricultural schemes has contributed to a comparatively higher
degree of mechanization which ranks first among all other
provinces. Accordingly, it is the province with the highest
in-migration since early in this century, with the result
that it is one of the most densely populated provinces,
containing almost one fifth of the contry's total population. Furthermore, it ranks third to Khartoum and the
Northern province in number of educated people (A. M. S.
SWAR EL DAHAB, 1978, p. 145). All these factors work together to generate a base for continous population circulation into and out of the province. The early adoption
of irrigated and rainfed mechanized agriculture and its
steady expansion have created a solid foundation for
technical training and mechanical work. The establishment of functional locations of mechanization in each
scheme formed a centre of modernization and training
which stimulates young males, particularly school-leavers,
to participate in agricultural mechanization as an alternative to traditional occupations or urban employment.
Although elementary education in this province is more
widespread than in other provinces, the acquisition
of higher education level has been and continues to be
restricted by the limited number of higher schools. Thus
acquiring a technical skill is regarded as compensation
for a discontinued formal education. [14]

---

14) The role played by agricultural mechanization as a
    sort of informal education will be treated in chapter
    VII as part of the whole assessment of its socio-economic
    effects.

The longer tradition in agricultural mechanization coupled
with a good communication system favours a continous
diffusion of agricultural equipment and technical know-
how. Furthermore, the higher per capita income - ranks
second to Greater Khartoum- and the subsidization of
agricultural equipment has stimulated the wide spread
of tractors, cars and lorries among the tenants of the Gezira scheme. This may be taken as a further stimulus for
the sons to learn a new vocation on the father's owned
vehicle. This was confirmed by a number of respondants,
who reported that they had been trained at the father's
own workshop before they join the stream of skilled la-
lour circulation between the various agricultural schemes.

A comparison of the distribution of respondants originating in this province among the three schemes under study
reveal clear spatial preferences. Table 5.4 shows that
El Rahad scheme attracts more skilled tractor drivers
originating in this province (68 %) as compared with
El Suki (37.1 %) and the Khashm el Girba (16.8 %) schemes.
Reasons for these preferences may be related to their
technical skills which facilitate employment in El Rahad
scheme where comparatively higher wages are offered.
This confirmed our hypothesis that 'the better the qualifications of a person trained as a result of the
mechanization of agriculture, the better are his chances
of finding a job even in the newly implemented schemes
with relatively higher incentives'. This is quite evident
if one crosses the level of training and experience gained
with the income offered in each of the three schemes
separately. Our inquiries revealed that the higher the
level of training and experience of a tractor driver the

higher is his income. [15]

Table 5.4:   Distribution of the Sample of Tractor Drivers
              in each Scheme According to their Province of
              Origin (in % of total respondants in each
              scheme)

Agric. Sch.	Khashm el Girba		El Suki		El Rahad	
Prov. of birth	N. of resp.	%	N. of resp.	%	N. of resp.	%
Blue Nile	25	16.8	49	37.1	102	68.0
Darfur	71	47.7	8	11.0	6	4.0
Kordofan	21	14.1	2	2.7	16	10.7
Kassala	23	15.1	--	----	3	2.0
Khartoum	2	1.3	1	1.4	4	2.7
Northern	4	2.7	12	16.4	19	12.0
Bahar el Gazal	1	0.7	1	1.4	---	----
Equatoria	1	0.7	--	----	---	----
Upper Nile	1	0.7	--	----	---	----
T o t a l	149	100.0	73	100.0	150	100.0

Source: Our own investigation (tractor driver survey, 1980)

---

15) It has been recorded that El Rahad scheme offers the
    highest income level to tractor drivers compared
    with the other two schemes. This may be taken as a
    reason for the drift of trained tractor drivers to-
    wards this particular scheme rather than others.

The Northern Province with less than 10% of the total respondants is found to be underrepresented in comparison to
the Blue Nile province. Although it is regarded as the most
uninhabited province of the Sudan with only 7 % of the total population, it is believed to be the province with the
longest tradition of out-migration. The history of the Nubian
migration to the towns of Egypt and the Sudan, and the
circulation of the Gaaliyyin in the different provinces
of Sudan has been well documented elsewhere (M. E. ABU SIN,
1975; M. E. GALAL EL DIN, 1979). It is relevant here to
mention some factors which we believe to be pertinent to
agricultural mechanization.

From an agro-economic point of view, the privince is one
of those least favoured with arable land. According to
G. A. DISHONI (undated mimeo, p. 2), the cultivable area
is less than 500 square miles out of the total of 240,000.
In addition this small arable area is continuously dimini-
shing because of desert encroachment and Nile erosion. Its
effective use is further limited by continuous fragmenta-
tion due to the Islamic system of inheritance which, with
few exceptions does not favour the introduction and expansion
of agricultural mechanization to the extent of the Blue Nile
and Kassala provinces. Thus the chance to acquire a technical skill through agricultural mechanization as a matter
of course are quite limited.

A well-established system of education and an inherited
culture which despises manual labour may explain the small
proportion of the tractor drivers originating in this
province. But this attitude seems to be gradually changing,
since our findings revealed that there is an increasing
tendency toward participating in agricultural mechanization.
As shown in Table 5.4   El Rahad scheme, the most

recently implemented one, attracted more than half of the tractor drivers originating in this province (19 out of 35) as compared with 34.3 % and 11.4 % in El Suki and the Khashm el Girba schemes, respectively. An explanation of this increasing tendency may be the further deterioration of the agro-economic conditions and the high rate of population increase in the home area. Furthermore, there is increasing competition among migrants from other parts of the Sudan for employment traditionally practised by persons from this province, e. g. employment in the urban areas, particularly in the informal sector. The same could be said for Khartoum province which also contributes a very small proportion of the skilled labour relative to agricultural mechanization. As the smallest province in terms of area and arable land, and with a comparatively higher per capita income than the other provinces, it is neither expected to depend on agricultural mechanization nor is it likely that the people in it will attempt to acquire skills through it. On the contrary, by including the capitol Khartoum with its expanding industrial and service sectors, it becomes a centre of gravity for all other regions, attracting people who are in search of occupation outside their traditional areas. Thus it is continuously gaining at the expense of the other provinces, particularly with respect to the skilled labour force. In a later chapter an attempt will be made to disclose the relationships between Khartoum as the centre of attraction for many qualifications and the other regions of the Sudan as sending areas for different population groups including skilled labourers.

It remains to consider the case of the Western Provinces (Darfur and Kordofan). It is a special case because the proportion of the migrants in our case study, who

reported their origin to be this part of the country, is
33.3 % of all respondants tractor drivers, while it con-
tains only about one fifth of the total population of the
country. Although the region is separated by hundreds of
miles from the north-eastern Sudan, where the modern agricultural and industrial sectors are concentrated, its natives
are to be found in all parts of the Sudan, particularly
in the irrigated and rainfed mechanized agricultural
schemes. As casual unskilled labour, they have a long tradition of out-migration, a case to be elaborated in chapter
eight in relation to population movements indirectly caused
by agricultural mechanization. Generally, lack of government investment in industrial development and services
together with the deteriorating environmental conditions
have created push factors that induce people to change their
habit of seasonal migration to permanent stay in the places
of destination. The construction of the railway line to
Neyala at the western border of the country and the increased transport, are both the outcome of prosperity in the
north-eastern Sudan and, as an essential means of tapping
the human and natural resources of this region, have greatly contributed to speeding up the process of out-migration
due to reduced physical and financial difficulties of movement. Furthermore the steady expansion of the modern agricultural sub-sector in other parts of the country and the
resultant demand for labour force has greatly reduced the
risk of unemployment for migrants from this particular
region, who proved capable of undertaking the hardest type
of work, contrary to migrants from other parts of the country.
These conditions were and still are the cause of increased
in-migration of 'Westerners' in the most developed regions
of the Sudan and the tendency toward permanent settlement
in areas of destination, a feature of the Sudan's regional
development policy to be treated in the last chapter of

this study.

What is striking in this context is the high proportion of
skilled labour originating in this region. This seems to
refute our hypothesis that 'proximity to long-established
functional location of mechanization is decisive in stimulating young people to acquire new skills'. An explanation
for this phenomenon can be found by comparing the distribution of the tractor drivers in the three schemes (Table
5.4). The relatively high representation of the Westerners
(61.8 %) in the Khashm el Girba scheme in comparison to
the 13.7 % and 14.7 % in El Suki and El Rahad respectively
could be interpreted as follows:

The Khashm el Girba scheme, second largest after the Gezira
scheme, has attracted a huge number of Westerners since the
early days of its implementation in 1963. [16] They participated at first as daily workers on the scheme construction
works and later as agricultural workers. Their number is
not exactly known, but BLANKENBURG, P. von and HUBERT, K.
(1969, p. 345) placed it at approximately 80,000 - 100,000
as seasonal workers in excess of the agricultural workers
who have taken up residence in camps scattered among the
irrigation canals. This last group, relevant to our interpretation here, was not only composed of newly recruited
workers from the western provinces, but mainly of families
who had been working before in the Gezira scheme and
Gedarif mechanized rainfed cultivated area. The drift of
in-migrant flow in the scheme was justified by the relatively higher material gains, since the tenants were igno-
rant of the comparative cost of agricultural operations in

---

16) 'Westerners' is a vague designation of migrants from
western Sudan and west African countries.

other schemes. [17] Moreover, both the Halfawis and the nomad tenants in the scheme were not acquainted with the type of agricultural operations instructed by the scheme administration. They have to depend on hired labour particularly those who had already participated in other agricultural schemes before arriving on the scheme. Consequently, a system of petty landlordism gradually emerged and spread among the new settlers of the scheme.

These favourable conditions have stimulated the Westerners to acquire more productive importance and encouraged them to exert some pressure on the actual tenant to increase their material gains from the scheme. As the actual producers in the scheme, they began to be dissatisfied with the wages they received from the tenant and demanded to have a share in the produce as legal partners of the tenants. [18] As a consequence of this new partnership system, the Westerners began to take up permanent residence in scattered settlements close to the Halfawi villages [19].

---

17) The Halfawis, being displaced and resettled in this project, were at first rewarded with a lot of compensations, which partly served to ease the hardships of the new environment, particularly to cover the cost of agricultural operations to be carried out manually and which they could not accomplish themselves (see EL MANGOURI, 1978).

18) For more elaboration on this new form of partnership see EL MANGOURI (1978 pp. 96 - 103).

19) This type of partnership was not practised in El Suki scheme and it is gradually emerging in El Rahad scheme and for this reason the Westerners are still practising seasonal labour in these schemes without being permanently settled as are those in the Khashm el Girba scheme.

In order to tap the maximum benefits from all available
opportunities, they brought their families to the scheme,
thus reducing the chances of counter-migration in a home
area. As settlers in the scheme, they have developed a
continuous contact with the other population groups. Such
contacts were necessitated by daily contacts in the New
Halfa town market, the social services, the field and the
scheme Head- and Subquarters. The town offers them a complementary income through participation in other occupations
as porters, home or office servants, street sellers and
the like. All these types of contact, however, were not
enough to produce the expected homogeneous society in the
scheme, since each group in the scheme preserved its own
identity a feature of the Khashm el Girba scheme's social
setup which is argued to be one of the factors which rendered all development planning in the region to be considered a failure (AGOUBA, M., 1980, pp. 65 - 80).
It is relevant to point out, from the viewpoint of our
study here, that through the contact with agricultural
machines and equipment, the young male Westerners were
enabled to attain technical skills. Many of them had already attained this technical know-how before joining
the Khashm el Girba scheme as the result of their previous
exposure to the machines in other agricultural schemes,
particularly the Gezira and the Gedarif mechanized schemes.
Being prepared to do the hardest and dirtiest work, they
were given priority over the young nomads and young
Halfawis for whom high-rewarding and pleasant jobs were
reserved. Thus the skilled worker Westerners were considered
as second class after the Halfawis and the nomads. This
may explain their higher representation among the tractor
drivers in the sugar farm and the sugar factory of the
Khashm el Girba scheme which employ mainly junior and
less skilled tractor drivers who are ready to take the

job of transporting the sugar-cane to the factory at minimum wage to reduce the cost of production. Such a rare
opportunity did not prevail in other agricultural schemes
where highly skilled tractor drivers were demanded, and
higher wages and additional incentives were offered. A
comparison of the wages offered to the tractor drivers in
the sugar factory (average LS. 33)[20] and in both El Suki and
El Rahad schemes (average LS. 55) may confirm our explanation of the phenomena of the high representation of
the Westerners in the Khashm el Girba scheme rather than
in the other two schemes, a result of which is by no
means to be generalized.

This new tendency of the Westerners to acquire a technical
skill which is not yet widely spread may be expected,
in a short time to come, to grow steadily if the present
stage of agricultural mechanization further develops.
The spread of information among the Westerners, both in
their places of origin an destination, about the prevailing
occupational opportunities for skilled workers, the prevailing regional disparities, the high turn-over among
employed persons, particularly among skilled labour
caused by the drift towards urban centres and the oil-rich
Arab countries, and the readiness of the Westerners to
work under the difficult rural socio-economic conditions -
in contrast to people from north-eastern Sudan - are all
factors which confirm our assumption.

5.2.2   Rural-urban Composition of the Tractor Drivers

Before going into more detail, it should be noted that
more than 90 % of the Sudanese population live in rural
areas with settlements of less than 20,000 persons (A.
SWAR EL DAHAB, 1978, p. 137). It must be noted that

---

20) LS = US $ 2 (Apr. 1980)

the percentage of those reporting a town as their place
of origin should be taken with caution, because some of
them, shy to reveal their rural origin, give the name of
a nearby town as their place of birth.

According to our data, 82.8 % of all respondants gave a
village as their place of birth, 14.8 % a town and only
2.4 % reported themselves as nomads. The relatively high
proportion of tractor drivers of urban origin in the
Khashm el Girba scheme (23.5 %) as compared with that in
El Rahad (10 %) and El Suki (6.8 %) may be attributed to
the higher number of Westerners in it, who most likely
gave inaccurate answers. This is explained by the Westerners'
inability to differentiate between a town and a village
and his shyness to state his actual rural origin so as
not to be further discriminated against by his colleagues,
particularly those who really originated in urban centres.[21]
The relatively low participation of the townsfolk points
to an almost one directional population movement, namely:
rural-rural-urban. The reason for this may be readily
found in the income disparity between urban centres and
rural areas even apart from the 'bright lights' of the town.
Other factors remaining the same, it is expected that
skilled labour moves from areas with low economic incentives
to areas with relatively higher economic incentives as
will be shown later on.

---

21) Rural origin is conceived by the Sudanese people to
be a sign of primitiveness and is a cause for discrimination. This attitude is justified by the prevailing rural-urban development disparity to be discussed in chapter VI.

The very low participation of the nomads in agricultural
mechanization (2.4 %) reflects their negative attitude
towards innovation in general and paid manual work in particular. Moreover, a nomad may also be shy to state his
nomadic origin as a sign of primitiveness as compared with
rural or urban origin. But a change in the attitude of the
nomads towards occupations other than livestock keeping
may be expected in the future through further contacts
with other population groups, particularly the more sophisticated townsfolk and skilled workers from other areas.
The spread of development schemes and the relevant infrastructure in areas which were hitherto dominated by nomadic groups is expected to stimulate a change in their
attitide by stimulating the young to accept innovations,
a step which is essential in integrating them into a
settled life. This step could be facilitated not only
through political decision based nearly on economic achievements, but most important, by recognizing the perception of
the nomads themselves of the issue of development.

5.2.3   Educational Composition

Table 5.5 shows that the majority of the interviewed tractor drivers (71 %) have formal education. Elementary education was reported by 57.8 %, intermediate and secondary
education by only 12.9 % and 0.3 % respectively.

Table 5.5:   Distribution of the Sample Tractor Drivers
              According to their Level of Education

Education Level	N. of Resp.	% of Total
Without Education	27	7.3
Non-formal Education	81	21.8
Adult Education	6	1.6
Koran School	75	20.2
Formal Education	264	71.0
Elementary Education	215	57.8
Intermediate Education	48	12.9
Secondary Education	1	0.3
T o t a l	372	100.0

Source: Our own investigation (tractor drivers survey, 1980)

This shows a relatively higher percentage of those with
formal education as compared with the countries formal
education ratio. According to the ILO (1976, p. 128) the
enrolment ratio at the primary level in rural areas is 30
to 35 %. This shows that agricultural mechanization is
highly selective in terms of education standard, since it
attracts people with at least primary education. The low
proportion of highly educated persons among the respondants
may be due to their disdain of manual work and their pre-
ference for the 'white-collar' jobs.

If the above findings were crossed with the rural-urban
place of origin it would appear that there is a relationship between education level, place of origin and the rate

of participation in agricultural mechanization. The townsfolk, with a probable higher education level are underrepresented among the tractor drivers. [22] This is mainly because townsfolk are more likely to be attracted by
'white-collar' jobs or other jobs in the formal or informal sectors in the town rather than in rural areas.

An explanation of the dominance of those with formal education over those with informal education may be sought in
the composition of respondants according to their province
of origin. Since the majority of respondants originated
from the Blue Nile, Northern, and Khartoum provinces with
the highest enrolment of children in primary schools in
the country (75 %) according to ILO (1976, p. 128), it is
not strange to reach such a result. This could be seen by
comparing the distribution of respondants with primary
education in the three schemes under study, whereby in
the Khashm el Girba scheme, the majority of whose respondants originated from Darfur and Kordofan provinces - both
with relatively low enrolment. The proportion of the
primery-educated people in Darfur and Kordofan provinces
is 50.3 % in comparison to 84.9 % and 84.7 % in El Suki
and El Rahad respectively. The majority of respondants
originated from the three above mentioned provinces with
the highest enrolment (Table 5.6).

---

22) This may also be said of the rural folk who succeeded
in achieving a higher education level.

Table 5.6:   Distribution of Respondant Tractor Drivers in
               Each of the Three Schemes According to Education
               Level

Agric. Scheme	Khashm el Girba		El Suki		El Rahad	
Education Level	N. of Resp.	%	N. of Resp.	%	N. of Resp.	%
Non-formal	74	49.7	11	15.1	23	15.3
Formal	75	50.3	62	84.9	127	84.7
T o t a l	149	100.0	73	100.0	150	100.0

Source: Our own investigation (Tractor drivers survey, 1980)

5.3   Previous Mobility

5.3.1   Mobility as an assistant driver

In this section the analysis will be confined to the factors
that induced previous mobility of the present tractor drivers
and the motivation for further mobility.

Our data shows that the sample of tractor drivers interviewed presents a varied migration history, which began
for many with their joining a workshop connected to one
of the mechanized agricultural schemes which was located
(for 61.8 % of all respondants) some miles away from the
parents' residence, a distance which necessitated a temporary stay there (Table 5.7).

Table 5.7:   Distribution of the Sample Tractor Drivers
              According to the Distance Between Parents'
              Residence and the Nearest Workshop (in km)

Category label	N. of resp.	% of total
0 - 5	97	26.1
6 - 25	165	44.4
26 - 50	42	11.3
51 and more	68	18.3
T o t a l	372	100.0

Source: Our own investigation (tractor drivers survey, 1980)

As Table 5.7 shows, the distance between the parents'
residence and the nearest workshop varies considerably.
It could be said generally that those who originated
from the Western provinces, where traditional agriculture
is practised, had to cover longer distances than those
originating from North-eastern Sudan, where the modern
agricultural sector is concentrated. Although such distance
is important as a decision-making factor in relation to
the physical and financial friction, other working factors
stimulate a person to out-migrate. The availability of
other occupational opportunities in the urban centres of
the North-eastern Sudan, for example, divert the young males
from participating in agricultural mechanization even if
its functional locations are adjacent to one's parents'
residence. The distance factor works effectively only in the
diffusion process of innovations, since the more a place
is affected by innovations (i. e. the nearer it is situated to the functional location of innovation) the greater

is the possibility of increased participation of its
people. Thus for respondants originating from the North-
eastern Sudan, both the nearness and the long tradition
of agricultural mechanization were factors of the steady
diffusion of technical know-how, particularly among the
increased number of school-leavers. Of particular importance in this context is the role played by pioneer
participants in transmitting technical skills through
continuous contact with their home area. They act not only
as a source of information about the opportunities offered
by agricultural mechanization, but also as points of
contact for close relatives and friends still living in
a home village. Our survey shows that 78.8 % of all respondants reported a close relative as a driver or mechanic
at the time of starting work in a functional location of
agricultural mechanization. Thus to join a relative elsewhere was regarded by many respondants, as a stimulus to
leave the home village at this early stage of a carreer
ladder. For many this was the first step in their mobility
process, apart from a school visit.

This early movement of the young males, as unskilled
workers, continues in a period of assistantship for the
sake of better training and job opportunities. 69.1 % of
our respondants reported a change of workplace (one or more
times) as assistant driver, mostly for material reasons.
A relative or friend was given by 79 % of the respondants
as the source of their information about working conditions
in the places to which they moved. Unlike the tractor
drivers, as will later on be shown, the assistant drivers
have limited circulation because of their still limited
skills and the limited number of vacancies offered to them
in other places. In normal cases, a vacancy for an assistant
driver will be occupied by a person from the same place
rather than from a distant one, to reduce their living cost

which could not be covered by the very low wage offered to him (presently LS 29.5 as compared with LS 13.90 a few years ago). However, sometimes an assistant driver may be compelled to search for employment elsewhere, because of the temporal nature of this particular occupation due to the seasonal nature of the agricultural mechanical operations.

During a period of assistantship, ranging from one to five years, an individual becomes gradually trained to do some mechanical operations. To escape the risk of being displaced as assistant driver, he strives for a driver's licence as a prerequisite to employment as a tractor driver, a step which necessitates, for many, the first visit to an issuing place, which is, in most cases, identical with the provincial capital (95.7 % of all respondants reported a place of issue to be outside the parents' residence and 64.8 % to be even outside the birth province).

This incidence of a first visit to an issuing place probably affects one's further movement decision, particularly the move into a town, since for many this was the first personal visit to a big town where one could change his place utility matrix due to increased information about the surrounding world.

5.3.2   Previous mobility as a driver

According to our investigations, there is a higher demand for tractor drivers than for assistant drivers. This can be seen in Table 5.8 which shows the length of the waiting period for employment as a tractor driver. Nearly three quarters of all respondents were employed immediately after being issued a driving licence. A proportion of

12.6 % were even employed before being issued a driving
licence. This may reflect the rapid expansion in agricultural
mechanization on the one hand and the high rate of turn-over
among the older tractor drivers on the other.

Table 5.8:   Distribution of Respondants According to the
              Length of Waiting Period to be Employed as a
              Tractor Driver

Category label	N. of resp.	% of total
Employed before being issued a licence	47	12.6
Employed immediately after being issued a licence	270	72.6
Employed a short time after being issued a licence	55	14.8
T o t a l	372	100.0

Source: Our own investigation (Tractor driver survey, 1980)

For a proportion of 61 % the step of being employed as a
tractor driver made it necessary to move away from the
parents' residence or from the place where he worked as
assistant driver, since qualified tractor drivers have
little or no job opportunities at their place of origin. To
make use of the qualifications they gained through agricultural mechanization they are compelled to move to other
places (Table 5.9).

Table 5.9:　　Distribution of Respondants to the First Place
　　　　　　　of Working as Tractor Driver

Category label	N. of resp.	% of total
Parents' residence as a first place of work as a driver	33	8.9
Same place where he worked a assistant but not parents' residence	112	30.1
Other places	227	61.0
T o t a l	372	100.0

Source: Our own investigation (Tractor driver survey, 1980)

This step, however, is reported to be a further stimulus
to circulate between the different agricultural schemes.
In fact, the tractor drivers circulate more frequently
than the assistant drivers, due to the high rate of turn-
over created by the increased rural-urban drift of qualified persons (Table 5.10).

Table 5.10:　　Distribution of Respondants According to
　　　　　　　the Number of Changes in the Place of Work
　　　　　　　as a Driver

Agricultural schemes	Khashm el Girba		El Suki		El Rahad	
N. of changes	n. of resp.	%	N. of resp.	%	N. of resp.	%
0	40	26.8	3	4.1	7	4.7
1	48	32.2	11	15.1	7	4.7
2 and more	61	41.0	59	80.8	136	90.6
T o t a l	149	100.0	73	100.0	150	100.0

Source: Our own investigation (Tractor driver survey, 1980)

The reasons for variation in mobility frequency may be sought in the composition of the group of drivers in each scheme. Whereas in both El Suki and El Rahad schemes the interviewed tractor drivers are relatively older, more experienced and possess licences issued some years ago, the drivers in the Khashm el Girba scheme are younger, with newly issued licences. In the Khashm el Girba scheme nearly two thirds of the tractor drivers possess newly issued driving licences (1 - 3 years old only), whereas in El Suki and El Rahad schemes the corresponding proportions were 5.4 % and 14.7 % respectively (the rest having licences longer than three years). This means that the respondants in the latter two schemes had a longer circulation history than those in the former scheme. The relationship between the length of employment period and the frequency of mobility may be sought in the degree of qualification attained in that period. Thus it may be argued that the longer the period of employment of a person the more he is liable to be qualified; and the better his qualifications, the better are his chances of finding a job quickly when he moves away. The low risk of unemployment at the place he moves to increases his readiness to out-migrate. This may explain the higher concentration of respondants in El Rahad scheme (91.6 %) with high (0.42 - 0.54) to very high (more than 0.55) mobility rate by virtue of being the most qualified persons among the respondants in all three schemes. [23]

---

23) Mobility frequency was calculated by dividing the number of moves by the age of a driving licence which gives the number of moves in a year. The resultant mobility frequencies were then aggregated in four categories referred to as low (0. - 0.20 moves / year); medium (0.21 - 0.41 moves / year); high (0.42 - 0.54 moves / year) and very high (0.55 and more moves / year).

Table 5.11:   Distribution of Respondants According to
Mobility Frequency   in a Year (in Each
of the Three Schemes)

Agricultural Scheme	Khashm el Girba		El Suki		El Rahad	
Mobility Frequency	N. of resp.	%	N. of resp.	%	N. of resp.	%
0. - 0.20	40	26.8	3	4.1	7	4.7
0.21 - 0.41	50	33.6	17	23.3	7	4.7
0.42 - 0.54	44	29.6	18	24.7	28	19.5
0.55 and more	15	10.0	35	47.9	108	72.1
T o t a l	149	100.0	73	100.0	150	100.0

Source: Our own investigation (Tractor driver survey, 1980)

5.4   Mobility Frequency of Tractor Drivers as a Factor of Different Variables

In this section we shall attempt to present some of the de-
terminant factors which work together or separately to
affect the mobility frequency of this particular population
segment. Our method was to cross the aggregated four categories of mobility frequency with different variables as
will be shown in the following presentations.

5.4.1   Birth place and mobility frequency

The birth place, whether a town or a village seams to have
some influence on the rate of mobility of a tractor driver.
Accordning to our investigations, the majority of those
born in a town (52.7 %) reported a high to a very high

mobility rate, whereas the majority of the villages (53.3 %)
reported a low to medium mobility rate (Table 5.12).

Table 5.12:   Distribution of Respondants According to a
               Combination of Birth Place and Mobility Frequency

Birth Place	Town		Village	
Category label	N. of resp.	%	N. of resp.	%
0 - 0.20	14	25.5	58	18.8
0.21 - 0.41	12	21.8	106	34.5
0.42 - 0.54	18	32.7	78	25.3
0.55 and more	21	20.0	66	21.4
T o t a l	55	100.0	308	100.0

Source: Our own investigation (Tractor driver survey, 1980)

This may be attributed to the low level of qualification
among the villagers together with their limited contacts
with the key figures in the different agricultural schemes
who work out new applications. Through such contact persons
the townsfolk are able to evaluate the working conditions
prevailing in different regions and accordingly, they are
always ready to shift to a more rewarding job offered in
another locality, before a villager has been able to
gather the needed information about it. Moreover, it is
harder for a person originating from a town to fulfill
his aspirations by confining his movements to a limited
number of working places in the rural areas. By virtue of
being born in a town with different place utility matrix
than that of a villager, he always tries to achieve his
goals by changing his place of work whenever a more rewarding opportunitiy becomes available. The relatively

lower risk of unemployment at a new place of destination
- in contrast to a villager - increases his readiness
to change his place of work.

5.4.2   Birth Province as a variable of mobility frequency

By relating the mobility frequency of a tractor driver and
his province of origin, some variations will be apparent.
Whereas two thirds of the people originated from north-
central Sudan (Blue Nile, Gezira and Khartoum provinces),
reflects a high to very high mobility rate (0.42 and more),
the majority of those originating from the northern, eastern
and western provinces fall within a low to medium mobility
rate (below 0.41) as shown in Table 5.13.

Table 5.13:   Distribution of Respondants According to the
              Combination of the Geographical Origin and
              Mobility Rate

Geographical regions	Western		Central		Eastern		Northern	
Mobility Frequency	N. of resp.	%	N. of resp.	%	N. of resp.	%	N. of resp.	%
0 - 0.20	32	25.8	29	15.8	9	34.6	3	8.6
0.21 - 0.41	38	30.6	34	18.6	7	26.9	21	60.0
0.42 - 0.54	36	29.0	47	25.7	8	30.8	7	20.0
0.55 and more	18	14.6	33	39.9	2	7.7	4	11.4
T o t a l	124	100.0	183	100.0	26	100.0	35	100.0

Source: Our own investigation (Tractor driver survey, 1980)

This result seems to confirm our previous hypothesis that
'the more primitive the place of origin, the lower is the

possibility of contact with key figures of employment
boards and hence the lower is the frequency of changing
the place of work. As previously mentioned, the Westerners,
by virtue of their being less qualified and in lower demand, are always ready to accept the lowest-paid job in
contrast to the people originating from other regions of
the Sudan. They often enter temporary occupations, such
as the sugar farm in the Khashm el Girba scheme. They are
prepared to do seasonal work, as they had done in their
capacity as unskilled seasonal labourers before joining
agricultural mechanization. Their readiness to work under
hard conditions increases their chance of occupying seasonal
jobs particularly in the rainfed mechanized areas around
Gedarif. The fact that the peak demand in the mechanized
rainfed agricultural schemes alternate with the peak demands for junior tractor drivers in the sugar farm of
the Khashm el Girba scheme offers them a sort of complementary employment which is reflected in the relatively higher
mobility frequency in the above table, as compared with
persons who originated from the eastern and northern
Provinces.

In comparing the remaining regions, it becomes evident
that the tractor drivers originating from the middle Sudan
have a higher mobility rate than those originated from
the two other regions. The relatively lower mobility rate
of the respondants from the eastern and northern regions
may be attributed to their relatively recent participation
in agricultural mechanization as compared to people from
middle Sudan. This confirms our hypotheses that 'the more
a place is affected by mechanization, i. e. the nearer
it is situated to the functional occasion of mechanization
(workshop) or the longer such location already exists, the
greater is the probability of increased mobility rates of

skilled labour, other factors remaining constant.

5.4.3   Age as a variable of mobility frequency

It is obvious that there is a correlation between age and
the mobility frequency of a tractor driver. According
to our investigations among the sample tractor drivers
in the three schemes under study, the highest mobility
frequency is reached by the age group of 17 - 25 years,
since more than half the respondants in this group registered
a high to very high mobility frequency. If we consider the
age group 26 - 30 the mobility rate will gradually drop
until it reaches a minmum by the age group 31 years and above
in which more than two thirds of the respondants registered
a low to medium mobility frequency (Table 5.14).

Table 5.14:   Distribution of Respondants According to Age
                and Mobility Frequency

Age group	17 - 25		26 - 30		31 and above	
Mobility frequency	N. of resp.	%	N. of resp.	%	N. of resp.	%
0 - 0.20	35	31.9	29	20.3	11	15.9
0.21 - 0.41	39	24.4	45	31.6	36	52.3
0.42 - 0.54	45	28.1	38	26.4	15	21.7
0.55 and more	41	25.6	31	21.7	7	10.1
T o t a l	160	100.0	143	100.0	69	100.0

Source: Our own investigation (Tractor driver survey, 1980)

The explanation for the relatively higher mobility rate
registered by the younger tractor drivers may be sought
in the degree of dissatisfaction of this particular group
with the working conditions prevailing in most of the agricultural schemes. Full of aspiration and expectations, they
feel dissatisfied staying in one place. This attitude is
created by the recent expansion in agricultural mechanization with an increased demand for skilled labour, in
contrast to the older generations, whose circulation had
been restricted by the limited employment chances for
qualified drivers. Another explanation may be sought in
the fact that almost all the Westerners, who registered a
relatively high mobility frequency, fall within this age
group.

By correlating the marital status, number of children and
the rate of mobility it becomes evident that the single
drivers with no children, who mostly fall in the younger
age group, registered a relatively higher mobility frequency
than those who are married - both with and without children
(Table 5.15).

Table 5.15:   Distribution of Respondants According to the
                Marital Status, Children and the Mobility
                Frequency

Marital status	Single (no child)		Married (no child)		Married (with child	
Mobility Frequency	N. of resp.	%	N. of resp.	%	N. of resp.	%
0 - 0.20	45	28.1	3	18.8	27	13.9
0.21 - 0.41	27	16.9	6	37.4	86	44.3
0.42 - 0.54	36	22.5	4	25.0	57	29.4
0.55 and more	52	32.5	3	18.8	24	12.4
T o t a l	160	100.0	16	100.0	194	100.0

Source: Our own investigation (Tractor driver survey, 1980)

An explanation for this variation may be sought in the prevailing living conditions in the various agricultural
schemes. According to our own investigations most of the
agricultural schemes offer only limited accommodation facilities for skilled labourers and their families. Thus the
less a working place is equipped with living accommodations
the smaller is the probability of increased mobility
frequency of married persons, particularly with children,
who prefer to stay with their families in one place where
social services and accommodation are offered by the scheme
authority. This is confirmed by the fact that the tractor
drivers who could afford to leave their families behind, registered a comparatively higher mobility frequency than those
who were accompanied by their families. (Table 5.16).

Table 5.16:   Distribution of Respondants According to
                Familiy Accompaniment and Mobility Frequency

Family accompaniment	Yes		No	
Mobility Frequency	N. of resp.	%	N. of resp.	%
0 - 0.20	8	7.6	20	19.0
0.21 - 0.41	59	56.2	15	14.3
0.42 - 0.54	25	23.8	37	35.3
0.55 and more	13	12.4	35	34.4
T o t a l	105	100.0	105	100.0

Source: Our own investigation (Tractor driver survey, 1980)

5.4.4   Education as a variable of mobility frequency

By correlating the mobility frequency registered by the
respondants in the sample to their level of education, it

appears that respondants with formal education are likely to
circulate more frequently than respondants with non-formal
education. According to our findings, the majority of
those who attained at least elementary education (63.7 %)
fall within the mobility frequency category high to very
high, while the majority of those with only non-formal education (54.6 %) fall within the category of medium to low
as shown by the Table 5.17.

Table 5.17:   Distribution of Respondants According to
               Education Level and Mobility Frequency

Education level	non-formal education		formal education	
Mobility frequency	N. of resp.	%	N. of resp.	%
0 - 0.20	34	31.5	41	15.5
0.21 - 0.41	25	23.1	55	20.8
0.42 - 0.54	25	23.1	73	27.7
0.55 and more	24	22,3	94	36.0
T o t a l	108	100.0	264	100.0

Source: Our own investigation (Tractor driver survey, 1980)

This may be explained in that formally educated persons are
likely to be more aware of the range of alternatives in the
surrounding world than the persons with non-formal education.
Such awareness is argued to be one of the catalysts that increase the rate of circulation among the tractor drivers.
This is found to be true in the case of persons originating
from an urban centre, who are presumed to have a relatively
higher education level and hance greater awareness of the

different offers than the villagers. Moreover, educated persons, by virtue of their higher aspirations, always try to search for new alternative working places with expectation of betterment of their socio-economic conditions unlike non-educated persons with limited perception and aspirations.

The degree of training attained by a person is also found to be a factor affecting mobility frequency. According to our inquiries, the majority of those with vocational training (67.4 %) registered a high to very high mobility frequency while the majority of those without vocational training (72.6 %) fall within the mobility frequency category medium to low. This may confirm our hypotheses that 'the better the qualifications of a trained person, the better are his chances of finding a job quickly when he moves away'. The low risk of unemployment at other destinations increases his readiness to change his place of work. Thus by the expansion in vocational training, which is now stressed by the development planners, it is expected that the mobility frequency among this particular group will be increased.

5.4.5   Income as a variable of mobility frequency

It is generally argued that income disparity is one of the most important factors which induce labour force circulation, with the hope of attaining the maximum possible income. According to our own investigation, it has been noticed that the mobility rate of the tractor drivers decreases proportionally with the increase in income. While the mobility frequency reaches its maximum at an income level of less than LS 49, it shows a slight fall at an income level of LS 50 - 69 and becomes more remakable by an income of more than LS 70 (Table 5.18).

Table 5.18:   Distribution of Respondants According to
                 Income Level and Mobility Frequency

Income level	Lowest to LS 49		50 - 69		More than LS 70	
Mobility frequency	N. of resp.	%	N. of resp.	%	N. of resp.	%
0 - 0.20	44	32.6	20	11.6	11	17.2
0.21 - 0.41	18	13.3	70	40.5	32	50.0
0.42 - 0.54	34	25.2	51	29.4	13	20.3
0.55 and more	39	28.9	32	18.5	8	12.5
T o t a l	135	100.0	173	100.0	64	100.0

Source: Our own investigation (Tractor driver survey, 1980)

An explanation of this phenomenon may be sought in the degree
of satisfaction or dissatisfaction with the material gain,
other things remaining the same. Thus persons with relatively
lower income are likely to change their places of work more
frequently than those with higher income, with the hope of
additional gain at a new destination. This could be confirmed by correlating the motive stated for changing a place
of work and the mobility frequency. As shown in Table 5.19
the mobility frequency is higher among the respondants who
reported material reasons as a motive for changing a place
of work, than among persons motivated by non-material reasons.

Table 5.19:   Distribution of Respondants According to
                Motives for Changing a Place of Work and
                Mobility Frequency

Stated motives	Material		Non-Material	
Mobility frequency	N. of resp.	%	N. of resp.	%
0 - 0.20	18	9.3	7	5.4
0.21 - 0.41	53	27.5	54	41.9
0.42 - 0.54	66	34.2	45	34.9
0.55 and more	56	29.0	23	17.8
T o t a l	193	100.0	129	100.0

Source: Our own investigation (Tractor driver survey, 1980)

The relatively higher-paid drivers are often identical with
the older, married persons who, as previously noted, tend to
circulate less frequently than the comparatively lower-paid,
younger unmarried persons.

Most decisive in the variation in mobility frequency, however,
is the degree of information received by a person about better opportunities in other places. According to our inquiries among the sample tractor drivers, the highest mobility frequency was registered by persons who possessed adequate information about other destinations, since it was
argued that adequate information reduces the risk of unemployment there. This means that through the exchange of
information a person becomes aware of the differences in
material and non-material gains in the various regions. In
this respect the presence of a relative or a friend in

another location or periodical visits may be taken as a
means of increasing one's information about that location.
At present the expanded means of communication (transportation, radio, television, telephone, newspapers),particularly
for those with at least elmentary education, is contributing
much to the increase of information about other places,
a factor which is to be treated in relation to the rural-
urban movement of skilled labour in the following
chapter.

So far we have been presenting the findings of our questionnaire-based investigation among the tractor drivers in three
selected agricultural schemes. It becomes evident that the
agricultural mechanization, by virtue of its qualifying
effect, has directly contributed to the mobilization of
the rural population. The mobility of persons trained as
the results of agricultural mechanization is found to be
more selective than other types of population mobility
as far as sex, age, and education level composition of the
movers is concerned. Our findings show that above all, young
active males with relatively higher education and training
than the rest of the residual population are participating
in agricultural mechanization. For many the participation
in a functional location of mechanization marks the first
real step in a long migration process. We have so far been
confined to the circulation of skilled labourers between
the different agricultural schemes within the rural areas.
Generally speaking, the movement was directed from the
older to the relatively recent agricultural schemes. The
factors which work to stimulate persons to change their
place of work and induce a variety of mobility Frequencies
among this particular group have been presented. Above all,
material reasons were found to induce this type of rural-
rural population mobility which were reflected in the
disparity of income between the different agricultural

schemes. But disparity in income is to be observed not
only between the different agricultural schemes but to
a greater extent between the latter and the urban centres.
Such a prevailing disparity in material gaines has been
often treated as the main cause of the rural urban movement of unskilled labour. Whether this is also true or
not for the skilled manpower is the theme of our following
discussion which concentrates on the rural-urban movement of the tractor drivers, as a further stage of their whole
mobility process. The fact that more than two thirds of
the interviewed tractor drivers (69.4 %) stressed their
intention to move to an urban centre for both material an
non-material reasons, makes it apparent that there is a
continuous rural-urban migration of this particular group.
This may confirm our hypothesis that measures to develop
rural areas, including agricultural mechanization, do not
stabilize the population situation there but, on the
contrary, cause a mobilization of the rural population
thus intensifying in-migration pressure on the towns.
To prove this hypothesis empirically, it was thought necessary to follow the migrant tractor drivers in one of their
urban destinations, namely Greater Khartoum, which was
stated by the majority of our respondants (86.3 %) as the
first urban target. As drivers, the majority of our respondants
(72.7 %) were intending to join the tertiary sector as
taxi or bus drivers in the town as an occupation before
joining another occupation or going abroad to the oil-rich
Arab countries. Thus it was thought necessary to conduct
a questionnaire-based survey among a sample of taxi drivers
in Greater Khartoum to find out whether they have had any
participation in agricultural mechanization before they
join this occupation. In the following we present our
findings which, we hope, shed some light on the whole
spectrum of rural-urban population mobility, particularly of
the skilled manpower.

VI.   RURAL-URBAN MIGRATION OF SKILLED LABOUR AS RE-

PRESENTED BY A CASE STUDY AMONG A GROUP OF TAXI

DRIVERS IN GREATER KHARTOUM   (see map 2)

1.   INTRODUCTION

In this chapter our analysis will be mainly confined to
male migrants who joined the tertiary sector as taxi drivers.
A special questionnaire was designed and adressed to a
sample of taxi drivers in Khartoum by means of a complete
covering of some of the taxi collecting centres. [1]
Our questionnaire was designed to reveal the demographic
structure, social structure, economic structure, previous
mibility, motive for in-migration, and the intentions
and opinions of this particular group. It was not possible
to obtain the actual number of all taxi drivers working
in Khartoum conurbation because accurate registration
is completely lacking, let alone the high rate of turn-
over among this group. To reach an approximate number
we have to consult the chief director of the vehicle transportation headquarters in Greater Khartoum. According to
this source there were over 17,000 vehicles registered as
public transport vehicles and permitted to work in the
town at the beginning of 1980. If we assume that each vehicle
provides a job for a driver we could assume that the above
figure may be taken as the number of working taxi drivers
in Greater Khartoum in 1980. Of course, sometimes, particularly in the case of mini-buses, a co-driver or assistant
driver is needed to assist in doing the job, which sometimes
lasts for more than 18 hours a day. If we also consider
these workers, then the number of skilled and semi-skilled

---

1) The whole number of in-migrants among the interviewed taxi
   drivers amounted to 87 persons (75.7 %). The rest were non-
   migrants born in Khartoum.

workers joining this particular sub-sector may rise
to about 30,000 persons, which would be very difficult to
cover in any single study. Thus we have to pick up samples
which, though far from being representative, may give at
least an idea about the most important characteristics and
attitudes of the whole group, and most importantly how
this group is related to the group of skilled labour participating in agricultural mechanization.

We attempt to prove our assumption that most of the skilled
labour, particularly the vehicle drivers, had been participating in agricultural mechanization in one way or another
before they decided to migrate to Greater Khartoum or other
big towns. Our aim was to test the validity of the hypothesis that 'measures to develop rural areas, including agricultural mechanization, do not stabilize the population
situation there, but on the contrary, cause a mobilization
of the rural population, thus intensifying in-migration
pressure on the towns and increasing the tendency to polarization.' In this sense migration to Greater Khartoum or any
other town is nothing but a continuation of the circulation
process started by joining the agricultural modern sub-sector as unskilled labour and continued in the form of rural
circulation of skilled workers who finally enter the stream
of rural-urban migration as qualified drivers or mechanics
(see fig. 1). But migration to Greater Khartoum should not
be understood as the final destination for all Sudanese
skilled labour, since for many, as we shall reveal in this
study, this is only a preparatory step before finally migrating abroad, particularly to the oil-rich Arab countries.
The most effective factor in this process is the degree
of qualification acquired by participating in the functional locations of mechanization or the technical institutions
related to it, since the better the qualifications of a

person trained as a result of the mechanization of agriculture, the better are his chances of finding a job quickly when he moves into a town or abroad. The low risk of
unemployment at the new destinations increases his readiness
to migrate further, particularly if at the places of origin
no job opportunities for qualified workers are available.

2.   DEMOGRAPHIC STRUCTURE OF THE TAXI DRIVERS IN GREATER
      KHARTOUM

2.1 Age Composition

According to our investigations about 75 % of all interviewed taxi drivers were young adults in the age group 18 to
30 years (Table 6.1).

Table 6.1:   Age Composition of the Sample Taxi Drivers in
             Greater Khartoum

Age groups	N. of resp.	%
18 - 25	31	27.0
26 - 30	55	47.8
31 and over	29	25.2
T o t a l	115	100.0

Source: Our own investigation (Taxi driver survey, March
        1980)

If this composition is compared with that of the tractor
drivers in Table 5.1 it could be noticed that the tractor
drivers are relatively younger than the taxi drivers, since
the proportion of the former in the age group under 25 years
is 43 % while it is only 27 % in the case of the latter.

The corresponding proportions for the age group 'above thirty' is 21 % and 35.7 %, respectively. This may confirm our assumption that the taxi drivers are (in-migrated) former tractor drivers. To prove this we have to consider the age at the time of arrival in Khartoum by deducing the time spent in Khartoum from the age of a respondant at the time of investigation.

As shown by Table 6.2 more than half of all respondants had arrived in the past three years and less than one fifth reported a stay in Khartoum of more than 7 years.

Table 6.2:   Distribution of the In-migrant Taxi Drivers According to the Time Spent in Khartoum (in Years)

Time category	N. of resp.	% of in-migrant
1 - 2	50	57.5
4 - 6	23	26.4
7 and more	14	16.1
T o t a l [1]	87	100.0

Source: Our own investigation (Taxi driver survey, March 1980)

[1] The rest were born in Khartoum.

We come later to consider the relationship between this age group composition and the previous mobility on the one hand and the intention to return to the places of origin or to leave the country on the other hand. At present we shall attempt to relate age to marital status in the case of the taxi drivers.

2.2   Marital Status

By comparing the marital status of the two groups we found
that there was a higher proportion of married persons among
the taxi than among the tractor drivers.(64.3 % as compared
with 56.5 %). If we consider age as a factor which influences the incidence of marriage in the Sudan, it will not be
strange to find the result above, other factors remaining
constant. By virtue of being relatively older than the
tractor drivers still participating in agricultural mechanization at the time of investigation, the taxi drivers can be
expected to be in a position to afford marriage at least in
the first one or two years after arrival at Khartoum.

This last assumption may be supported by the assumed higher
income received by a taxi driver as compared with the tractor driver. The validity of the assumption of an increased
income will be discussed as part of the economic structure
of this group in the following pages.

3.   SOCIAL STRUCTURE OF THE TAXI DRIVERS IN GREATER KHARTOUM

3.1 Birth Place Composition

It should be noted here that 24.3 % of all interviewed
taxi drivers (28 out of 115) were in-migrants born in
Khartoum. About 40 % of the in-migrants gave another
town as their place of birth. But these figures should be
accepted with great caution since it is possible that, as
previously noted, some respondants may have stated an
incorrect place of birth. Nevertheless, this proportion
is far higher than that among the tractor drivers (14.8 %),
as an indication that Greater Khartoum attracts not only

persons from rural areas but also from other relatively
smaller towns. It is not strange, however, to find that
the majority of Khartoum in-migrants were villagers, since
more than 90 % of the country's population live in rural
areas (SWAR ELDAHAB, A., 1978, p. 137).

If, instead of the birth place, we consider the latest
place of out-migration to Khartoum, it will be found
that about 20 % of all in-migrants came to Khartoum from
another urban place and 30 % from a rural one. The rest,
almost half of all in-migrants, stated an agricultural
scheme as their last place of out-migration, not identical
with a village or an urban centre (Table 6.3). This means
that some of the respondants originating from a village
or an urban centre first migrated to one or more agricultural schemes before they finally migrated to Khartoum.
In this sense agricultural schemes serve as a preparatory
step for many before they decide to join the rural-urban
migration stream, a case to be elaborated further when we
discuss the role of agricultural mechanization in intensifying rural-urban population mobility.

Table 6.3:   Distribution of In-migrant Taxi Drivers
              According to Latest Place of Out-migration

Latest place of out-migration	N. of resp.	% of In-migr.
Urban	17	19.5
Rural, without agricultural scheme	27	31.0
Agricultural scheme	43	49.5
T o t a l	87 [1]	100.0

Source: Our own investigation (Taxi driver survey, March 1980)

3.2   Birth Province Composition

To find out the intensity of migration flows directed towards Khartoum it is vital to determine the geographical
regions from which the in-migrant taxi driver in Khartoum
originated. The first remarkable point is that all of them
are Sudanese citizens, contrary to the findings of Prof.
G. HEINRITZ (1981) in his observations about the squatter
settlement of Hay-Maio in Khartoum. He stated that a
third of all respondants are foreigners who migrated to
the Republic of the Sudan from neighbouring countries. Of
course, since Hay-Maio, as a squatter settlement, where
he conducted his study, receives migrants with different
characteristics and qualifications, it is not strange that
it presents such a composition of Sudanese citizens and
foreigners. In our case study, however, we confined ourselves to a particular employment sector (the transport
sector) which excludes the foreigners (only Sudanese citizens are able to receive driving licences), thus they
are not expected to be represented.

Unlike the ways of the tractor drivers the geographical
origins of the taxi drivers are found to be more widely
distributed over the country but showing concentration in
some regions over others. As Table 6.4 shows, the middle
Sudan (presently Blue Nile, Gezira and Khartoum provinces)
contributed almost one half of all taxi drivers in Khartoum,
the northern Sudan (presently Northern and Nile provinces)
20 %, and the western Sudan (presently Northern and
Southern Kordofan and Darfur) 12 %. The contribution of
the eastern Sudan (14 .8 %) and the southern Sudan (7 %)
are far higher than their contribution to the tractor
drivers.

Sample

Table 6.4:   Distribution of the Taxi Drivers in Khartoum
According to the Geographic Region of Origin

	N. of resp.	& of total
Middle Sudan	52	46.2
Blue Nile	10	8.7
Gezira	15	14.0
Khartoum	27	23.5
Northern Sudan	23	20.0
Eastern Sudan	17	14.8
Western Sudan	15	12.0
Southern Sudan	8	7.0
T o t a l	115	100.0

Source: Our own investigation (Taxi driver survey, March 1980)

The middle Sudan ranks first among all the other geographical regions as a supply region for skilled labour to both
agricultural schemes and Greater Khartoum, although it is
the region with the highest per capita income in the country after Greater Khartoum, for it was the area of the huge
Gezira scheme, the backbone of the Sudanese economy and other
important public investments. As the largest gainer in internal migration, it has become the most densely populated
region, apart from Khartoum province with the three towns
- Khartoum, Khartoum North and Omdurman.   It is also a
region where agricultural mechanization is widely distributed
and has a longer tradition than in any other region, thus
facilitating the adoption and diffusion of many innovations,

particularly technical skills. This factor has been aided
by a higher level of education, particularly elementary
education and a comparatively well developed communication
system, a factor which allows for regular contact with the
capitol town. Continuous population movements reflect the
socio-economic disparity between Greater Khartoum and this
particular region, which is regarded as the most effective
stimulus to out-migration. Thus it is not surprising to
find such a high proportion of in-migrants from this region
among the taxi drivers in Khartoum.

As previously mentioned, the northern Sudan contributes a
comparatively lower Proportion to the number of skilled
labours participating in the agricultural modern sector.
Still, it ranks second to the middle Sudan in contributing
to the taxi drivers in Khartoum. This may be due to the
nearness of this region to Greater Khartoum and/or due
to the inherited spatial preferences of an individual of
this province particularly for the large towns. The prevalence of this attitude is expected to decrease in the
near future, if the present trend of development in the
region continues and the present inflow of migrants from
other regions in Greater Khartoum increases. The first condition may increase the opportunity to be employed within
the same region and the second condition may decrease the
chances previously available for the in-migrants of this
region in Greater Khartoum.

The contribution of the western Sudan, to the taxi drivers
in Khartoum, despite its remoteness may be an effect of a
regional disparity, since this region is said to be one
of the most economically depressed regions of the country,
with a negligable government investment programme. The
proportion of the in-migrants from this region to Greater

Khartoum as taxi drivers is found to be far lower than
its proportion of the taxi drivers in agricultural schemes.
This finding is quite logical since it is assumed that
Westerners have comparatively limited chances of acquiring
technical skills in their home areas und thus they circulate
between other relatively developed regions, where after
a long stay, they could acquire a new qualification necessary to allow for their participation in an occupation related to a town. Hence, a Westerner leaving his home area
may first join the agricultural modern sector as an unskilled worker, and after a long stay and due to a continuous
contact with innovations, he may attempt to learn a new
skill, as a tractor driver or a mechanic, for example.

The large number of Westerners presently participating in
agricultural mechanization, as previously shown, may be
taken as a cause for their participation as taxi drivers
in Khartoum. Another cause may be the enormous increase
in lorry transport in western Sudan, particularly in the
past few decades, which has stimulated the young males
to search for a job as assistant lorry driver. In this
capacity he may be able to acquire further qualification
which would stimulate him to join the rural-urban migration
stream of skilled labour. Even the tractor drivers may
work as lorry drivers in the agricultural off-season before they finally decide to join an occupation in Greater
Khartoum or any other large town.

The proportion of the Westerners working as skilled labour
in Greater Khartoum can be expected to grow steadily due
to their continuing and increased participation in the
modern agricultural sub-sector.

The relatively small contribution of the eastern Sudan to
the taxi drivers in Khartoum, despite its long tradition

in agricultural mechanization may be attributed to the
nature of the nomadic tribes dominating there, who only recently started to join work outside their traditional occupations. As previously stated, the nomads used to be
disgusted at any paid work, preferring independent occupations. But this attitude is gradually changing due to increased government efforts to sedentrize the nomads by
superimposing modern agricultural schemes on their traditional grazing areas, such as the Khashm el Girba irrigated
scheme, the mechanized rainfed scheme around Gedarif town
and the recently implemented Rahad irrigated scheme.
Accordingly, they feel deprived of their previous grazing
and rainfed cultivated areas with the result that some
changes in their socio-economic life are taking place. The
young males can expect nothing more from their fathers,
they have to look after themselves, so that the authority
of the father is continuously declining. Such disintegrating families are more liable to lose their younger generation, who perceive the change quite differently from the
older generation. But such an interpretation is not enough
to explain the comparatively higher participation of the
people of the eastern Sudan as taxi drivers in Greater
Khartoum rather than as tractor drivers in the agricultural
schemes under study. It could be added that, the change in
the regional economy, as a consequence of the recently
implemented development schemes, has greatly stimulated a
change in attitude towards livestock among the nomads. As
the result of an increased demand for animal products due
to an increased per capita income, perticularly in central
Sudan, livestock has acquired a new qualitative, rather
than the previous quantitative, value. The revenue gained
by selling part of the animal wealth, is invested in new
economic fields, particularly for the purchase of transport
vehicles and agricultural machines, which are in some cases

regarded as a symbol of social rather than economic status. Nevertheless, the importance of this change could be seen in the new opportunities created for the young generation to operate these machines, a step which stimulates them to join new occupations within the region or in the urban centres.

Another reason for the relatively higher participation of the Easterners as taxi drivers rather than as tractor drivers may be the value of the region as a centre of attraction for migrants from all over the country, particularly from Western Sudan (MATHER, D. B., 1956). Accordingly, it is probable that some of the in-migrants in this region, may attempt to join the stream of rural-urban migration and for one reason or another they gave this region as their origin rather than the actual region of origin. SWAR EL DAHAB (1978, p. 142) suggested that it is those migrants who came to Greater Khartoum rather than the indigenous tribes of the area, who constitute less than 2 % of all in-migrants in Khartoum.

It remains to consider the southern region which accounts for only 7 % of all taxi drivers in Khartoum. Small as it is, this proportion is found to be relatively higher than the contribution of this part of the country to the skilled labour force in connection with the modern agricultural sub-sector (Table 5.3). Our findings deviate only slightly from other findings which showed the proportion of the migrants from this region in Khartoum to be 15 % (SWAR EL DAHAB,1978,p.140). This means that the participation of this region is negligibly low, not only in the modern agricultural sub-sector, as shown by its lower participation in agricultural mechanization, but also in the other modern economic sub-sectors in connection with an urban

centre,despite the fact that it accounts for more than
a quarter of the total population of the country. Unlike
the case of the Westerners it has been observed that
most of the Southerns migrated directly to Khartoum without
any sort of participation in the agricultural schemes of
the north central Sudan. Most of them arrived during the
past decade and according to SWAR EL DAHAB, A. (1978, p.
141), more than two fifths during the past five years. This
means that the trend is towards increasing flow in Khartoum,
which is expected to grow steadily in the near future if
the present political and socio-economic conditions per-
sist.

3.3   Educational Composition

As shown by Table 6.5, more than two thirds of the sample
taxi drivers are formally educated as was the case for the
tractor drivers. Although the in-migrant taxi drivers were
distinctively better educated than those still living in
the sending areas they were far less educated than the
natives of Khartoum. It was found that Greater Khartoum
attracts those with formal rather than non-formal education,
by virtue of having the secondary and tertiary sectors of
the economy concentrated in it. It offers some alternatives,
particularly for the school-leavers, to the traditional
occupations in the rural areas. Thus, as in a case of
the agricultural mechanization, it draws off a particular
segment of the active labour force which pessess certain
characteristics including education level and skills. This
is confirmed by the high proportion of those with technical
and vocational training among the interviewed taxi drivers
(45.2 %). The rest were trained on the job. This proportion,
however, is noticed to be far higher than the proportion
of the tractor drivers with technical and vocational

training, which hints that Greater Khartoum attracts not
only educated but also the most highly trained persons.
(Table 6.5)

Table 6.5: Distribution of the Sample Taxi Drivers
            According to Education Level and Training

Education Level			Training		
Category Level	N. of Resp.	% of Total	Category Level	N. of Resp.	% of Total
Formal Education	80	69,6	Technical and vocational	52	45.2
Non-formal	35	30.4	on the job	63	54.8
T o t a l	115	100.0	T o t a l	115	100.0

Source: Our own investigation (Taxi driver survey, March 1980)

4. PREVIOUS CIRCULATION

It seems that the taxi drivers had a longer migration
history than the tractor drivers still working in agricultural schemes. Apart from their circulation during the
period of assistantship, which sometimes necessitated their
stay in a location outside their birth places, the majority
of them have reported a number of moves, as skilled workers
within the rural areas before finally arriving in Khartoum
(Table 6.6).

Table 6.6: Distribution of the Sample Taxi Drivers
According to the Intensity of Circulation
Between Agricultural Schemes before Arriving
in Khartoum

Category Level	Absolute Frequency	Relative Frequency (%)
No Previous circulation	36	31.3
1 - 2	25	21.7
3 - 4	32	27.8
5 and more	22	19.2
T o t a l	115	100.0

Source: Our own investigation (Taxi driver survey, March 1980)

The Table above shows that more than two thirds of all
respondants (90 % of in-migrants) have previously circulated between agricultural schemes before they arrived in
Greater Khartoum. This means that the majority of the interviewed taxi drivers came indirectly to Khartoum from their
places of origin, which confirms the step-like rural-urban
migration assumption (see fig. 1). Thus the factors that
induce such a step-like movement are not expected to be
different from the factors which cause the circulation of
the tractor drivers already mentioned at the beginning of
this chapter. In the following discussion an attempt will
be made to uncover the forces which cause a deviation from
the rural-rural population mobility to a rural-urban population mobility.

A comparison between age and previous mobility shows that
the majority of those who had not joined any agricultural

scheme before arriving at Khartoum are in the age group
18 to 25 years, those who had circulated among several
schemes are in the age group 26 to 30. The highest frequency
of mobility is registered among the age group above 31 years.
This means that the older a taxi driver is the greater is
the probability of a high previous mobility rate.

A correlation of the age composition of the tractor drivers
in the selective agricultural schemes with that of the
taxi drivers in Greater Khartoum reveals that the former
are relatively younger than the latter. While 73 % of all
interviewed taxi drivers were in the age group above 25
years, nearly half of all respondant tractor drivers were
in an age group under 25 years. This may confirm our hypothesis that the taxi drivers, as part of the skilled labour
force in Khartoum, were in-migrant older tractor drivers,
who were replaced by relatively younger and less qualified
persons (fig. 1).   A direct question about the previous
occupation revealed that almost 75 % of all interviewed
taxi drivers had been working in occupations related to
the mechanical part of the agricultural sector. (see Table
6.7)

Table 6.7:   Distribution of Respondant Taxi Drivers According to Previous Occupation

Previous Occupation	Absolute Frequency	Relative Frequency
Peasant agr.	5	4.3
Mechanic.	26	22.6
Tractor driver	30	26.1
Ass. driver	25	21.7
Lorry driver	23	20.0
Other Occup.	6	5.2
T o t a l	115	100.0

Source: Our own investigations (Taxi driver survey, March 1980)

As shown by Table 6.3 only a small proportion of respondants came to Khartoum from another urban centre. This indicates that the idea of a chain migration which assumes that 'the movement of the villiagers is toward smaller towns at first before they finally take the step to migrate to a larger urban centre' is not functioning in this particular case. To explain this we have to uncover the factors which induce more migration to Greater Khartoum and to other urban centres in the country.

5.   SOME IN-MIGRANT DETERMINANTS

As shown by Table 6.8 two thirds of the in-migrants stated material resons to be the motive for their migration to Greater Khartoum; more than a third came with the hope of working in an industry which is thought to offer a relatively higher income than a job in the rural areas; one fifth stated that they came to Khartoum only to have a means of leaving the country for the oil-rich Arab countries; and almost one tenth were intending to work in non-technical fields of the urban centre. The rest of the in-migrants reported the 'bright lights' of the town and the educational possibilities to be the main reasons for their in-migration.[2]

---

2) Our questionnaire is designed to reveal only the main-reasons behind in-migration. We believe that nearly all reasons are interrelated. We aggregate all the motives, stated by respondants for in-migration in three main categories: non-material reasons (education, a 'bright light' of the town, join a family or friend), material reasons (work in industry and earn more income), and leaving the country.

Table 6.8:   Distribution of Sample Taxi Drivers
              According to Motive of In-migration

Motives	Absolute Frequency	Relative Freq. (%) of In-mig.
Material Reasons	39	44.8
To join industry	31	35.6
To join non-technical work	8	9.2
Non-material Reasons	29	33.4
'Bright lights' of the town	26	29.9
Education	1	1.1
To join a friend	2	2.3
To go abroad	19	21.8
T o t a l	87	100.0

Source: Our own investigation (Taxi driver survey, March 1980)

The proportion of those reporting the 'bright lights' of
the town to be the motive for their in-migration is found
to be lower than expected, inspite of the prevailing disparity between Greater Khartoum on the one hand and the rest
of the country on the other with regard to the concentration of social services and means of recreation (television,
cinemas, dance halls, gardens and national parks as well
as other recreational centres). Contrary to what had been
supposed, the 'bright lights' of the town are less attractive
to the villagers than the material gains expected, since
it is illogical to think of entertainment if the material
possessions are limited to the necessities as is the case
for the majority of the villagers in our case study. This

may be taken as an explanation for the relatively higher
proportion of in-migrants who came to Greater Khartoum
for the purpose of improving their material situation,
either by working in Khartoum itself or by emigration
to other countries. This last motive, for one reason or
another is not always directly stated, and we believe
that the actual proportion of those intending to leave the
country is far higher than could be stated here. Although
the above mentioned motives by no means include all of
the motives for in-migration, they can be regarded as the
most influential 'pull' factors which are aided by the
'push' factors prevailing in the sending areas (see chapter 2.2).

5.1 Income Level And Employment Opportunities In Khartoum

In fact the regional income disparity prevailing in the
country is probably the most decisive factor which induces population mobility, particularly among the skilled
labour force. As Table 6.9 shows 87 % of all taxi drivers
receive an income of more than LS 70 a month, about the
third of those reported a monthly income even higher than
LS 100.

Table 6.9: Distribution of the Sample Taxi Drivers in
Khartoum According to Income Level in LS

Income Cate-gory Label	Absolute Frequency	Relative Frequency (%)
Lowest to 69	15	13.0
70 - 84	32	27.8
85 - 99	29	25.2
100 and more	39	33.9
T o t a l	115	100.0

Source: Our own investigation (Taxi driver survey, March 1980)

These results are found to be not only in sharp contrast
to the average per capita income in the whole country,
but even to the per capita income of the skilled labour
force still working in the rural areas. According to our
own investigation among tractor drivers, only 17.1 % of
all respondants stated a monthly income of more than
LS 70 (Table 5.18). But this does not mean that this
wide disparity is valid in all cases. Sometimes an individual may earn more money in rural areas than in urban
centres. But it is not always possible to calculate the
actual income of an individual, since some sources of income are difficult to be converted in terms of money.

Although the case of the taxi drivers in Khartoum is an
exceptional one which offers a comparitively far higher
income than any other equivalent occupation, it reflects
an economic disparity which is likely to stimulate both
regional and sectoral population mobility. As part of the
tertiary sector in Greater Khartoum, taxi driving becomes
an increasingly important occupation which attracts part
of the skilled labour which might have been directed to
cover the demand for skilled labour in the rural areas,
particularly in the mechanized modern agricultural sub-
sector. The absurdity of this sort of population mobility
will be dealt with in a seperate chapter in relation to
the effect of agricultural mechanization on the Sudanese
economy with regard to skilled labour force mobility.

For our purposes in this context, it could be added that
the growing transport sector in Greater Khartoum is not
only the cause of an intensive rural-urban migration
and emigration but also an effect of the latter, since
emigrants, as skilled workers, are likely to collect and
transfer some money to be invested in this particular
economic sub-sector rather than in other sectors (see

chapter 9). Thus the demand for additional drivers is
steadily growing, aided by a high turn-over among relatively older persons created by the increased demand for
skilled labour in the oil-rich Arab countries, particularly in the last decade, as will be shown below. Our own
findings confirm both the expanding nature of this particular occupation and the higher rate of turn-over in it.
About two thirds of all interviewed taxi drivers (65.2 %)
stated that their occupation is only a terporary one, which
means an expected turn-over. This turn-over is confirmed
by the short time required to find a job as a taxi driver
in Khartoum. More than three quarters of all taxi drivers
reported less than four months (Table 6.10).

Table 6.10:   Distribution of Sample Taxi Drivers According
to Duration of Searching for Work as Taxi
Driver (in months)

Duration of Searching for Work as a Taxi Driver	Absolute Frequency	Relative Frequency % of Total
Months		
0 - 1	36	31.3
2 - 3	54	47.0
4 and more	25	21.7
T o t a l	115	100.0

Source: Our own investigation (Taxi driver survey, March 1980)

Further evidence of the high rate of turn-over among the
taxi drivers is the high tendency to emigrate. 79.1 % reported an intention to emigrate to one of the Arab countries.

5.2 Presence of Contact Persons in Khartoum

Apart from the economic reasons as pull factors inducing
rural-urban population mobility there are other working
factors which speed up the mobility rate. Previous knowledge of the working and living conditions in areas of
destination, for instance, may increase an individual's
aspirations by affecting his 'place utility matrix', since
it can be expected that more persons will decide to make
the move if they are informed about other destinations.
According to our investigations, all of the interviewed
taxi drivers had been informed by one means or another
before they joined the rural-urban migration stream.
About 40 % of in-migrants reported a relative or friend
as their source of information, 24 % knew Khartoum from
their previous visits, the rest reported publicity from
other sources (Table 6.11).

Table 6.11:   Distribution of Respondant Taxi Drivers
              According to Source of Information About
              Khartoum Before In-migration

Source of Information	Absolute Frequency	Relative Freq. (%) of In-migr.
Relatives	35	40.3
Friends	12	13.8
Previous own visit	21	24.1
Publicity (Radio-Newspapers)	12	13.8
Other sources	07	8.0
T o t a l	87	100.0

Source: Our own investigation (Taxi driver survey, March 1980)

The above table indicates the importance of the presence
of a pioneer migrant in a destination as a point of
contact for secondary migrants as previously discussed.
Pioneer migrants not only inform their relatives and
friends still living in the sending areas, but also
modify the hardships of the first stay for a secondary
migrant by covering most of his needs including accommodation and maintenance. Furthermore, they mediate to find
them a job without any sort of commission. As shown by
Table 6.12 more than 80 % of the in-migrants reported
mediation by pioneer migrants in finding their first
job in Greater Khartoum.

The presence of points of contact, in Greater Khartoum
for newly arrived in-migrants confirm the idea of a
continuous population movement process which was started
in the last century and intensified particularly in the
past two decades. But this does not mean that all geographical regions are equally represented by points of
contact in Greater Khartoum, since the influence of
the latter is unevenly dispersed among the various regions
of the Sudan.

Table 6.12: Distribution of Respondant Taxi Drivers
             According to Mediation to Find a Job as a
             Taxi Driver

Type of Mediation	Absolute Frequency	Relative Frequency (%)
Relative	56	48.7
Non-relative tribe member	31	27.0
Friend	10	8.6
Personal effort	18	15.7
T o t a l	115	100.0

Source: Our own investigation (Taxi driver survey, March 1980)

Of course, the nearer a region is to an urban centre, and
the better the communication systems within it, the greater
is the probability of increased in-migration to that urban
centre and hence the higher is the number of pioneer migrants
who act as points of contact for following migrants. Thus
it can be expected that the provinces of the north-eastern
Sudan (Blue Nile, Gezira, Khartoum, Kassala and the Northern
Provinces) have more contact with Greater Khartoum than
the provinces of the western and southern Sudan. These
last two regions have been, through a deliberate policy
of the colonial administration, deprived of all development plans, to the extent that they could neither provide
their people with a high enough level of income nor offer
them the employment situation to allow them to make temporary
trips to the capital town before finally moving there.
Accordingly, they are found to be less represented by
pioneer migrants than other regions with a relatively
higher prosperity (Table 6.4).

The importance of points of contact in a particular destination can be seen in the degree of reliance of a potential
migrant on the information received from those contact
persons. As Table 6.12 shows, it is not the previous personal visit to Greater Khartoum that provided the needed
information about it but rather, the presence of a relative or a friend there.

6. INTENTION TO EMIGRATE

Our inquiry about the intention to emigrate revealed that
more than three quarters of all interviewed taxi drivers
(79.1 %) were intending to leave the country for one of
the oil-rich Arab countries as soon as possible. Material
gain was stated by almost all of them as the most stimulating factor. A close relative or friend was stated by 64.3 %
of all those intending to emigrate as their main source
of information about the working and living conditions
in their respective foreign destinations.

By applying Chi-test we could not reveal any significant
correlation between the intention to emigrate and variables
such as place of origin, province of origin, age, marital
status, duration of stay in Khartoum, intensity of previous mobility, income level and the motive for emigration.
One thing was evident that the majority of those intending
to emigrate (57.2 %) were well aware of the higher material
rewards in the oil-rich Arab countries as compared with
that in Greater Khartoum. The awareness of the income
differentials appear to be the most decisive factor which
worked out the socio-economic differences between them.
By crossing the degree of awareness with the level of
education and age it appeared to be higher among respondents
with formal education than among those with non-formal or
no education (65.7 % of those intending to emigrate were
formally educated as compared with 23.6 % of those who did
not state the intention to emigrate). This feature
of education selectivity was found to be coupled with age
and qualification selectivity. Nearly half of those intending to emigrate (44.2 %) were in the age group 26 - 30
years as compared with 29.7 % and 26.3 % in the lower and
higher age groups respectively. The age composition of

those who were not indending to emigrate was found to be
37.7 %, 14.1 % and 48.2 % in the age groups 18 - 25, 26
- 30, 31 years and more, respectively. This meant that
emigration was intended by the most dynamic persons among
the skilled labour force who presumably acquired a higher
degree of qualification than the relatively younger generations. The relatively lower representations of those
above 31 years old among those who were intending to emigrate despite the probability of being highly qualified,
could be explained by the probable working 'pull factors',
mostly in terms if socio-economic and political obligations which were expected to limit their further migration.
In some cases older taxi drivers were found to constitute
part of those who had been previously abroad and who had
managed to start a promising occupation in Khartoum.

The interrelated factors which have been working to induce
the emigration of the skilled labour force in the Sudan
and the result and effects will be further dealt with in
the concluding chapter. To our concern in this context
is to stress the point that, for the majority of the interviewed taxi drivers, Greater Khartoum was by no means
the ultimate target for their migration process.
It appeared that, in the majority of cases, Greater Khartoum
was regarded as a preparatory station before they enter
the emigration stream. Thus it was found difficult to
predict an end for the whole migration process, at least in
the short view, as long as the regional socio-economic
disparity prevails. In the following we attempt to reveal
whether the migrant taxi drivers are intending to return
back to their rural origin or to take up permanent residence in the places of destination and what are the factors which work to induce this or that decision.

7. INTENTION TO JOIN THE COUNTER-STREAM OF MIGRATION

The question of remigration in the rural area was found to
be difficult to answer by the majority of respondants,
since no one could say with a high degree of certainty
whether he would join the remigration stream or would
stay permanently in a particular destination. According
to our inquiries no one among the respondants stated his
intention to remigrate in a year's time; 14 % were intending to remigrate in two to three years; 23 % in four
to five years; 29 % did not know at all what time they
would stay in their destination and the rest (34 %) stated
their intention to take up permanent residence in Khartoum.
Nevertheless, the proportion of those who intend to remigrate was found remarkably higher than expected. This appeared,
from the first sight, to refute the hypothesis that 'the
rural-urban population movement is a cause and effect of
the prevailing rural-urban income disparity'. To clear
this dilemma an attempt was made to investigate the reasons behind the intention to stay in a destination or return to the rural areas.

By classifying the proportion of those who were intending
to return according to their province of origin we found
that 62.5 % originated in the north-east Sudan, a relatively developed region. But this variable alone would not
have explained the desire to return to the rural areas,
since even the relatively developed regions of the
country were far behind the capital Khartoum in terms of
the level of income and the attractivity of the urban
life. Only by relating the intended remigrants to their
places of origin could we find a somewhat soundable explanation. The high representation of those originated
in an urban centre among the intended remigrants (56,4 %)

gave a clue that townsfolk by virtue of their relatively
higher education and material wealth in comparison to
the villagers, were in a better position to accumulate
the needed capital for an investment in a rural location.
This was evident from the income composition of the whole
group which showed that 72.3 % of those who were intending to remigrate were in the income group LS 81 and more,
while those who were not intending to remigrate were dominantly in the income group of less than LS 81. This
assumed accumulated capital was reflected in the desire
of the intended remigrants to start a business away from
Khartoum. Our inquiries revealed that 53.9 % were intending
to start a business in one of the small urban centres,
particularly those in connection with the recent development schemes, where services were increasingly needed;
23 % were intending to invest in the mechanized rainfed
agriculture and the rest did not exactly know what type
of occupation they would join in the rural areas. Thus it
might be inferred that remigration was stimulated by the
financial ability to start a business in locations other
than Greater Khartoum where all branches of the most
rewarding occupations were monopolized by individuals and
companies who possessed the means to protect themselves
against any new competition. In small urban centres the
vertical mobility might probably be easier than in Khartoum.
This might be the reason why some of them prefered to invest in the modern agricultural sub-sector. However, the
desire to invest in this particular sub-sector might
be seen from the first sight, as a healthy tendency which
might have worked to counteract the prevailing regional
disparity which had originally caused the rural-urban
population mobility. This might have been the case if the
remigrants would have joined their previous occupation
as skilled workers to help develop the existing public

agricultural schemes which suffer a remarkable deficit of
qualified manpower as reflected in their declining contribution to the national income. The intention of the
remigrants to start an independent business would be
expected to intensify the existing disparities between
the different population groups and hence it might cause
an additional rural-urban mobility. But to convince them
to do otherwise would not be an easy task under the prevailing socio-economic and political setup of the Sudan,
since everyone would strive to improve his socio-economic
situation irrespective of the negative impacts which might
accrue to others. Perhaps the best way might have been
the mobilization of this particular group in a way that
they have to build cooperation in the rural areas whereby
their qualification and experience would be utilized for the
benefits of their respective regions to promote change
and development. Only then could it be rational to speak
about the merits of the rural-urban population mobility of
the skilled labour for their areas of origin or for the
rural areas as a whole. This subject will be part of our
concluding remarks in the last chapter.

Our concern in this context is to stress the point that
remigration of skilled labour force involves, in the majority of cases, persons who originate in the relatively
developed regions in the country. By contrast, persons
from backward regions tend to stay longer, in some cases
even permanently, in their areas of destination, probably
because the conditions which had originally induced
their out-migration were still prevailing in their areas
of origin. Unlike the case of those originating in the
relatively developed regions, this group has to support
financially the relatives who are still living in a home
village as long as the means of production there are not

improved. Accordingly, it would be difficult for them to accumulate the needed capital to start a business like one who originates in a developed region. Moreover, for skilled workers originating in backward regions there are no or only limited chances to make use of the qualifications and the experience they gained through their migration process. By virtue of their increasing aspirations and their continually changing place utility matrix they are reluctant to return to their places of origin where their needs are hard to be locally satisfied. For the unskilled persons it is the matter of better income oportunities to cover the necessities of life that induce them to leave their home areas for other locations rather than to satisfy their growing aspirations. As has been shown by HEIN-RITZ, G. (1980) and SWAR EL DAHAB, A. (1978) there was a high tendency among the unskilled persons to remigrate to their respective regions after a short or long stay in the areas of destination. This is probably because of their failure to achieve economic progress in the destinations and the need to secure a life within their traditional social setup. But this should not imply that the skilled labour, by virtue of the socio-economic status they have reached, are completely detached and uprooted from their traditional societies, since there are concrete evidences of strong relations between them in terms of repeated visits and/or financial help, even if they chose to take up permanent residence away from their origin. In the next chapter we attempt to show, by means of a concrete example, how the migrant skilled persons were retaining a good relationship with their relatives still living in the home area in spite of the geographical and social displacement and the effects these relations have on the residual communities.

VII. MOBILIZATION EFFECT OF AGRICULTURAL MECHANIZATION

ON THE RURAL POPULATION: A CASE STUDY IN EL SUKI

DISTRICT

1. A FRAMEWORK FOR MOBILITY IMPACT STUDY

The following chapter deals with the possible effects of
agricultural mechanization on the rural areas of the
Democratic Republics of the Sudan. We attempt to prove
the hypothesis that the rural development measures, including the adoption of agricultural mechanization, do
not stabilize the population situation in the areas concerned, but rather cause a mobilization of the rural population, thus intensifying in-migration pressure on the
towns and increasing the tendency towards polarization.

Within the general inter-disciplinary field of population
mobility study, the dominant pattern has been a concern
with three particular branches: analysis of the spatial
patterns of movement, investigation of the motivations
for movement and description of the effects of migration
on the places of destination. There is, however, one
further aspect of population mobility which has been
neglected for the most part, namely, the study of the
effects of population mobility on the places of origin.
As LOWENTHAL and COMITAS (1962, p. 196) have pointed
out: 'people who move are much more frequently considered
as immigrants than as emigrants'.

Within the scope of a single chapter such as this it is
impossible to consider a complete mobility repercussions
study, but an attempt will be made to redress the customary
imbalance of interest by providing a case study of the
areas and communities left behind by rural emigrants.
Our attention will be mainly directed to loss of population
through migration, since this is the most measurable result in comparison to others. Moreover, we believe that all
other effects are a functional volume and attributes of
the persons who leave the rural areas. However, although
the study of net migration loss from rural areas has a
long history, particularly in the developed world (SAVILLE,
1957; BEALE, 1964), the measurement of migration loss has
often created problems in defining 'rural' or 'non-metropo-
litan' areas as well as in collecting data in the case of
the deloping countries. In the latter, including our case
study, lack of accurate census reports and population registration methods has caused statistics on population
gain and loss to be based on estimation rather than actual
information. More important than a quantitative and
qualitative examination of migration loss is examination
and explanation of the interrelated factors causing that
loss. Among the factors which have been most frequently considered are improved rural educational standards, regional
and sectoral wage differentials, dissatisfaction with
rural community life, the displacement effect of agricultural mechanization and deteriorating environmental conditions. Attempts have often been made to explain the general large scale reduction in rural population levels
against the background of major social, economic and
demographic changes occurring in other sectors on the
local or national level. In the developed countries, population loss from rural areas has been recognized within

the context of a major transformation in the national
way of life within the past century. This transformation
is presently taking place in the developing countries,
including our case study. Thus any analysis of the effect
of large-scale rural out-migration on the communities
left behind is made more complex by the need to relate
change in the rural areas to those on the broader national
level, separating the effects of other variables. The
phenomenon of counter-streams, as noted in the studies
of the developed world by SCHOFIELD (1970) is not yet a
factor in the developing world, since large-scale population
mobility, relative to socio-economic transformation, is
a relatively recent phenomenon. Until now there has been
no study on the developing countries which concentrates
on the flows of incoming population with suggestions
for possible reduction of the negative effect of net
population loss.

Consideration of the effects of migration on the residual
communities left behind with respect to the selectivity
of the process has been the greatest attention in nearly
all of the mobility impact studies. It has been generally
found that net migration loss from rural communities
has certain common features (MERLIN, 1971, pp. 67 - 92),
the two most common being that most migrants are young
and that males generally outnumber females. Other aspects
of selectivity which have been investigated include educational achievement (HANNAN, 1969, pp. 206-207), position
in the local rural social hierarchy (ISZAEVICH, 1975,
p. 304) and whether or not the migrant is a social inno-
vator (GALTUNG, 1971, pp. 190-191).

Selectivity in migration is a function of socio-economic
transformation in both sending and receiving areas. Thus it
should not always be taken as a negative effect of population

mobility, since a net loss of migrants from a rural area
may be either beneficial or detrimental to the residual
community. It is often argued that the fertility declined as a result of age - and sex-selective out-migration has caused rural migration loss to become a problem
rather than a safety valve which acts to stabilize the
rural social structure, partucularly in times of economic difficulties.

Studies of the residual communities have shown very similar effect on the sending areas, the most frequently considered being the two demographic effects of increased
relative age of the population (DRUDY, 1978, p. 58) and
the creation of a sex imbalance. These two aspects often
manifest themselves in the socio-economic performance of
the residual community. Socially, selective rural loss may
result in a loss of potential innovators and social leader-
ship (JONES, 1965, p. 42). Economically that loss may re-
strict the scope and viability of commercial activity
which may induce further emigration (REITER, 1972, p. 42).
On the whole, it may be argued that the effects of migration loss may be so severe that demographically, socially
and economically there is little possibility of future
stabilization, let alone growth and development.

2.   AN APPROACH TO THE STUDY OF POPULATION MOBILITY IMPACT

It is the aim of the present chapter to make a detailed
study of recent migration changes in a rural region of
the Democratic Republic of the Sudan with a view to
identifying the actual patterns of selectivity that have
operated among migrants of some selected villages and to

examine the way in which the observed patterns of selectivity have altered the structure of the residual community.
We attempt here to discriminate between the mobilizing
effect of the agricultural mechanization and the mobilizing effect of other working factors.

We approached the subject by selecting a number of villages in a particular region where agricultural mechanization
is wide spread and is generally accepted as the one innovation which has contributed most to bringing about
the present socio-economic transformation in the region.
Lack of adequate information, particularly on the population, and the restricted time for investigation have
limited the scope and depth of the study. Data concerning
the demographic structure of the rural areas as well as
that about in- and out-migration is utterly lacking in
the Sudan, particularly at the village level. Accordingly,
our study is based on a field survey on the micro- rather
than the macro-level. We attempt to measure the pull-effect
of a functional location of agricultural mechanization
on the young males of the surrounding villages. Our aim
is to prove the hypothesis that the more a place is affected by agricultural mechanization (i.e. the nearer it is
situated to the functional location of mechanization or
the longer such a location exists), the greater is the
probability of increased participation and hence increased
out-migration.

In our analysis we confine ourselves to the qualifying
effect of agricultural mechanization whereby the rural
population is stimulated to acquire technical skills,
causing a rise in aspiration which in turn induces out-
migration. Thus it is attempted to examine whether the
acquiring of technical skills through this type of

outmigration may be used to measure the contribution of agricultural mechanization to rural transformation. The argument is prefaced by a brief discussion of the changes which have overtaken the place in the last two decades and an analysis of the extent of rural out-migration, as caused by agricultural mechanization and its impact on rural developed. Our approach is to give a brief historical background on the expansion of the modern agricultural sub-sector in this particular district as part of its expansion in the whole Blue Nile Province to help explain, by means of a concrete case study, the effect of this process on the rural transformation there.

The administrative region of El Suki consists of a number of small- to large-sized villages with El Suki town (some 20,000 persons) as its largest central town. The area of study lies roughly in the centre of the former Blue Nile Province and some 40 km south of Sennar on the eastern bank of the Blue Nile. It is predominantly settled by a group of Fulani refugees who had fled Nigeria as a consequence of the British colonial invasion (DUFFIELD, 1977). The favourable natural conditions of the region (extensive unexploited lands with good quality soils as part of the central Sudan alluvial plain, extendable irrigation possibilities) have attracted other groups, particularly from the Northern Province, since the beginning of this century. As in other parts of the country's rural areas, there was no exact information available on previous in- and out-migration. Short-range but extensive population movements in the past, particularly to market centres, were reported to be fostered by the nature of land holding and by the existence of local crafts and rural industry. Although developments in other parts of the province had been communicated long before the actual transformation in this region

vocational training contributes to the rise in aspiration
in the same way as formal education. It may generally be
suggested that improved qualification increased an individual's chances of finding a rewarding job quickly when he
migrates. The fact that qualified workers have few or no
job opportunities at their places of origin induces them
to move to other locations.

3.   METHODOLOGY

We followed a method of complete coverage of all participants in a particular workshop with the aim of investiga-
ting their geographical origin, their age composition,
their educational level, their motives in joining the workshop and their intention with respect to future migration.
To investigate the problem of out-migration, as caused by
agricultural mechanization, a comprehensive survey was
carried out among the residual population in two selected
villages which were supposed to be directly affected by
agricultural mechanization according to the criteria described above. The study concentrated on the group of the
out-migrants in terms of sex, age, qualification and previous occupation in comparison to the residual population.
The main findings of the study are described in the following.

4.   THE CASE STUDY AREA: EL SUKI DISTRICT (see map 2)

Within the context of rural depopulation, this study seeks
to show how the population structure in one of the Sudan's
most impoverished provinces - the Blue Nile Province -
has undergone pronounced changes. An important theme developed in this section is the way in which the pattern of

began to take effect, interregional population movements had remained low due to limited aspirations, long distances and a primitive transport system. It was only after the Second World War that transformation gradually began to become apparent in the region. Like other regions in the country which have come into contact with the modern agricultural sub-sector, this region has experienced socio-economic transformation on a large scale since the beginning of this century.

The regional peasant economy of the nineteenth century, in which the village or sub-tribe defined the limits of social intercourse for the majority, communication was limited and markets were highly localized, gave way to a new phase of rural transformation. An essential element of change was and still is the mobilization of regional resources, particularly human resources, to participate in production for the world market. As elsewhere, the basis for this change does not lie in the agricultural sector itself but is the outcome of a prior expansion of non-agricultural sectors.

The main feature of change in this region, however, is the superimposition of pump-irrigated agriculture on the traditional rainfed agriculture. As a result of the rise in world cotton prices in the early fifties, the British administration attempted to promote the development and expansion of an indigenous private sector within the prevailing dependent formations. To realize this policy, land previously under communal use was newly registered and sold by the government to local merchants and companies (OSMAN, D.M., 1958, p. 40). Consequently, a number of small pump schemes appeared along the banks of the Blue Nile between Sennar and El Roseires more or less along the same lines as the tenancy system of the Gezira scheme. Few area residants

participated as tenants, rather the majority were degraded
to the status of agricultural labourers on the same land
which had hitherto been under their communal use. The incentive for their participation was the need for money to
pay the taxes imposed by the colonial government and to buy
non-agricultural commodities which began to flood the rural
central markets. Thus the change in land tenure and land
use may be regarded as the first real transformation of the
economy of this region. The gradual spread of wage labour
has been encroaching upon the traditional forms of labour
process based on the cooperation of family and village members, as a result of a gradual appearance of an indigenous
relatively wealthy group within the existing formations.
Thus two distinct social groups appeared in the region,
namely the commercial group largely based on the transport
business and trade transaction and the group of paid agricultural workers. This new form of economic involvement
has provided the indigenous population with the cash necessary for investment or to buy non-agricultural commodities.
The effect of capital accumulation has been a gradual change
in the individual's place utility matrix (see chapter 1.4),
a cause of out-migration. This change has manifested itself
in the gradual disappearance of the cooperative work system
and the phenomenon of contempt for agricultural manual work
among the peasant youth, an attitude which was further intensified by the spread of formal education.[1] As a consequence of this development some groups, particularly the
school-leavers, began to join the stream of rural-urban

---

1) The desire of a tenant to raise his socio-economic status
   has stimulated him to encourage his sons to join formal
   education at the same time that 'white-collar' jobs were
   highly appreciated.

migration.[2] This tendency has increased particularly since the early sixties when revenue from cotton began to fall.[3]

Parallel to the process of out-migration of the school-leavers, there has been a gradual increase in participation in the mechanical headquarters of the agricultural schemes in the same region, for the purpose of acquiring technical skills as a substitute for discontinued formal education. This effect of agricultural mechanization had more impact than merely skimming off the surplus population and began to dig deeply into the roots of the rural population. This type of population mobility reflects the deep-rooted socio-economic upheaval of shifting from a peasant-subsistant to a centralized urban-oriented way of life. The expansion of the urban centres and the attraction of their 'bright lights' was met by rising aspirations and growing discontent with rural conditions. Increased training opportunities, limited chances for employment in the region, prevailing regional wage differentials and increased information exchange were other effective factors which have been inducing the out-migration of the peasant youth. This process was highly selective in terms of sex, age, education and training level. This selectivity and its expected effect on the residual population is to be considered and tested empirically in the following discussion.

4.1　Findings of the Study Conducted Among the Participants of El Masara Workshop (see map 2).

To test the validity of our hypothesis that 'the intensity of rural population participation in the functional points of agricultural mechanization is a function of the distance

2) Due to the limited vacancies in higher schools (bottle-neck system of education) and because of limited chances for employment in the region the school-leavers were compelled to move away to make use of the level of education they attained.
3) As a consequence of a continuous drop in the tenant revenue, off-scheme interests became the main pursuit.

between those points and the parents' place of residence, we conducted a case study in the largest and oldest workshop in the region called El Masara workshop.[4]

4.1.1   Social composition

All participants were found to be males of Sudanese nationality.[5] They were in age-groups from 14-45 years as shown by Table 7.1.

Table 7.1:   Age Composition of Participants of El Masara Workshop

Age group	Absolute number	% of total
Less than 15	6	2.5
15 - 20	114	46.9
21 - 25	53	21.8
26 - 30	25	10.3
31 - 35	19	7.8
36 - 40	17	7.0
More than 40	9	3.1
T o t a l	243	100.0

Source: Our own investigation (Sending areas survey. Jan. 1980)

4) El Masara workshop was installed by Abullela Group Companies in the early fifties to serve a number of private pump schemes in the region. It is located at the site of El Masara scheme about halfway between Sennar and El Suki towns and is surrounded by a number of small and middle-sized villages. The number of participants in January 1980, in the technical branch only, was 243 persons, the majority of whom were tractor drivers and assistant drivers.

5) Although there were some participants from the Fulani ethnic group, they were still regarded as Sudanese, since they possess the Sudanese nationality by virtue of being supporters of some political groups in the past.

It is apparent from the above table that the majority of
participants were concentrated in the age groups 15-25
(68.7%), which reflects the attraction of the workshop particularly for young people. This was found to be manifested
in the higher number of assistants among the participants
(34.2%).[6] The markedly lower representation of persons in
the age groups 30 years and above may be attributed to the
out-migration of this particular age-group soon after acquiring the qualification necessary to compete for a job
elsewhere, since for qualified persons there are usually no
or only limited employment opportunities in the region and
there is an increasing demand for them particularly in
newly implemented schemes in other regions. The remaining
older persons were either highly paid or they were bound
by social obligations which compel them to stay. In fact,
some of this group were found to be in-migrants, who had
been purposely recruited from other locations to instruct
junoir technicians and to maintain the mechanical fleet.
They were accommodated in a separate quarter built especially for them and provided with the required services as
an incentive to stay. It is relevant to stress the importance of this particular group in providing a model of
urban life among the indigenous population (in their mode
of life, dress and communication), since they were predominantly originated from urban centres. They contribute
to a change in the population's place utility matrix, thus
stimulating the move to other places to acquire the same
standard of living.

Concerning the educational composition, we found that more
than three quarters of all participants have received at
least elementary education (Table 7.2). In comparison, the
majority of the rural population were without a formal education (informally educated). This suggests that this

---

6) The job of an 'assistant' was created to attract young
peasants to help in the technical work and at the same
time to be instructed in order to build up a potential
working cadre for further development of the scheme. It
offers training with very limited financial incentives
(LS. 13,900, presently LS. 29,500).

particular occupation is highly selective in terms of education level. The relatively lower representation of individuals with a higher education level may be due to the desire of the highly educated to join 'white-collar' jobs rather than working as assistant drivers or assistant mechanics. The small proportion of persons with a high secondary school level (6.2%) and holders of university degrees (1.2%) was exclusively composed of in-migrant highly skilled workers who occupied the directional posts of the workshop.

Table 7.2: Educational Composition of the Participants in El Masara Workshop

Educational level	Absolute number	% of total
Informal education	54	22.2
Elementary education	129	53.2
Lower secondary level	42	17.3
Higher secondary level	15	6.2
University level	3	1.2
T o t a l	243	100.0

Source: Our own investigation (Sending area survey.Jan. 1980)

As for the marital status of the participants it was found that almost two thirds were unmarried. Such a result appeared, at first sight, to be unusual in the rural areas, since usually marriage from the age of 18 to 25 years is quite common. The explanation for this finding may be sought in the rise of aspirations which renders marriage to be an endeavour which is to be well planned and thoroughly calculated. The accumulation of the money required to get married was impossible for many as long as they were still in the lower ranks of the economic ladder.[7] This was evident by crossing marital status and income level which revealed that those of higher income level had an increased propensity to marry (Table 7.3).

Table 7.3 A Combination of Marital Status and Income Level of the Participants in El Masara Workshop

Income group	Married N.of pers.	%	Unmarried N. of pers.	%	Total	% of total
Less than LS 30	4	4.8	79	95.2	83	34.2
31 - 40 LS	16	25.8	46	74.2	62	25.5
41 - 51 LS	28	68.3	13	32.7	41	16.9
51 - 60 LS	21	77.8	6	22.2	27	11.1
61 - 70 LS	14	87.5	2	12.5	16	6.6
71 - 80 LS	10	90.9	1	9.1	11	4.5
More than LS 80	3	100.0	0	00.0	3	1.2

Source: Our own investigation (Sending areas survey, Jan. 1980).

The table above shows that 76.6% were in the income level of LS 50 and lower which is comparatively lower than the average income of the tractor drivers in the agricultural schemes already discussed in chapter five (Table 5.18).[8]

7) It should be noted that all assistants in the workshop (almost one third of all participants) received the minimum wage of LS 29,500 at the time of investigation in 1980. Only two years ago the minimum wage had been LS 13,900.

8) The reason for this wage differential may be explained in terms of the relatively lower experience level of the participants of this workshop in comparison to those in other agricultural schemes. Another reason may be the fact that most of the participants of this workshop were still living with their parents, thus the cost of living is relatively lower than for a person who migrates to another location and has to accomodate himself independently.

Perhaps the perception of this wage differential and the inability to accumulate the money needed to marry induce some of them to move to other places despite the fact that even the minimum wage of skilled workers in-situ was far higher than the wage received by an agricultural worker.

4.1.2   Participants' place of origin

Our investigation revealed that 47.3 % originated from the village where the workshop is located (Um Durraba village), 23.9 % in El Busata village, 2 km apart. The rest originated from other locations within and outside the same district. As Table 8.4 shows the degree of participation of the young villagers in the workshop is a function of distances between parents' residence and that workshop. (Fig. 2).   This confirms our hypothesis that the proximity of the place of origin to the functional location of agricultural mechanization (workshop) increases the probability of participation. The most convincing explanation is the desire of the scheme's private owner to employ persons from the adjacent villages to eliminate the costs of accommodation and transportation and hence to be able to offer lower wages. [9] In this sense the rural places of origin contribute to the development of such functional locations not only by providing the needed reserve of potential skilled workers but also by assuming the

9) There were 15 houses which were meant to accomodate senior technicians who predominantly originated from distant places. House rental in the villages surrounding the workshop was still an investment seldom practised. The majority of participants commute daily between workshop and their parents' residence.

responsibility for accomodating them.

Table 7.4:   Number of Participants From Each Origin and
             its Relation to the Distance Between that
             Origin and the Workshop (see Fig. 2)

Place of origin	Distance in km	N. of pers.	% of total
Um Durraba village	less than 1 km	115	47.3
El Busata village	2 km	57	23.5
Zein el Abidin village	5 km	10	4.1
Abu Tamra village	7 km	6	2.5
Hamadnalla village	10 km	2	0.8
El Suki town	12 km	1	0.4
Other distant places	more than 12 km	52	21.4

Source: Our own investigation (Sending areas survey, Jan. 1980)

4.1.3   Previous occupation

The majority of participants (57.2 %) had participated
in the agricultural sector as unskilled labourers prior
to participating in the workshop. Their motive for participation was readily given as comtempt for agricultural
work (particularly in the case of the school-leavers),
the desire to acquire a skill in order to be able to
compete for a rewarding job elsewhere and the lack of
employment opportunities outside the agricultural sector. The effect of this fact is to reduce the number
of potential agricultural workers available, in compensation for whom other groups were recruited seasonally by
the scheme authority in more distant places. The fact
that the daily earnings of a semi-skilled worker in the
workshop, however low, are far higher than the daily
earnings for physically exhausting agricultural work

stimulate the rural youth to compete for such a job. The
high turnover among the skilled workers increases the possibility of their participation, thus decreasing their
readiness to do any sort of manual work. In fact, participation in the workshop provides the only opportunity to
break through the existing rigid socio-economic conditions
prevailing in their places of origin. This was confirmed
by our finding that 76.7% of all participants were intending to move to other places as soon as they acquired the
necessary qualification. under such conditions it may be
expected that the places which come into contact with the
agricultural mechanization are suffering a continuous decrease in their active labour force. To examine this expectation it was thought necessary to conduct a demographic
study in two randomly selected villages in the same district.
In the following we present our findings in El Kurmuta[10]
and Abu Gara [11] Villages.

---

10) El Kurmuta is a small-sized village (136 persons) and
one of three villages surrounding El Masara workshop
(collectively called Um Durraba village) inhabited by a
group of people who originated in the Northern Province
and who in-migrated to the region as early as the eve
of this century.

11) Abu Gara is a middle-sized village (675 persons) which
lies about 15 km south of El Suki town at the site of
Abu Gara irrigated scheme. By contrast it is inhabited
predominantly by a group of people originating from
Western Sudan who have in-migrated into the area since
the late nineteenth century as part of the Westerners'
settlement of the north-east Sudan. By contrast the
workshop adjacent to this village is smaller and more
recent than El Masara workshop near El Kurmuta village.

4.2   Findings of the Study Conducted Among the Residual
       Population of El Kurmuta and Abu Gara Villages of
       El Suki District (see map 2)

4.2.1   Aims and methodology of the study

In this study we attempted to reflect the mobilizing effect
of agricultural mechanization on the rural population whose
members, by virtue of its proximity to the functional locations (workshops) were able to acquire technical skills
which stimulated them to emigrate. Our approach was to investigate the demographic structure of the residual population
and the socio-economic composition of the emigrants. Here,
too, we followed a method of complete coverage whereby all
householders in each village were directly interviewed. This
was the only practical method in the absence of any sort of
demographic registration in the district.

4.2.2   Sex composition

Our investigation revealed that the female element dominated
in both villages among the residual population. This was found
to be in contrast to the sex composition of the emigrants
which was found to be dominated by the male elements (Table
7.5).

Table 7.5: Sex Composition of the Residual Population and the Out-
           migrants of El Kurmuta and Abu Gara' Villages

| Village | All Population | | | | | | | | | |
| | Total | Out-Migrant | | | | | | Residual population | | |
		Total	% of all pop.	Male N.	% of all Male	Female N.	% of all Fem.	Male N.	% of all Male	Female N.	% of all Fem.
El Kurmuta	136	48	35.4	39	50.0	9	15.5	39	50.0	49	84.5
Abu Gara'	675	98	14.5	81	23.5	17	5.2	264	45.8	313	94.8

Source: Our own investigation (Sending areas survey, January 1982)

The findings in the table above may be taken as the first
sign of the selectivity effect of agricultural mechanization on the population left behind, since usually only males
participate in the technical work in rural areas. The small
proportion of females among the out-migrants was reported to
be dependant householders.

4.2.3   Age structure

Our findings revealed that the selectivity effect of agricultural mechanization was not only manifested in the in-
balanced sex composition but also in age structure. As
shown in Table 7.6, the majority of the residual population
was composed of older persons (over 35 years) and children
(under 20 years). In contrast, the out-migrants were predominantly persons in the age group 21 - 35 years, who probably by this age had managed to acquire the necessary qualification to compete for more rewarding jobs in other locations.

Table 7.6 Age Composition of the Residual Male and Female
          Population and Out-migrants of El Kurmuta and
          Abu Gara Villages (in % of total number of each
          group)

Village	Residual population					Outmigrants				
	0-20	21-25	26-30	31-35	35+	0-20	21-25	26-30	31-35	35+
El Kurmuta	23.9	17.0	9.1	6.8	43.2	0.0	16.7	31.3	39.5	12.5
Abu Gara	21.7	16.8	8.5	6.2	46.8	2.3	18.3	29.2	37.1	13.1

Source: Our own investigation (Sending areas survey, Jan. 1980)

The finding above may be regarded as the most dangerous phenomenon as regard to the future socio-economic development

of the villages under discussion. If this trend continues
it may be expected that both villages will be depopulated,
since even the present younger residents (under 20 years)
stated their intention to leave the village as soon as they
acquire qualification in the workshop. the low representation of persons over 35 years of age among the out- migrants was not an effect of counter-migration, as is usually
the case in the developed countries, but rather a reflection
of the recentness of the out-migration of this particular
group of skilled labourers.

4.2.4   Educational composition

Our enquiries revealed that the outmigrants were selected
from the most educated elements of the male groups in the
two villages. As shown by Table 7.7, more than two thirds of
the out-migrants had at least elementary education, an education level similar to that of the interviewed tractor drivers and taxi drivers in the previous cases of study. In
contrast, the residual population was predominantly composed of presons who had only informal education.

Table 7.7: Distribution of the Residual Population and Out-
migrants According to the Level of Education (in
percentage of the total number of each group)

Village	Residual population			Outmigrants		
	Informal Education	Elementary Education	Higher Education	Informal Education	Elemen. Educat.	Higher Educat.
El Kurmuta	78.4	19.3	2.3	12.5	70.8	16.7
Abu Gara'	84.9	13.0	2.1	27.5	64.3	9.2

Source: Our own investigation (Sending areas survey, Jan 1980)

The importance of this type of selectivity, however, may
be seen in the tendency to deprive the rural areas of the
innovators who might be expected to contribute to the transformation in the social, economic and political set-up of
the rural community.

4.2.5   Economic composition

In order to reveal the relationship between agricultural
mechanization and the prevailing out-migration trends, an
attempt was made to classify the occupation structure of
the out-migrants prior to joining the stream of out-migration.
According to our findings there was a higher participation in
the mechanical part of agricultural mechanization, in both
villages, than in other occupations (Table 7.8).[12]

Table 7.8 Distribution of the Out-migrants in Each of the
           Two Villages According to Occupations Prior to
           Out-migration[13]

Village	Mech. work		Peasantry		Commerce		Personal serv.		No Occu.	
	N.	%	N.	%	N.	%	N.	%	N.	%
El Kurmuta	28	58.3	7	14.6	3	6.3	1	2.1	9	18.7
Abu Gara'	37	37.8	27	27.6	11	11.2	6	6.1	17	17.3

Source: Our own investigation (Sending areas survey, Jan. 1980)

12) Since there was a possibility of having more than one oc-
    cupation at the same time we consider only the prime oc-
    cupation of each person to the exclusion of any secondary
    occupation.
13) The occupational structure has been broken down into four
    categories: Mechanical = all activities in relation to
    the technical part of agricultural mechanization; peas-
    antry = all non-technical activities in relation to the
    agricultural sector; commerce = mainly shop-keeping, food
    processing such as baking, butchery and restaurant keep-
    ing; personal service = housekeepers, servants, cooks
    and the like; dependant wives = unemployed women.

The table above shows that more than half of the out-migrants of El Kurmuta had been participating in occupations related to agricultural mechanization before they left for other locations. This means that some individuals had left their previous occupations to join the mechanical sector while they were still in the same region of origin. Such a change of occupation, enforced by the adoption of agricultural mechanization, should be interpreted as a sign of an early stage of economic transformation in such rural areas. But a change in occupation, in situ, does not automatically mean that an individual is lost to his community; on the contrary, his value may be even higher than before. The real loss appears at the time when highly qualified persons feel compelled to emigrate, particularly in cases where the out-migrant is intending to take up permanent residence in areas of destination. At that stage it becomes evident that the whole region is suffering from a drain of its most innovating elements, as is the case of the two villages under discussion. The ultimate result will be an economic stagnation or even retardation.

It is paradoxical that persons with other occupations were poorly represented among the out-migrants despite the fact that these occupations offer lower economic incentives than occupations related to agricultural mechanization. The effect of the factor of aspiration on an individual's place utility matrix (chapter 1.4) may offer an explanation for the low respresentation of this group. By virtue of their education and experience, the skilled persons may be expected to be more motivated to move than others with less qualification. Moreover, qualified workers have a lower risk of unemployment when they move away than unqualified persons.

The comparatively lower proportion of those with mechanical
occupations in Abu Gara village may be explained by the
recentness and size of the functional location of agricultural mechanization there rather than in the reluctance
to move away. [14] The relatively higher representation of
persons with other occupations may be due to the ethnic
composition of the people in this particular village who,
predominantly originated in the western Sudan, have a
longer tradition of out-migration of unskilled persons,
particularly to urban centres, than the Northerners of
El Kurmuta village.

4.2.6   Period of out-migration

By retracing the period of out-migration among the members
of both villages we found that out-migration increases
with time (Table 7.9). It was apparent that the intensity
of out-migration through time was a function of the length
of existence of the functional locations of agricultural
mechanization. Accordingly, El Kurmuta village seems to
have a longer out-migration history of skilled labour
than Abu Gara village as evident from its higher proportion of out-migrants in the period prior to 1970 as compared with that of Abu Gara village.

---

14) In comparison to El Musara workshop, the workshop of
    Abu Gara scheme is smaller and more recently installed.
    The former was installed in 1953 and, at the time of
    investigation, it offered employment to 243 persons in
    the technical branch alone, while the latter was in-
    stalled in 1960 and offered employment for 78 persons.

Table 7.9:   Distribution of Out-migrants According
              to the Period of Out-migration

Village	El Kurmuta		Abu Gara	
Period of Out-migration	N. of respondants	% of total	N. of respondants	% of total
Before 1960	8	16.7	6	6.1
1960 - 1970	11	22.9	18	18.4
1971 - 1975	13	27.0	36	36.7
1976 - 1980	16	33.4	41	41.8
T o t a l	48	100.0	98	100.0

Source: Our own investigations (Sending areas survey,
        January 1980)

The   increasing demand for qualified persons, particularly
vehicle drivers and mechanics, both in the urban centres
and in the oil-rich Arab countries where higher economic
incentives are offered, has served as a main catalyst
to out-migration in the last few years. Were it not for
the qualifying effect of agricultural mechanization, it
would not be possible for the rural population to compete
for relatively high-paying jobs in other destinations,
which is illustrated by the relatively lower proportion
of out-migrants with non-technical occupations. In this
sense agricultural mechanization contributes to upgrading
the qualification level of the rural population, thus increasing their chances of finding a job quickly when they
move away. Such an upgrading effect, however, would have
been of significant importance for the process of rural
development were it not for the prevailing wage differentials between the latter and the urban areas which compel

the qualified persons to move.

By disintegrating the group of out-migrants in each of
the two villages according to their places of destination
at the time of the investigations it became evident
that the qualified rural youth did not only abandon their
places of origin but also left the agricultural sector.
(Table 7.10).

Table 7.10: Distribution of the Group of Out-Migrants
According to their Places of Destination
at the Time of Investigation

Destination	Still in agric. schemes		in Greater Khartoum		in other towns		abroad	
Village	n. of pers.	%	n. of pers.	%	n. of pers.	%	n. of pers.	%
El Kurmuta	6	12.5	22	45.8	8	16.7	12	25.0
Abu Gara	26	26.5	38	38.8	19	19.4	15	15.3

Source: Our own investigation (Sending areas survey, Jan. 1980)

The table above revealed that the end effect of the
qualifying process of agricultural mechanization was the
concentration of the most qualified of the rural population in the urban centres, particularly Greater Khartoum,
as a step towards leaving the country entirely. [15]

---

15) The majority of those who were in Khartoum, other towns
and abroad at the time of investigation were reported
to have circulated between the different agricultural
schemes before they finally arrived at these destinations (see the circulation of skilled and semi-skilled
workers in chapter 5.).

The fact that only a small proportion of out-migration
(11.3 % and 13.4 % in El Kurmuta and Abu Gara respectively)
were reported by the interviewed relatives to have succeeded in taking up permanent residence in the places of
destination indicates that this particular type of
population mobility has not reached a mature stage. For
the majority, Khartoum was a preparatory station in the
continuing the mobility process. [16]

4.2.7   Contact with the place of origin

To show the reflexive effect of this type of population
mobility on the places of origin, an attempt was made
to reveal the degree of contact of an out-migrant in the
different destinations. We generally noticed that increased
spatial an social displacement (horizontal and vertical
mobility) of a person decreases the degree of contact with
his place of origin (Table 7.11).

---

16) It was not possible for a third person to define the
    intended new destination of out-migrants, but there
    was good reason to consider them potential movers.

Table 7.11:   The Relationship Between the Different
                Destinations and the Degree of Contact
                of an Out-migrant with his Origin (as
                a Percentage of Out-migrants in Each
                Destination) [17]

Destination	Agricul. schemes			Small Urban			Khartoum			Abroad		
Degree of contact	Strong	Weak relation	no	Strong	Weak relation	no	Strong	weak relation	no	Strong	Weak relation	no
El Kurmuta	83.3	16.7	00	57.1	42.9	00	40.9	50.1	9.1	25.0	58.3	16.7
Abu Gara	80.7	19.3	00	67.9	36.6	5.3	44.8	47.4	7.8	33.3	46.7	20.0

Source: Our own investigation (Sending areas survey, Jan. 1980)

The highest degree of contact (regular visits and regular
financial aid), however, was reported among persons who were
still joining the agricultural sector. At the other end of
the spectrum, the out-migrants abroad were reported to
have the lowest degree of contact, even in relation to the
migrants in Khartoum. But even so, at least a quarter of
the out-migrants still keep strong relations with their
home area in spite of the physical distance and inefficient
means of communication. The fact that out-migration is
still viewed as a temporary move for the purpose of the
bettering of their socia-economic situation, induces the
out-migrants to maintain strong contacts with their home
areas with a view to socio-economic security at the age
of retirement. Whether or not these strong family relations,

17) We aggregated all types of contacts in three distinct
    categories: Strong = regular visits and/or regular
    financial aid; Weak = irregular visits and irregular
    financial aid; No contact = No visits and no financial
    aid.

a feature of the Sudanese extended family system will continue to prevail is a function of the rate of community socio-economic transformation in the sending areas and the rate of integration of out-migrants in their places of destination.

At this stage of out-migration process it was impossible to measure the resulting effect of such contacts on the places of origin. Although there were apparent changes in the way people live, dress and communicate, it was not possible to quantify this effect due to the difficulty of collecting the necessary information. It was evident, however, that in both villages there was not a single case of a return migrant. Even those who had joined the stream of counter-migration prefered to take up residence in the urban centre nearest to their place of origin as a compromise between their desire to satisfy increasing socio-economic needs and the need to be attached to the traditional community. [18)]

5. SOCIAL AND ECONOMIC IMPACT OF POPULATION MOBILITY ON AREAS OF ORIGIN

The two villages under study have been experiencing continuous socio-economic changes in the past two decades, a situation which is not untypical of many rural areas where the population for one reason or another has been induces to join the stream of rural-urban migration. The most apparent effect manifested itself in the tendency

---

18) At the time of investigation there was a small number of return migrants who had taken up residence in Sennar and El Suki towns.

toward depopulation which has been occurring as an effect
of the negative migration stream rather than through national population loss (no evidence of birth control
measures or of abnormally high mortality rate). With the exception of the few skilled workers who were brought in on a
temporary basis from other distant localities to direct
and maintain the technical work at the functional points
of agricultural mechanization, there was no sign of in-
migration which could play a vital role in reversing the
general trend of population evolution and maintaining
the demographic balance.

Because of the lack of any sort of registered data, it
would be difficult to quantify the demographic effects
of out-migration on the communities left behind. It is
also difficult to distinguish between the effects of
out-migration and the effects of other external factors.
Furthermore, it is difficult to evaluate the demographic
impact at this stage of population out-migration, since
out-migration effect is likely to become evident only
after a long period of time. This means that the out-
migration of adult males now, though having an immediate
effect on fertility, will deplete a particular age group
for years to come.

By analysing the demographic structure at the time of
investigation, it was found to be characterized by a pre-
dominance of females over males, and generally of persons in the age groups over 35 years old and children
under 20 years. In contrast, the group of out-migrants
was found to consist predominantly of males in the age
group 20 - 34 years (Table 7.6). This suggests an enhance-
ment of the relative importance of the elderly and a
reduction in the importance of young adults, particularly

of the middle-aged, which inevitably contributes to an increase in the age ratio of the population which leades to a strain on welfare facilities and/or instability of the social structure.

We have already pointed out the selectivity effect of out-migration in terms of education level and economic occupation (Tables 7.7 and 7.8). It is relevant in this context to stress the point that in areas where the population falls numerically and structurally far short of local demand for manpower, as is the case in the area under study, out-migration is likely to have disastrous effects, particularly where the process is highly selective. In the longer term, pronounced changes in the population structure, as found in both villages under study, are likely to be accompanied by difficulties in the provision of various forms of local government services. The fact that certain facilities become redundant with a consequent loss of capital investment, such as the closing of private shops in both villages, may be taken as a reflection of the structural and numerical changes in the population resulting from selective out-migration. Such closures, however, are inevitable in a situation where buying power is reduced due to decreasing revenue from traditional occupations and the out-migration of the relatively higher-paid persons. The suggestion that this situation may be counteracted by expected remittances is not yet applicable in these particular cases, since out-migration is still a recent phenomenon and most of the out-migrants, with the exception of the few abroad are still on the lower rungs of the occupational ladder. Even those remittances sent back were found to have been chiefly invested in buildings, giving the eroneous impression of increased village population and a higher economic standard.

Occupational transfer in situ, i. e. displacement of the
labour force in a particular sector, coupled with increased employment in another sector in the same region,
which might have stopped or at least slowed the migration
speed from such villages, has not yet been put into
practice on a sufficient scale. Thus it may be inferred
that population stability and the provision of social
welfare facilities will be further threatened if present
trends of selective out-migration continue. Inasmuch as
continued out-migration on the present scale will result
in a reduction in further viability and stability of
rural communities, more large scale preventive and correc-
tive measures are needed. At the present stage of socio-
economic transformation in the rural areas, it should be
recognized that only by halting urban growth and reducing
the regional and sectoral income disparity can the rural
exodus be controlled. One-sided measures to foster the
development of the rural areas, such as expansion in the
modern agricultural sector, as shown by this study, do
not stabilize the population, rather they intensify the
deleterious effects of past population mobility on the
rural communities left behind. The argument that rural-
urban migration contributes to the socio-economic transformation of the sending areas should, accordingly, be
accepted with great caution. Of course, there are some
advantages to out-migration such as the diffusion of
innovations and the increase in the rate of social trans-
formations which are manifested in the two villages under
study in the way people live, dress and communicate. These
gains are highly valuable to the residual population,
in the shorter term only, since without such gains the
rural population would remain primitive and isolated.
But these gains should not obscure the long-term negative
effects, since these very short term gains are likely to

cause further instability in the rural communities as
a result of their stimulating potential movers to join
the stream of out-migration in the absence of local employment opportunities with an effect of depopulating
the rural areas, a situation which would prove disastrous
for the economy of a developing country like the Sudan.

VIII. AGRICULTURAL MECHANIZATION AS AN INDIRECT FACTOR

OF POPULATION MOBILITY

In this chapter we present briefly other types of population mobility which we believe have some relation to
agricultural mechanization. We distinguish between two
main types of population mobility, namely: rural-rural
population mobility (movements of the seasonal agricultural labourers, the inter-and-intra-regional curcula-
tion of the nomads and the government controlled type
of population movements) and ural-urban population mobility of unskilled labourers. Both types have been dealt
with by a number of writers elsewhere. [1] All we need
here is to consider agricultural mechanization as a variable
which induces these types of population mobility.

1. RURAL-RURAL POPULATION MOBILITY

1.1 Rural-Rural Circulation Of Unskilled Labourers

This type of population movement is often referred to as
the movement of seasonal agricultural labourers which is
necessitated by the existence of a highly localized modern
agricultural sub-sector, centred around mechanization,
resulting in the creation of actual economic systems, a
feature of the Sudan's economy.

The significance of this particular type of population
mobility lies both in its magnitude with regard to the

---

1) Both types have been treated by a number of scholars, who attempt to
reflect their magnitude and effects on both sending and receiving
areas (GALAL EL DIN, M. E., 1973, 1979; EL BUSHRA, 1976; ABU SIN, M.
E., 1975 and SWAR EL DAHAB, A., 1978).

number of people involved and to its socio-economic impact both on sending and receiving areas. It reflects the main mechanism of the basic socio-economic changes and the transformation of the contemporary Sudanese society. It is often represented as a function of two major factors, namely, the structural nature of the country represented by diverse environmental and cultural conditions and the adoption of agricultural innovations, particularly agricultural mechanization (chapter 4), which are concentrated in some regions rather than in others. The former is regarded as a 'push' factor, which induces people to search for compensation for their deteriorating environmental conditions by moving to more rewarding localities. The latter is a 'pull' factor which stimulates people to participate in the sort of seasonal occupation offered in the modern agricultural sub-sector. Both factors are working together, resulting in a regional and sectoral population mobility.

As previously stated, the Sudan is characterized by diverse environmental conditions reflected in a diverse pattern of land use. The people in the different geographical regions used to adapt themselves to the available resources to ensure their living, but as time goes on and due to natural and human factors, a deterioration in the environmental conditions becomes apparent and it is obvious that it is no longer possible to maintain the previous way of life with their limited knowledge and primitive production tools. Thus the only alternative, in the absence of government intervention, is the movement to other regions. This is particularly the case of the provinces Darfur and Kordofan where the off-region interest becomes a pursuit of life. The people in this province are compelled to move not only within the same region but to participate

in a long-distance, interprovincial type of movement.
In this context the government as the mean decision-maker
in the whole process of modernization, plays a leading
role in locating and relocating the different resources
including manpower.

In chapter IV we attempted to give a brief review of
the process of developing the modern agricultural sub-
sector. We emphasized the fact that the development trend
in the Sudan was and still is towards more localized development projects which concentrate on market-oriented
products. The favourability of the north-eastern Sudan
centered around the Nile axis, (in terms of agro-ecological conditions and its central location to communication
systems) has rendered it a centre of gravity for all
types of population mobility, particularly that of seasonal
agricultural labourers. In this context mechanization is
the most important agricultural input which determines
the scope and intensity of resource utility in the region
including manpower. Mainly for economic reasons (abundance
of cheap labour force, scarce capital) it was thought
necessary to adopt partial rather than full mechanization
practices. Thus a huge number of unskilled workers has to
be mobilized from backward regions toward development poles,
i. e. from the traditional sector to the modern agricultural sector. Frankly, the exact number of persons involved in this type of population mobility is not precisely
known. According to ILO (1976, p. 106), there are approximately one million persons circulating annually between their
home area and the different mechanized agricultural schemes.
Other authorities stated that the rainfed mechanized
schemes alone attract about one million workers annually,
apart from the irrigated mechanized schemes which attract
approximately 750,000 persons annually (GALAL EL DIN, M. E.,
1979). But even if we consider the figure of one million

as the actual number participating in the agricultural
modern sub-sector it becomes evident that this particular
type of population mobility is of significant importance
as far as population redistribution is concerned, since
it constitutes 14 % of all the country's labour force and
6 - 7 % of the total population of the Sudan.

This type of population movement started as early as the
first quarter of this century when the colonial government was confronted with the problems of labour shortage
in the newly implemented Gezira project. The inability of
the tenants and their families to do the needed manual
work has induced the scheme administration to recruit
agricultural workers from other regions. Thus it was thought
necessary to build up recruitment committees and to
open recruitment offices in a number of towns to help
mobilize and persuade the indigenous people to join the
work in the modern agricultural sub-sector centred around
the Gezira scheme.Many devices were introduced to convince people to participate in the process (provision
of food, loans and free transport). In addition, instruc-
tions were given to the local authorities to close the
public drinking-places during the peak demand season
to help induce the indigenous population to join the cotton-
picking campaign. The recruited people have to be accompanied by the police, the tenant delegates and the labour
contractors to make sure that they go where they are supposed
to go (ABU SIN, M. E., 1975, p. 254).

At first the majority of the recruited people were from
the West African countries who were on their way to Mecca.
For this group the participation in the picking campaign
was essential to collect some money for the completion of
the journey. This was often argued to be the reason for
the huge waves of in-migrating West-African people who

at present constitute a high proportion of the Sudanese
population.[2] But due to some in-migration restrictions,
this source was no longer capable of covering the increasing demand for agricultural workers in the Nile axis.
Thus the main emphasis was laid on the people from Western
Sudan, who by no means voluntarily participated in the
process. Has it not been for the recruitment measures
pursued by the government authorities, and the overwhelming environmental conditions prevailing in a region
they would not have participated in the process at all.
Thus it is not justified to relate their movements to the
functioning of a free-labour market system according to
supply and demand as has been suggested by the ILO (1976).[3]
The majority of migrants were neither selective to particular occupation nor to particular destination.

Our concern in this context is to stress the fact that
developments in the modern agricultural sub-sector, which
centred around mechanization, have substantially widened
the existing regional disparity which gives this type of
population mobility more importance in regard to volume,
frequency, interregional convergence and socio-economic

---

2) The study of the in-migration of the West-African people
   in the Sudan has been well dealt with by a number of
   scholars elsewhere (BARNETT, 1977; GAITSKELL, 1959;
   HENIN, R. A., 1961; GALAL EL DIN, 1973; MATHER, D. B.,
   1956; Mc LOUGHLIN, P. F. M., 1963).

3) The ILO (1976) suggested that the movement of seasonal
   unskilled labourers is evidence that the theory of labour supply and demand functions well between the less
   developed region in western Sudan and poles of development in north-eastern Sudan.

impact. It has gained momentum particularly since the
sixties as the result of the tremendous expansion in both
irrigated and rainfed mechanized schemes. The concentration
of development poles in north-central Sudan has given
this type of population mobility its converging nature,
while the coincidence of the period of high demand for
labour in the schemes with the period of idleness in
other regions has reduced it to seasonality rather than
the whole year round. But this seasonal nature does not
imply that the move is exclusively a temporary one, since
some of the movers, particularly in recent times have
decided to stay in their areas of destination for a number
of years before joining the counter-stream of migration.
This decision is governed by the geographical distance
between areas of origin and areas of destination, since
it is unlikely that the long-distance movers will be
able in one season to collect the money needed to cover
the return journey and the needs of the family members in
the home village. Moreover, availability of employment
opportunities even in the agricultural dead season, particularly in the towns within or near the schemes, stimulates
them to increase their income or to sustain themselves
til the coming season. This possibility, we believe, is
of significant importance, since it gives this type of
population mobility its socio-economic magnitude, to be
discussed in relation to the rural-urban population mobility.

1.2   Intra- And Interregional Movements Of The Nomads
      As Related To Agricultural Mechanization

Circulation of nomads as caused by external factors has been
well treated by ABU SIN, M. E. (1975). We attempt here

to relate this type of population movement to the phenomenon of agricultural mechanization to see whether it is
similarly affected by its geographicel distribution. It
may be suggested that the expansion of the modern agricultural sub-sector has not only deprived the nomads of their
traditional grazing lands and hence compelled them to
search for new locations but also stimulated them to pursue a settled way of life. The experience of the Gezira
scheme to sedentrize the mobile semi-nomadic tribes proved
to be incapable of being widely practised in the region.
Recent attempts to stimulate the nomads of eastern Sudan
to adopt a settled life proved to be unsatisfactory.

Although some of the nomads participate in the modern
agricultural sub-sector as tenants or agricultural workers,
the time is not yet ripe to speak about a successful
transformation process. The experiences of the Khashm
el Girba, El Suki and El Rahad schemes show that the
nomads participate in these schemes at present not because
of their positive attitude towards innovations but only
because they see this as the only way to secure their
rights on their previous territories. They are not yet
convinced of the good of such innovations, since
their material gains lay far behind their expectations,
which are governed by their own inherited perception of
the positive nature of any change. Even the present measures to integrate the nomads in the modern agricultural
sub-sector by providing settlements and social services
have not yet proved successful for the very simple reason
that the nomads were not asked to present their own
perception of a settled life. If this does not occur, all
other measures will be bound to fail like the functional
literacy programme experiment in the Khashm el Girba scheme
(AGOUBA M., 1980, p. 65 - 81).

1.3   The Government Controlled Population Movement In
       Relation To The Agricultural Mechanization

By this type of population movement we mean the attempt
of the government to mobilize some groups from distant
areas to the newly implemented irrigated or rainfed
mechanized schemes. In this context we refer to the direct
government involvment in large-scale resettlement projects such as that of the Khashm el Girba and El Suki
projects. The implementation of the first project in the
early sixties coincided with the search for a suitable
alternative place to resettle the Halfawis whose home area
was to be flooded by the proposed Lake Nasir in connection
with the construction of the Aswan High Dam. As a means
to make use of the human resource factor for the development of the newly implemented scheme the government decided
to transfer the Halfawis from their home area at Wadi
Halfa to the Khashm el Girba area in the Butana Plain some
600 miles away, irrespective of the reluctance of the people
involved. The government's choice was based on the assumption that this particular group, with its long settled life
and its agrarian experience, was likely to establish an
example for the indigenous population, mainly the nomads, in
developing an integrated regional economy. In this
sense an attempt was made to exploit the available resources, irrigation water from the Atbara river by means
of a dam, and enough land with good quality soil for
modern agricultural practices, through mobilizing the Halfawi group and some of the nomadic tribes. Thus 50,000
Halfawis were induced to move in spite of their objection
to the idea of transfer in general and to this particular
destination in particular. It was the first experience in
the country of mass resettlement. The process started in

1964 and was completed in 1968 whereby the transferred
people were resettled in 25 villages with sizes varying
between 175 - 250 houses with a main town (New Halfa) in
the centre. The cost of the whole operation was over
LS 58.3 million including the dam (7.5 million), other
irrigation installation (24.8 million) and the rest (26
million) was spent on housing, compensations, provision of
services etc. (EL MANGOURI, H., 1978). The study of
the resettlement of the Halfawi group has been well dealt
with elsewhere (DAFALLA, H., 1975; EL BAGIR, H., 1972;
FAHIM, H. M., 1972 and EL BADRAWI, M., 1972, to mention
a few).

Our concern in this context is to stress the fact that the
expansion in the agricultural modern sub-sector has induced
the government to organize and complete a transfer of this
particular group. Although the Halfawis traditionally participated in the waves of internal and external migration,
it is not justified to regard their transference to Khashm
el Girba as a continuation of their traditional migration
process, since the action was against their will. Everything
was arranged for them and they had no say but to accept what
the government regarded as beneficial for them. The consequence of this type of government-controlled population
movement is well manifested in the unsatisfactory performance of the scheme, an assessment of which was made
by the writer elsewhere (EL MANGOURI, H., 1978).

It is worth mentioning in this context that this particular
scheme was not only responsible for the transference of
the Halfawi group but also caused the mobilization of over
100,000 persons from different parts of the country, as
tenants, traders, officials or agricultural workers. Unlike
the Halfawis, ex-nomad tenants and their families were

stimulated to move to the scheme area with the hope of
improving their living standard. In this sense the government measure to develop the region by means of a modern
agricultural scheme was the cause of the mobilization of
the nomads in the region, a process which is still going
on with questionable results.

Most striking was the attempt to resettle part of the Beja
tribe whose home area had considerably deteriorated due
to the severe drought conditions. As part of the solutions
proposed, 600 tenancies were allocated to this group and#
the government increased pressure to induce them to migrate
them to the new destination chosen for them. The success
of the experiment is manifested in their poorest agricultural performance in comparison with other tenant groups.
In spite of this negative result the government continued
the process of resettlement of this group as a result of
the further deterioration of the home region and the difficulty of offering them a secure way of life there. In
another attempt, the government directed the educated members of this group to mobilize their tribe to accept the
transfer to two other proposed schemes, namely Setit
scheme some 70 miles south-east of Gedarif town and
El Suki scheme on the Blue Nile. Both sites are over
400 miles from the Beja area north of Port Sudan. Although
the majority of people objected to the idea of a transfer
as such, the government succeeded in persuading a minority
to move.

Thus some were transfered to Setit site in 1971 and others
to El Suki site in 1971/1972. Although in both cases the
government has attempted to provide them with the necessary services and helped them to overcome the difficulties
of the first seasons, the whole operation proved to be a

failure particularly in El Suki site where the migrants
deserted their planned villages and remigrated to their
places of origin. It should be noted that in both cases
a modern agricultural performance is pursued whereby
agricultural mechanization decreases the drudgery of work,
a sort of stimulation to the newly settled nomadic elements. Thus the government has been fully involved in
all processes of controlled mobility. It acted not only
as a decision-maker for the transfer of a particular
group but also as a demarcator for the destinations, time
of move, the way and its financing. Even the modes of
living in areas of destination is pre-determined for the
migrants by the government whose main objective was to
mobilize the available resources for the sake of the modernization of the country. Hence, contrasted with other types
of population mobility, this type is characterized by its
involuntary nature since the decision to migrate and the
whole process of migration has been made and implemented
by the government. This means that it involves in the majority
of cases non-potential migrants for whom the constraints
of movement are modified or overcome by the government.
They are influenced more by 'push' factors than by 'pull'
factors and move in a group rather than as individuals,
thus the normal push-pull model governed by supply and
demand and freedom of decision does not function in this
case. The persons involved in this mass displacement have
to follow the government instruction irrespective of their
own objectives. The effect of this type of population mobility may be more profound than other types of mobility since
it involves a transfer of a whole group with its characteristic culture to another region with other culture groups.
Whether a homogeneity will result from this cultural
heterogeneity is questionable as is the case of the present
situation in the settlement schemes under study. The

uprooting of such groups will affect the socio-economic
set-up of the sending area, since in this case, the possibility of a counter stream is reduced to a minimum unlike
in other types of population mobility.

2. RURAL-URBAN POPULATION MOBILITY

In the following discussion we confine ourselves to the
rural-urban population mobility of unskilled labour which
is, we believe, indirectly caused by expansion of the
use of agricultural machnization. As elsewhere in the
developing countries, this type of population mobility
is becoming one of the main features of the developing
Sudan. Its main characteristic is its converging nature,
since all moves from different parts of the country converge in the big towns particularly Greater Khartoum. Its
main effect is the depopulation of the rural areas and
the growing of squatter settlements in the urban centres,
both are a cause and an effect of regional disparity. Thus
it attracts the attention of planners and technocrats to
uncover its dimension and result. These have been presented
in many studies, each from a particular viewpoint. Hence
we need not go into more details here, all we need is to
clarify the role played by agricultural mechanization in
mobilizing the group of unskilled labour from their rural
exodus to the urban centres.

Like other types of population mobility, this one started
as early as the last quarter of the nineteenth century
as a result of the gradual rise of small urban centres,
particularly in the Northern and Khartoum provinces, as a
result of a gradual change in the Sudan economy as it

began the primary stage of economic development. The gradual
substitution of the steam- and diesel-drawn machines for
the traditional agricultural equipments, necessitated
land accumulation and land consolidation for the sake of
producing for the internal and external market. Consequently,
some groups, particularly the poor, who could not afford
the cost of modernization, were obliged to search for alternative chances elsewhere. The first targets were the
towns of western and central Sudan where the hinterlands
were still practising a sort of subsistance economy. Well
experienced in agriculture and trade, the riverain people
began to introduce a cash economy in their new destinations
which enabled them to accumulate wealth and to be distinct-
ly differentiated from the indigenous populations.
This was manifested in their way of living, their relatively modern houses which were grouped in quarters close to
the core of the town, contrasted sharply with those of
the indigenous population.

This stage, however, gained momentum by the gradual structural change of most of the Sudanese towns, due to the
process of upgrading from purely local market centres, into
centres with more urban amenities, service and seasonal
or permanent employment opportunities, in a larger hinter-
land than before. This change was an effect of the gradual
expansion of the modern agricultural sub-sector, particularly in the Nile axis and its tributaries, which differentiates
the development of models of the modern style of life
sharply from the rural style. This was further facilitated
by the development of other economic fields such as small-
scale industries, commerce and public utilities, all related to agricultural development, which induce further rural-
urban population mobility with the hope of reducing the
income disparity between the different regions.

Table 8.1: Balanced Net In-migration of the Urban Areas by Province - 1966 *

(e. g. in-migration into the urban areas of province A minus out-migration from province A into the urban areas of province B)

Province of In-migration	Blue Nile		Kassala		Khartoum		Darfur		Kordofan		Northern Province	
	total gain or loss	%	total gain or loss	%	total gain or loss	%	total gain or loss	%	total gain or loss	%	total gain or loss	%
Blue Nile	+35510	+34.5	- 4450	- 2.4	-13190	- 5.4	+ 7380	+ 5.6	+ 7440	+ 3.5	+17830	+16.1
Kassala	+ 4450	+ 5.1	+21250	+23.5	+ 2040	+ 4.1	+ 3120	+ 2.4	+ 4860	+ 4.9	+38580	+39.9
Khartoum	+13190	+ 5.4	- 2040	- 4.1	+15020	+ 9.7	+ 9380	+ 0.8	+17590	+ 6.5	+56780	+27.9
Darfur	- 7380	- 5.6	- 3120	- 5.6	+ 9380	+ 0.8	+15320	+63.2	- 1980	- 1.3	+ 1550	+ 7.9
Kordofan	- 7440	- 3.5	- 4860	- 3.5	-17590	- 6.5	+ 1980	+ 1.3	+27040	+52.8	+ 3880	+ 6.1
Northern Province	-17880	-16.4	-38580	-39.9	-56780	-27.9	- 1550	- 7.9	-27040	- 6.1	+ 3850	+67.0

* Compiled from the Department of Statistics and Population and Housing Survey, 1964/66

Unlike the case of the government-controlled types of
movement, this one is vonluntary in nature since the migrants
carefully plan their movement according to the degree of
information they have about other destinations. It is a
chain-movement in the sense that each movement induced
a further one after a time-lag for information to be
transmitted. It involves individuals, in some cases families, rather than whole groups or whole tribes. Its exact
volume is difficult to assess,but one may refer to the
attempt of the Department of Statistics to give a balanced
Net In-Migration of the urban centres by province (Table
8.1).

The effect of this stage of the rural-urban mobility
may be seen in the urban model it sets among the indigenous population to which they respond positively. Daily
contacts and gradual spread of education were the cause
of cultural diffusion and rise in aspiration, which
brought about a change in an individual's place utility
matrix and hence a 'push' factor which induces him
to pursue an urban life. This is the cause of the huge
waves of unskilled workers, who desert their home village
and join the step-like migration process into a town
to secure a better life. The main stimulus for their
movements is the speedy economic transformation which is
presently taking place in North East Sudan. The continuous
increase in demand for agricultural workers to participate
in the modern agricultural sub-sector has greatly reduced
the risk of unemployment for a potential rural-urban
migrant. They joined the mechanized agricultural schemes
as seasonal agricultural workers with the hope of
collecting the money they need to improve their living
standard in the home village. But due to the disappointing
revenue, not more than an average of LS 15 a month, and

the seasonal nature of this occupation, they are compelled to search for other complementary alternatives.
Consequently, they have to move to the urban centres
particularly Greater Khartoum where industries - mostly
engaged in manufacturing agricultural products - and services are concentrated. At present this type of population
mobility is becoming more noticeable in size and effect.
It is gradually dominating the Sudanese internal mobility
as far as volume, convergence and impact are concerned.
The people involved are mostly unskilled, uneducated
from the least populated regions with the rural peasant
or nomadic background. They are less selective in their
choice of occupation and areas of destination than individuals of the previous stage. Depopulation of areas of
origin, sub-urban growth, appearance of squatter settlements, and ruralization of towns are some of the effects
of this type of population mobility, which we return to
later as part of the whole assessment of the problem of
population mobility in the Sudan.

The volume of the flow from rural areas to the big urban
centres is not exactly known, due to the dynamic nature
of the flow itself, and the primitive means of statisti-
cal registrations. Here we refer to some studies which
attempted to reflect the scope of this particular type
of mobility. According to ABU SIN, M. E. (1975, p. 364)
the 'cardboard' settlement dwellers increased in number
from 30,000 in 1965 to about 80,000 in 1972. In Port Sudan,
the second largest town in the country, the number of
illegal 'deims' dwellers has risen from 20,000 to over
60,000 during the same period. He further pointed out
that one settlement in southern Khartoum, now called
Hay Mayo, reached a number of 20,000 inhabitants within
4 years only. This shows that the rush is continually

increasing towards Greater Khartoum in which the population grew from about 50,000 in 1900 to about 1,000,000
in 1975 mainly due to internal migration (EL BUSHRA, E.,
1976, p. 75). This means that the population of the
three towns was multiplied by 20 times during a 75 years
period, because they have the highest concentration of
industrial and commercial enterprises as well as the
highest intensity of social services. According to ABU
SIN, M.E. (1975, p. 119) over 40 % of the total urban
population of the country in 1966 was concentrated in
Greater Khartoum.

Our concern in this context is to stress the fact
that the majority of Khartoum in-migrants arrived in a
step-like movement and very few of them came directly
from their places of origin. The survey of the Department of Statistics in 1971 quoted by SWAR EL DAHAB, A.
(1978, p. 139) shows that the province of birth and the
province of last previous residence are not always identical. For isntance, those who reported the Northern Province as their place of birth amount to 36.6 % of all
Khartoum in-migrants while the proportion of those who
directly arrived amounts to 29.4 % only. In contrast
to this the proportion of those who reported the Blue Nile
Province as their place of birth falls short of the
proportion of those who gave the same province as their
last place of out-migration. This means that, while some
provinces are losing part of their population to other
provinces before they join Khartoum in-migration, like
Northern Province, Kordofan and Darfur Province, other
provinces are gaining before they contribute to Khartoum
in-migration as is the case of the Blue Nile, Gezira and
Kassala Provinces (see Table 8.2). This has been recently confirmed by G. HEINRITZ (1981), who examined the mode

of in-migration in Hay Mayo in Greater Khartoum and village 17 of New Halfa town. He reached the conclusion
that a considerable proportion of the in-migrants in both
cases are Westerners who indirectly arrive at both destinations. This may confirm our assumption that part of the
rural urban migrants had been working in the agricultural
modern sub-sector before they decided to take up an occupation in an urban centre. In this sense the agricultural
modern sector is a transitional stage which prepares the
rural population for the move into the towns. In the absence of industrial development in rural areas, the urban
centres remain the only alternative to the less rewarding
agricultural employment. Of course, joining the rural-urban
stream of migration is not only an effect of income disparity but also of the whole regional socio-economic disparity, the seasonality of work in the agricultural
schemes, the long distance between areas of origin and
areas of destination which induce permanent stay in the
latter, the overwhelming 'push' factors still prevailing
in the former, the expanding secondary and tertiary sectors
in the towns and the recent development communication
systems which increase both the information flow about
other destinations and decrease the physical and financial
distance.

So far we have been discussing the different types of
population mobility which are indirectly caused by the
adoption and expansion of agricultural mechanization. We
conclude that measures to develop rural areas including
the modern agricultural sub-sector do not stabilize the
population there but, on the contrary, they cause different
population movements which tend in the end to converge
in the urban centres, thus intensifying the existing
pressure on the limited resources and contributing to

the depopulation of the rural areas and the marginaliza-
tion of rural population, a situation to be discussed
in the next chapter.

Table 8.2:   Migrants by Province of Birth and Province
              of Last Previous Residence (in Percent of
              all In-migrants)

Province	Born	In-migrated from	% of Provincial Population of the Sudan's total
Khartoum Rural	7.3	7.3	2.0
Northern	36.6	29.4	7.2
Blue Nile	17.3	18.9	20.6
Kordofan	15.3	15.2	18.3
Darfur	8.3	7.7	11.1
Kassala	5.0	8.5	10.6
Southern	4.1	5.0	26.1
Abroad	6.3	8.1	?
T o t a l	100.0	100.0	95.9 *

Source: Department of Statistics (estimate)

* This total does not add up to 100.0 % because the 'Three Towns'
   population are not included.

IX. PRINCIPAL FINDINGS, CONCLUSIONS AND PROPOSALS

1. PRINCIPAL FINDINGS OF THE STUDY

In this study an attempt was made to reveal the mobilizing effect of agricultural mechanization on the rural population. It has been shown that the installation of the functional locations of mechanization in relation to agricultural schemes stimulate the peasant youth, particularly the school-leavers, to acquire technical skills with the aim of being employed in highly rewarding jobs. Contempt for agricultural work and limited employment opportunity for school-leavers are the main 'push' factors which induce them to join such functional locations as assistant drivers or assistant mechanics. Soon after acquiring some skills they feel compelled to move to other locations, since in their places of origin there are only limited employment chances for qualified persons. The move to other localities is found to be a function of wage differentials, rise in aspiration, the amount of information about other places, the degree of social obligations, and the presence of a relative or a friend in the new places of destination. From all these, the wage differential is by far the most decisive factor. This was evident in the movement of the skilled workers from the oldest schemes such as El Masara in the Blue Nile province (1950) to the Khashm el Girba in Kassala province (1964) to El Suki in The Blue Nile province (1970) to El Rahad in Kassala province (1978) and from these to other recently implemented schemes and/or to the urban centres (fig. 1). A comparison of wages in the Khashm el Girba, El Suki and El Rahad schemes revealed that the more recently a scheme was implemented the higher was the material incentive for skilled workers.

This wage differential was created by the scheme authority to attract the most qualified persons from the older schemes in order to speed up the development process in the new ones. The effect of this policy is manifested in the concentration of the most qualified persons in some new schemes, as in the case of El Rahad scheme.

The study of the tractor drivers in the three selected schemes revealed that there is a high turnover, particularly among the highly qualified persons, since there is an increased demand for qualified persons to participate in the development of the newly implemented schemes. However, it became apparent that in most cases, qualified persons tend to move to the urban centres to join non-agricultural occupations rather than circulating among the various agricultural schemes. This was evident from the study of tractor drivers presently working in El Rahad scheme, the majority of whom were intending to join work in Greater Khartoum or abroad. This was taken to be evidence not only of the geographical mobility of skilled workers but also of a sectoral mobility. This rural-urban mobility of skilled workers is again a function of wage differentials between agricultural schemes and urban centres. This was evidence from the study of taxi drivers in Khartoum which revealed that the majority of the interviewed drivers stated their previous participation in agricultural mechanization (Table 6.6). Their main motive in seeking employment in Khartoum was, in the majority of cases the expected material incentives and the probable emigration to the oil-rich Arab countries (Table 6.8). This last motive was found to be the most effective 'pull' factor which stimulates skilled workers to leave their rural working places in the agricultural modern sector with the hope of a work contract in a foreign country. The fact

that all emigration formalities are to be completed in
the capital Khartoum necessitates their converging movement at this particular urban centre rather than others.
In this context the presence of a close relative or a
firend, as a point of contact is found to be of significant importance. Our findings revealed that the majority
of in-migrant taxi drivers had relatives or friends in
Khartoum who helped them to overcome the difficulties of
the settling-in period and mediated for them in finding
occupation. This may be taken as a sign of concentration
of particular ethnic groups from particular regions,
'snow-ball-effect', which can create powerful socio-
economic or political groups. Such a tendency was
apparent in the overrepresentation of persons from the Blue
Nile, Kassala, Gezira, Khartoum and Northern Provinces
both among the tractor drivers in the three agricultural
schemes studied (Table 5.3) and among the taxi drivers
in Khartoum (Table 6.4). Contributions of the other provinces, with relatively little economic development remain very low at present, though the trend is towards
increased participation. This implies that the more a
region or locality is affected by agricultural mechanization, i. e. the more it is dominated by the modern agricultural sub-sector, the higher is the probability of
increased participation of its population in the stream of
rural-rural and/or rural-urban mobility of skilled
labour. Our findings in the two selected villages in El
Suki District revealed that the rate of participation of
young rural elements in the functional location of agricultural mechanization is a function of distance between
that location and the place of origin of an individual.
The villages adjacent to the functional location (Umderra-
ba, and El Busata) were found to be overrepresented in
that location (fig. 2). This means that the direct effect

of agricultural mechanization as a mobility factor for
the rural population is confined to areas which come into
direct contact with the modern agricultural sub-sector.
The other areas where traditional agricultural is predominantly practised are only indirectly affected by agricultural
mechanization in terms of unskilled seasonal labourers.
It is paradoxical that the measures which were undertaken
to develop the rural areas are found to be incapable of
stabilizing the population situation there. On the contrary,
they are causing a mobility effect which intensifies the
existing regional and sectoral disparity.

Unlike the other types of population mobility this type involves a particular segment of the population, namely the
young and relatively well-educated elements. According to
our findings the majority of the taxi drivers and tractor
drivers were in the age group 20 to 30 years (Table 5.1
and 6.1), which implies that agricultural mechanization
attracts the most able-bodied persons. The tendency
of the young people to participate in agricultural mechanization was found to be a factor of the working 'push' factors
prevailing in the sending areas,such as the limited opportunities to continue in formal education and the lack of
local employment opportunities for school-leavers. This
was evident from the high proportion of those with elementary education among the tractor drivers in the three selected schemes (Table 5.5) and the taxi drivers in Greater
Khartoum (Table 6.5). The tremendous expansion of the modern agricultural sub-sector centred around mechanization
(chapter IV,) has stimulated the young school-leavers to
participate in the newly installed functional points as a
sort of vocational training to substitute for their discontinued formal education.

2. CONCLUSIONS

Population mobility, whatever its cause, has long been a major feature in the structure of Sudanese society which reflects a sort of adjustment to the regional and sectoral disparity. It began as early as the late nineteenth century and it gained momentum throughout the period of colonial administration and post-independence. In the last two decades it has reached a stage which began to strike hard at the socio-economic set-up of the whole country. It has been changing in form from traditional intra-regional, recently becoming inter-regional and inter-sectoral. It has been induced by the pre-industrial character of the society and the dualism of the country's economy. For a long time the mobility had remained rural-rural in form. Rural-urban population mobility, in the present magnitude, was kept low by the factors of limited transportation, the primitive stage of economic development in the urban centres, low aspiration among the rural population and limited information about the surrounding world. Only in the early sixties did the patterns of its old forms change as a result of the spread of communication systems, the spread of education in the rural areas, increased development in the urban centres and the prevailing 'push' factors in the rural areas. The most effective factor, however, was the fixing of a minimum wage for the labourer in government employment which was far above the average earnings of the agricultural worker, and in the most cases even above the average earnings of the peasant farmer. [1] Even the

---

1) In 1960 the annual minimum income of the unskilled labourer amounted to LS 127 including the cost of living (The New Workers Cadre: in Sudanese Economists, issue No. 122, August 1968, p. 26).

tenant farmer in the Gezira scheme, with the highest
per capita income after Greater Khartoum, did not earn
much more than the general worker in government employment. [2] For farmers in other modern agricultural schemes,
earnings were far less than those of the Gezira tenant.
Agricultural workers could hardly earn more than
75 piasters per day in the modern sector and even less
in the traditional agricultural sub-sector. [3]

This regional and sectoral income disparity has been
one of the main causes of the change in the nature,
pattern, type, intensity and convergence of population
mobility in the region. The process has been further

---

2) The average annual cash income per tenant in the
   Gezira was LS 162 for the year 1962/63. This cash
   income was estimated to make up at least 75 % of the
   total income of the tenant. But if one considers the
   money paid by the tenant of the Gezira to the agricultural worker, his net income will be considerably
   reduced (Ibd. p. 27).

3) In Darfur, for example, the average daily wage for
   an agricultural worker was estimated as about 10
   piasters or less in 1954 with employment lasting
   only a few month at most. (E. M. Mc LOUGHLIN, 1963,
   p. 19).

fostered by the recent measures to increase the urban
minimum wage. [4] The present minimum wage for a worker
in government employment is set at LS 29,500, while
the average earnings for both farmers and agricultural
workers remain comparatively lower. It should be noted
that substantial differentials in earnings are set in
accordance with differentials in education levels and the
degree of qualification. Thus it is not surprising to
find that the volume of rural-urban population mobility
is steadily increasing with the increase in education,
formal and informal. In this context agricultural mechanization, which offers a sort of informal education, contributes much to intensifying rural-urban population mobility.
Apart from its displacement effect on the rural population,
the spatial distribution of its functional points form an
important element in creating qualification opportunities
to satisfy widespread popular demand and to fulfil the
needs of hitherto underprovided areas. The movement of
young people, seeking qualification, to functional locations of mechanization represents for many, the first
significant break with parental authority and may be regarded as the initial stage in their life-cycle of migration. The rise of aspirations is considered to be among
the key factors inducing the circulation of qualified
persons and it is within this context that acquiring
skills through agricultural mechanization plays a vital

---

4) Due to the recommendation of a worker cadre committee
   in 1965 the minimum wage for a worker in government
   employment was set as LS. 12,500 which was increased
   by the councils of Ministers, probably for political
   reasons, to LS. 13,900 (Sudanese Economists, op. cit.,
   p. 25).

role in fostering existing rural-urban population mobility. Hence mechanization as a training institution resembles
formal education as the route to socio-economic status,
since acquiring new skills and additional experience inevi-
tybly affects the individual's place utility matrix and may
act as a catalyst to further mobility.

Although movements associated with qualification represent
only a mumerically small segment within the context of the
Sudanese population movement as a whole, it may be regarded
as the most important one. Its importance lies in the qualitative composition of persons participating in it. The
exact number of persons involved in the whole process is not
precisely known, since the mobility of qualified persons has
not yet been separately dealt with, even in the National
Census enumerations. According to the Six Year Plan (1977,
II, 18) there were approximately 12,000 tractors in 1977
participating in this particular agricultural sub-sector.
But if we consider the tremendous increase in mechanized
agriculture (chapter IV), particularly in the past few
years, which neccessitates an increased demand for tractors,
and if we consider the fact that more than one person is
needed to operate the same tractor (SHAKAK, 1977)[5], we
will come to a figure of more than 40,000 persons

---

5) For a mechanized scheme of 1,000 feddans the following
   staff is required:
   2 tractor drivers for 100 days between July and September
   1 tractor driver for 200 days between October and March
   2 service men for 100 days between July and September
   1 watchman for 360 days
   1 manager for 360 days

participating in the technical part of agricultural
mechanization in any particular year. Furthermore, considering the high rate of turnover, particularly among the
highly qualified persons, one may reach the conclusion
that this particular occupation is potentially capable
of attracting additional members of the rural population
to be prepared for further movement. The increasing demand for qualified persons in the urban centres and in
the oil-rich Arab countries will continue to speed up the
rate of turnover among the skilled workers in the rural
areas. Thus it may be expected that within a short time,
the number of those qualified through agricultural mechanization will increase substantially. Numerically this may
still continue to constitute only a small fraction of
the country's active labour force for a long time but
with a higher social, economic and political weight.

The fact that this small segment is highly selected from
the most dynamic elements of the population and that it
consists of persons with a relatively higher level of
education and qualification than the average population,
justifies our considering it as one of the most vital
population groups which might be expected to produce appre-
ciable socio-economic changes in both areas of origin and
areas of destination. Unlike other population groups, this
group could be organized and politically mobilized, so that
it could be expected to affect the political balance within
and between the different regions.

The concentration of this group in particular regions
which results from the concentration of development projects there, may lead to the domination of particular
ethnic groups over others, since skilled labour mobility
tends to reflect the familiar pattern of a chain-movement

whereby each participation event leads to another after
a time-lag in which information is sent back by a pre-
migrant to a relative who is still living in the home
area.

In this sense agricultural mechanization will add power
to particular ethnic groups with the discrimination
against others. This has been confirmed by our findings
that more than 75 % of all interviewed taxi drivers in
Greater Khartoum were able to find a job through the
mediation of a close relative and/or a tribe member (Table
6.11). In this sense joining agricultural mechanization
offers a continuation of the previous social structures so
that some social groups remain cohesive despite their spatial displacement.

Although migrants, particularly those from the socially and
economically more developed areas, maintain strong contact
with their places of origin through visits and remittances,
the impact of that contact cannot be quantified at this
early stage of the migration process. It may be argued that
through repeated contacts some socio-economic transforma-
tions in the areas of origin have become apparent (see case
study in El Kurmuta and Abu Gara villages), but this should
not suggest that the out-migration from such rural locations is always a temporary move. According to our findings,
47.8 % of all interviewed taxi drivers in Khartoum did not
intend to return to their places of origin, the majority
of whom originated in rural areas. This means that the
rural areas will continue to lose not only a large part of
its population but the most dynamic elements who are expected to be the initiators of change. It is not unrealistic,
therefore, to think that within a short period, the rural
areas will be deprived of their innovators if the present

development strategies prevail. Concentration of development projects in certain areas rather than others and ac-
centuation of developing particular sectors to the neglect
of others, will increase the existing disparity in social
welfare between the different regions and intensify the
prevailing rural-urban population mobility. The ultimate
effect of this process will then be a concentration of
the most energetic and creative elements of the population
in the big urban centres, particularly Greater Khartoum.
This will intensify existing pressure on the available
social services, creating an urgent need for investment
in the tertiary economic sector. Explosion of the transport sector in Greater Khartoum in the last few years to
cope with the increasing population numbers has further
aggravated the situation, since this particular measure
has further stimulated new in-migrants to compete for jobs
as vehicle drivers in the town. [6] Despite the tremendous increase in the number of public vehicles in Khartoum, there
is always an over-supply of vehicle drivers whose expectation of finding employment in Khartoum remains unfulfil-
led, thus intensifying the existing urban umemployment
and/or underemployment. Even measures taken by the government to decrease the rate of unemployment by creating temporary jobs have resulted in an additional rural-urban
rush, particularly of skilled labourers. In some cases it
is found to be a function of the assessment of the

6) According to the information received from Mr. Galal
   Suliman, the Director of Transport and Road Section in
   Khartoum, the total number of public vehicles registered in 1980 was over 16,000. About a quarter of this
   number were reported to be newly registered in the
   last two years. By now the total number of all public
   vehicles in Khartoum, apart from the private cars,
   may well be over 20,000.

individuals to the probability of finding a job rather
than the existing pay differentials that induce them to
join the rural-urban population mobility. Thus it may be
expected that every newly created job in the urban centre
will attract additional numbers of rural migrants to compete for it.

Fortunately for the Sudanese skilled labour force, there
is an increasing demand for their talents in the oil-rich
Arab countries. In fact the emigration of the Sudanese
labour force to foreign countries has long been known.
But in the early sixties it began to gain momentum due to
economic stagnation in the country. The process has further
been fostered in the early seventies by the appearance of
burgeoning opportunities for work in Saudi Arabia and the
Gulf States created by sudden rise in the price of oil. At
present throughout the oil-rich Arab countries as well as
in parts of the world further afield, the Sudanese skilled
workers are to be found working at all levels of society.
Although the phenomenon of the Sudanese emigration has been
touched upon by some authorities (M. E. GALAL EL DIN, 1979),
there ist still no comprehensive study which reflects its
magnitude, causes and impacts. All figures showing a number
of Sudanese working abroad are at best only estimates. Inefficient registrations in the different government institution, corruption and the reluctance of the receiving
countries to deliver exact information about Sudanese
immigrants have reduced any study to mere estimation. [7] It

---

7) M. E. GALAL DIN (1979, p. 19) gave a figure of 231,350
   as the number of Sudanese working at that time in a number of foreign countries with the highest concentration
   (95 %) in the oil-rich Arab countries. Although he succeeded in contacting all the internal and external official authorities which facilitate emigration of the Sudanese labour force, had admitted that his findings included by no means all the Sudanese emigrants, since some
   of them escape legal formalities.

remains undisputable that the number involved in this process is continuously increasing, especially among those
skilled or educated migrants who emigrate to obtain substantially more remunerative work in the Petro-Dollars-
Countries.

In a developing country like the Sudan with huge unexploited natural resources and a scarcity of capital, the suc-
ceeding waves of human resource emigration will no doubt
produce profound socio-economic effects. Even the expected material gains, if any, will contribute to social and
regional inequality, in itself the main cause of emigration. Creation of new consumption habits rather than planned
economic investment will continue to accelerate the rate
of inflation, which is also a prime cause of emigration.
Most dangerous for the country as a whole is the emigration of the top stratum of each profession, which leaves
the country at the mercy of its least efficient skilled
persons.

It is not our purpose here to convey all the expected impacts of the Sudanese emigration on the socio-economic
development of the country, but only to stress the statement of M. E. GALAL EL DIN (1977) that 'emigration will
eventually perpetuate the imbalance it appears to correct
and sustain the underdevelopment it claims to attack'
(quoted after SUDANOW, January 1981, p. 60). [8]

---

8) SUDANOW is a national news-magazine published in Khartoum every first day of the month by the Ministry of
   Culture and Information. The magazine contributed to
   the problem of the Sudanese emigration with three in-
   formative and evaluative articles which appeared in
   December 1976, October 1980 and January 1981.

Strangely enough, in spite of all perceived negative results, migrating abroad is increasingly becoming for many
not only a sophisticated endeavour but a socio-economic
necessity. All the government measures intended to control
the phenomenon have proven insufficient due to increased
illegal attempts to emigrate. The main reasons for the perpetuation of these intractable problems may be sought in
the financial reward expected abroad [9] as well as the
prevailing internal 'push' factors, such as limited employment opportunities, particularly for skilled workers,
rising cost of living, increasing inflation rates and the
desire to reduce the socio-economic disparity which is
primarily created by emigration itself. Furthermore, the
measures taken by the government to provide the emigration
with first and second class housing units in Khartoum
and other urban centres as a means of absorbing their hard
currency (directed by the critical situation in the balance of payments) has further aggravated the problem. As a
consequence of this policy, land prices have risen drasti-
cally, compelling some professional people to emigrate,
motivated by encouraging import facilities and rewarding
exchange incentives. Our concern in this context is to
stress the fact that turnover among the skilled labour
force in Khartoum will stimulate further rural-urban
population movement with the ultimate goal of emigration
thus making the process self-perpetuating. In the shorter
view this will create a defecit of skilled labour in some
rural localities as presently reflected in the unsatisfactory
performance of a number of the development projects. In

9) According to ALI A. ALI a Sudanese worker abroad earns
   2,500 % of his domestic wage. (Quoted after SUDANOW,
   January 1981, p. 60)

the longer view this out-migration process may cause
a drain-off of the most dynamic and creative elements potentially needed to produce a socio-economic transformation in the whole country. In this context the mechanization
of agriculture which was initially intended to develop rural
areas will indirectly contribute to the existing regional
and social disparity. By virtue of its effect of educating
the rural population, it prepares the qualified manpower
demanded in the urban centres and abroad. This side-effect
of agricultural mechanization could have been substantially significant for a developing country like the Sudan had
it not been for other working factors external to mechanization itself which induced a rural-urban drift of the skilled
and unskilled labour force. Limiting the magnitude of such
rural-urban drift does not lie in mechanization as such,
but rather in re-orienting the country's development plans
in accordance with available resources and to securing the
socio-economic equity between various regions. In the following we shall attempt to offer some proposals as to how
this may be achieved.

PROPOSALS

In a developing country like the Sudan with limited employment opportunities in the urban centres it would be wise to re-orientate all the available human and scarce capital resources to create employment opportunities in the rural areas where natural resources are located. Abundant unexploited cultivable land and irrigation water will continue to define the Sudan as an agricultural land for a long time to come. The agricultural sector will remain the main safety valve for the ever-increasing rural population which presently makes up over 70 % of the total Sudanese population. Thus the rational utilization of the agricultural potential at this stage of the Sudan's socio-economic transformation should still be given the utmost priority if the rising labour force surplus is to be more productively employed on the land. Although this priority has been stressed in almost all the development plans (The Ten Years, Five Years and the Six Years Plans) the results achieved so far have been far from satisfactory. The main reason has been the lack of integrated planning, which has previously concentrated on particular sectors in particular regions over others, creating as a consequence regional and sectoral disparity, a cause and effect of internal and external population mobility. Concentration on the modern agricultural sub-sector with a view to producing for the world market, while neglecting the traditional agricultural sub-sector from which the majority of the population derive their means of subsistence is in our opinion the main factor which produces the present economic vicious circle. This fact has been stressed by the ILO (1976) and ÖSTERDIECKHOFF (1980). The present tendency to expand the modern agricultural sub-sector at the expense of the traditional sector as recommended by the ILO and the World Bank in connection with the Arab

Investment strategy will not only deprive the rural population of the land which had been hitherto under their care
but it will also intensify the existing regional and social
disparity it claims to rectify. Instead a country-wise land
reform and land distribution policy should be introduced
to ensure more rational utilization of the available resources. This can only be achieved through intensified
and integrated research to explore the available potential of each region separately. Particular emphasis should
be placed on the improving of the food situation in the
whole country. But this should not imply that all production should be oriented to satisfy local needs. Export
commodity production should go hand in hand with production
for the internal market even in the largest modern agricultural schemes. Only so is it possible to improve the
internal food situation an to release the pressure on
the Sudan's balance of payments. The present high prices
for food induce a rise in urban wages, thus stimulating
the prevailing rural-urban population mobility. If the rural population is to be persuaded to stay where it is, it
would be wise to create employment opportunities for them
by encouraging rural industry based primarily on agricultural products to satisfy their socio-economic needs and
to minimize the rural-urban income inequality. The steps
often taken by the government to stabilize the urban
labour force by raising the minimum wages generates additional rural-urban population mobility. Instead, the
government should try to stabilize prices, not by additional subsidization but by encouraging increased production, particularly of foodstuffs. Even within rural areas
the present regional development disparity must be kept
to a minimum to ensure the participation of the population in the development process of their own regions. The
labour market should be organized to ensure rational

mobilization of human resources according to the principles of supply and demand. To achieve this, an overall educational plan is needed, based on the actual quantitative
and qualitative needs for labour in the different economic
sectors. The present educational system, inherited from
the colonial administration, contributes to the rise
of aspiration and is unsuited to the country's actual needs
for qualified persons, thus resulting in the prevailing
high unemployment and underemployment rates both in the rural areas and in the urban centres. An educational system
which will change the present negative attitude towards
manual work and rural areas is urgently needed if the
country's potentialities are to be fully and economically
utilized. The present wage differentials in favour of
'white-collar' jobs should be rethought to encourage the
school-leavers to participate in other productive vocational areas.

Finally, there remains the need to promote social services
in the rural areas in order to reduce the disparity in social welfare between rural areas and urban centres, as one
of the causes of the rural-urban population drift. However, the provision of services will only be possible if
the proposals to reorient the economic development are
carried out. Only by mobilizing the available resources
would it be possible to accumulate the needed capital to
promote social services in the whole region. This is achie-
vable only through a political will which perceives development as an integrated rather than as a disintegrated
issue.

AUSWIRKUNGEN DER MECHANISIERUNG DER LANDWIRTSCHAFT AUF
DIE BEVÖLKERUNGSMOBILITÄT IN ENTWICKLUNGSLÄNDERN:
FALLBEISPIEL - DIE REPUBLIK SUDAN

ZUSAMMENFASSUNG
_____

In der Diskussion über die geeigneten Maßnahmen zur För-
derung der ländlichen Entwicklung in den Entwicklungsländern wurde die Frage des Einsatzes von technischen
Mitteln in den letzten Jahren aktuell. Dabei sind die
gesamten sozialen und wirtschaftlichen Aspekte des
Mechanisierungsproblems in den Vordergrund gerückt. Be-
sonderes Gewicht in diesem Zusammenhang kommt der Auswirkung der Mechanisierung auf die Bevölkerungssituation
zu. Der Sudan macht in dieser Hinsicht keine Ausnahme.

Als Instrument zur Produktionssteigerung hat man bereits
in den zwanziger Jahren mit dem Aufbau staatlicher Schlep-
perstationen begonnen, die aber zunächst noch experimen-
tellen Charakter hatten und im neugeschaffenen Gezira-
Projekt zu finden waren. Dieses Projekt war das große
Entwicklungsvorhaben, in dem biologisch-technische und
mechanisch-technische Maßnahmen eingesetzt wurden, wo-
durch die Baumwollproduktion in der Zeit zwischen 1935 -
1955 sich um 70 % vermehrte und sich die Einnahmen aus dieser Produktion bis zu 800 % erhöhten, dank der enorm ge-
stiegenen Weltmarktpreise dieses Produkts besonders im
Jahre 1955 (SHARAK, K. I., 1977, S. 106). Als Folge dieser Entwicklung wurden Privatunternehmer und Kapitalgeber
zu Investitionen in der Baumwollproduktion motiviert, die
kleine Bewässerungsprojekte durchführten, die sich ebenfalls landwirtschaftlicher Maschinen bedienen. In der Tat

gibt es private Bewässerungsprojekte am Weißen Nil
schon seit Ende der zwanziger Jahre, die dann durch die
Errichtung des Jebel Aulia Damms im Jahre 1937 weitere
Impulse erhielten (Sudan Cotton Growers, 1964). Die Anbaufläche wurde von ca. 20.000 Feddan (8.400 ha) 1949/50
auf 215.000 Feddan (90.300 ha) 1967/68 ausgedehnt (ABDEL
SALAM, M. M., 1976, S. 51). In der Nordprovinz sind bis
1968 am Nil auf einer Anbaufläche von ca. 200.000 Feddan
(84.000 ha) ebenfalls Bewässerungsprojekte durchgeführt
worden (ABDEL SALAM, 1976, S. 49).

Schon bald nach Ende des Zweiten Weltkrieges wurden von
der Kolonialverwaltung im Sudan Pläne zur Entwicklung
der Landwirtschaft entworfen, die über eine Verbesserung
der Produktionsbedingungen im kleinbäuerlichen Sektor
zu einer raschen Steigerung der Agrarproduktion führen
sollten. Motive solcher Politik waren u. a. die Sicherung
der Versorgung des britischen Mutterlandes mit landwirtschaftlichen Rohstoffen, vor allem Baumwolle und die Er-
wirtschaftung und Bereitstellung von eigenen Finanzierungs-
mitteln für die im Lande vorgesehenen Entwicklungsvorhaben (ABDEL SALAM, M. M., 1976).

Da man in den traditionellen Anbaumethoden des Hackbaus
einen limitierenden Faktor für die geplante Produktionssteigerung sah, befürwortete man eine gesteigerte Mechanisierung.

Die 1950 erreichte Erhöhung der Baumwollproduktion, besonders bei Privatunternehmen, um bis zu 40 % im Vergleich
zu 1945, war der materielle Anreiz für die weitere Entwicklung der mechanisierten Landwirtschaft (Sudan Cotton
Growers, 1964).

Parallel zu dieser Entwicklung in der Bewässerungslandwirtschaft wurde die Mechanisierung auch in den nicht-
bewässerten Gebieten schrittweise eingeführt. Erste An-
sätze hierzu gab es kurz nach dem Zweiten Weltkrieg, als
Nahrungsmittel und pflanzliche Rohstoffe knapp wurden
(LAING, R. G., 1953).

Schon 1943 bekam der Sudan von der "Middle East Supply
Corporation" (MESC) ein Angebot, Sesam im Rahmen eines
relativ umfangreichen Mechanisierungsvorhabens im Raum
Gedarif anzupflanzen, wo bis dahin "Durrah" manuell ange-
baut wurde (HABASHI, W., 1966). Da die Sesamproduktion
bei der nicht-mechanisierten Ernte eine große Zahl von
Arbeitskräften voraussetzt, war der Sudan über das Angebot wenig begeistert, denn er verfügt gerade in diesem An-
baugebiet nur über eine begrenzte Zahl von Arbeitskräften,
und es war nicht problemlos, sie aus anderen Gebieten zu
rekrutieren. Trotzdem wurde das Projekt verwirklicht, denn
nach der Mechanisierung der Durrahproduktion wurden Arbeitskräfte frei, die dann im Sesamanbau eingesetzt werden konn-
ten. Daher wurden zum ersten Mal relativ moderne Traktoren
und Zubehör importiert. Diese Neuerungen hatten zur Folge,
daß sich die Anbaufläche ständig ausdehnte, sowohl in den
bewässerten als auch in den nicht-bewässerten Gebieten wie
Damazin, Dali, Mazoum, Kordofan und neuerdings Darfur
(The Ten Year Plan, 1961).

Nach der Erlangung der Unabhängigkeit 1956 wurden sowohl
die Erweiterung der Bewässerungsprojekte als auch der dafür benötigte Maschineneinsatz stark forciert, wobei der
Schlepperbestand beträchtlich ausgeweitet wurde, eine
Entscheidung, die nicht nur wirtschaftliche, sondern auch
politische Motive gehabt haben dürfte.

Im Kampf der Parteien um die Gunst des Wählers in den Parlamentswahlen von 1957 hatte das Versprechen an die bäuerlichen Wähler, den staatlichen Schleppereinsatz zu verstärken, eine wichtige Rolle gespielt. Es liegt also nahe, die neue Mechanisierungspolitik als die Einlösung eines Wahlversprechens und als Versuch der Regierungsparteien zu betrachten, sich die Unterstützung der Bauern zu sichern. In wirtschaftlicher Hinsicht wurde diese Entscheidungspolitik durch die Entwicklung der Baumwollproduktion beeinflußt, die wegen der erhöhten Weltmarktpreise (1951) stark zugenommen hatte. Es scheint, daß man in der Tat glaubte, angesichts der überragenden Bedeutung der Baumwolle für die wirtschaftliche Entwicklung des Sudans mit der Ausdehnung der Anbaufläche und dem großzügigen Einsatz moderner technischer Hilfsmittel, rasche Fortschritte erzielen zu können. Infolgedessen ist auf der Grundlage kapitalintensiver Bewässerungslandwirtschaft und staatlicher Leitung der Produktionsprozesse ein weltmarktabhängiger Sektor entstanden, der auch nach der Unabhängigkeit von den verschiedenen Regierungen übernommen und flächenmäßig auf Kosten des bisherigen traditionellen Sektors, in dem mehr als 80 % der ländlichen Bevölkerung leben, vervielfacht wurde, also eine immer größer werdende Enklave in ihm darstellte (Tabelle 4.1).

Es wurde also von Anfang an eine primär wachstumsorientierte Entwicklungsstrategie befolgt mit der Konsequenz einer Deformation der ländlichen Produktionsverhältnisse. Diese wird nicht nur durch die kapitalintensive Bewässerungswirtschaft verursacht, sondern auch durch die Mechanisierung des Regenfeldanbaus.

Den Entwicklungsplanern erschien die forcierte Veränderung durch die Anwendung hochentwickelter Produktionstechniken und massiver materieller Anreize eher wirksam zur

Produktionssteigerung als die allmählichen Verbesserungen
vorhandener Strukturen durch die Aktivierung und Mobilisierung der menschlichen Resourcen. Eine Folge dieser Ent-
wicklungspolitik ist die rasche Verbesserung des Maschi-
nenparks.

Dieser Mechanisierungsprozeß wurde dadurch beschleunigt,
daß - bereits in den sechziger Jahren - die "Agricultural
Bank" Kredite an Lohnunternehmer zum Schlepperkauf zur
Verfügung stellte. Allein in den Trockenfeldanbaugebiete
wurde die Zahl der Traktoren mit 4.000 angegeben. Diese
Zahl dürfte - nach dem "Six Year Plan" (1977, 2, S. 18) -
ein Drittel des gesamten Traktorenbestandes im Sudan dar-
stellen.

Die natürliche Ausstattung des Sudans - ungenutztes Ackerland, Bewässerungsmöglichkeiten - spricht für die
weitere Ausdehnung des modernen landwirtschaftlichen Sektors, vor allem in den Regelfeldgebieten. Nach Schätzun-
gen des "Ministry of Finance and National Economy",
1976/77 sind 50 Millionen ha als Ackerland und 32 Millionen ha für Viehzucht nutzbar. Bislang werden lediglich
13 % der nutzbaren Ackerbaufläche und 75 % der nutzbaren
Weidefläche bewirtschaftet (Ministry of Finance and National Economy, 1977, S. 18).

Der Staat, die einzige konzentrierte und organisierte Macht
der Gesellschaft, erschließt durch den Bau von Dämmen und
Kanälen, durch Rodung und Einebnung das Land und verpach-
tet es unter zentraler staatlicher Leitung und Kontrolle
weiter an ehemalige Kleinbauern bzw. Nomaden. Etwa die
Hälfte der gesamten bewässerbaren Fläche, die ca. 10 Millionen Feddan (etwa 5 Millionen ha) beträgt, wird zur Zeit
landwirtschaftlich genutzt (Ministry of Agriculture, 1978,
S. 2).

Die Betriebsgröße der Pachtstellen wurde auf maximal
40 Feddan (ca. 20 ha) festgelegt, was von vornherein den
Einsatz zusätzlicher Arbeitskräfte erforderlich machte.

Der mit der Ausweitung des modernen landwirtschaftlichen
Sektors schnell ansteigende Bedarf an zusätzlichen Arbeitskräften mußte mehr und mehr über die Region hinaus auf
Kosten des traditionellen Sektors gedeckt werden. Nach
Schätzung der ILO sind jährlich über 1 Million Saison-
und Wanderarbeiter unterwegs, die aus nicht-mechanisierten Regionen, wie Kordofan, Darfur, aber auch aus Zentral-
und Westafrika kommen. Allein im Gezira Scheme waren
1973/74 336.000 (mehr als die Hälfte der benötigten
Erntehilfen) Wanderarbeiter tätig. Dies bedeutet eine Art
von Abhängigkeit des modernen vom traditionellen Sektor
(ILO, 1976, S. 258).

Der mechanisierte Trockenfeldanbau wird hauptsächlich in
den Provinzen Kassala und Blue Nile (Ost-Sudan) auf über
4 Millionen Feddan betrieben. Davon sind etwa eine
halbe Million unter staatlicher Kontrolle, der Rest ver-
teilt sich auf private Farmen (ILO, 1976, S. 268). Trotz
des hohen Mechanisierungsgrades in diesem Sub-Sektor der
modernen Landwirtschaft (4.000 Traktoren) wird eine grös-
sere Anzahl von saisonalen Arbeitskräften benötigt, denn
im Sudan, im Gegensatz zu einigen Ländern Lateinamerikas,
wird nur Teilmechanisierung angewandt (hauptsächlich
für Feldbestellung und Ernte).

Eine wichtige Auswirkung einer derartigen Ausdehnung des
modernen landwirtschaftlichen Sektors ist in der tenden-
ziellen Auflösung der traditionellen Produktionsverhältnisse zu sehen. Die Produktion in der mechanisierten
Landwirtschaft, die hauptsächlich am Weltmarkt orientiert
ist, führt zur Entfaltung des Handels, der die

- 253 -

unterschiedlichen Produktionssphären in Beziehung zueinan-
der bringt, die Isolation des traditionellen landwirtschaftlichen Sektors aufhebt, neue Bedürfnisse unter der ländlichen Bevölkerung weckt, Regionen mehr und mehr durch
verkehrsmäßige Erschließung zu regelmäßigem Austausch
führt, die Produktion auf dem Markt Schritt für Schritt,
auch in Gebieten der traditionellen landwirtschaftlichen
Produktion fördert, und die Steuerung und Ausweitung der
Qualifikationsmöglichkeiten und damit der Ware-Geld-Be-
ziehungen bewirkt.

Die vorliegende Untersuchung befaßt sich mit sozialgeogra-
phischen Problemen der Mechanisierung in der Landwirtschaft. Konkret wurde nach möglichen Auswirkungen der
Mechanisierung auf die Bevölkerungsmobilität gefragt.
Derartige sozialgeographische Fragen wurden gegenüber den
technisch-ökologischen Fragen bei den bisherigen Untersuchungen über Mechanisierung der Landwirtschaft höchstens
beiläufig gestellt und, wenn überhaupt, dann vorzugsweise
auf Makroebene, d. h. für ein ganzes Land oder für einige
Länder. Ein wichtiger Grund dafür, daß bislang etwa Ent-
scheidungsprozesse und Arbeitsverhalten der Menschen in
der Landwirtschaft sozialgeographisch noch nicht gründ-
licher untersucht wurden, ist sicher darin zu sehen, daß
in der Regel das Sozialverhalten gerade in den Räumen,
in denen die Mechanisierung auf eine lange Tradition bzw.
eine stetige Entwicklung zurückblicken kann, völlig an
die jeweiligen Rahmenbedingungen angepaßt ist, so daß sie
eher als Selbstverständliches denn als etwas Untersuchungs-
wertes gelten (die für die Modernisierung des traditionellen
Sektors nötig sind, über den Handel versorgen zu können).
Ein solcher Grund entfällt sicher bei neugeschaffenen
landwirtschaftlichen Gebieten, in denen im Zuge umfang-
reicher politisch-wirtschaftlicher Aktionen Bevölkerungs-
bewegungen beschleunigt verliefen, vor allem dann, wenn

dort bis dahin keine Erfahrung mit mechanisierter Landwirtschaft vorlag.

Die Republik Sudan mit ihren umfangreichen landwirtschaftlichen Projekten, in denen Mechanisierungsmaßnahmen im
Vordergrund stehen, bietet ein gutes Beispiel dafür, daß
durch die Mechanisierung verschiedene Bevölkerungsgruppen
mobilisiert werden können (siehe Kapitel 8).

Diese Untersuchung beschränkt sich vor allem auf zwei Pro-
blemkreise, die zweifellos in einem engen gegenseitigen
Kontakt stehen und gerade in neugeschaffenen mechanisierten Agrarräumen von besonderer Bedeutung sein dürften.
Es geht dabei einmal um die Schaffung neuer Arbeitsplätze
innerhalb der Landwirtschaft, und es geht zum anderen um
die Frage, wie weit die verschiedenen Bevölkerungsgruppen
durch die Mechanisierung angezogen werden und welche
sozio -ökonomischen Auswirkungen sich aus solchen Bevöl-
kerungsbewegungen ergeben können. Über das Ausmaß dieser
Mobilität besteht freilich keine exakte Vorstellung.

Diese Untersuchung zeigt, daß die Entwicklung des
ländlichen Raumes, darunter auch die Mechanisierung nicht
zu einer Stabilisierung der Bevölkerungsverhältnisse führen, sondern im Gegenteil eine Mobilisierung der ländlichen Bevölkerung bewirken können, die den Zuwanderungs-
druck auf die Städte nur noch verstärkt und damit die Po-
larisierungstendenz vergrößert. Dadurch werden regionale
und sektorale Disparitäten sogar verstärkt, obwohl man
zunächst das Gegenteil angenommen hatte (siehe Kapitel
5, 6, 7).

Die Mechanisierung der Landwirtschaft spielt in diesem
Zusammenhang eine wichtige Rolle. Da der Einsatz technischer Hilfsmittel, vor allem kapitalintensiver und

arbeitssparender Maschinen, einen bedeutenden Teil der
Arbeitskräfte freisetzt, ist dieser gezwungen, andere
Beschäftigungsmöglichkeiten, auch in den Städten, zu
suchen. Über solche Mobilitäten wurde von vielen, die
sich mit der Mechanisierung der Landwirtschaft beschäfti-
ten, häufig berichtet (GALAL EL DIN, M. E., 1973; HEIN-
RITZ, G., 1977, 1982). Aber dies ist nur ein Teil der
verschiedenen durch die Mechanisierung verursachten Be-
völkerungsmobilitäten (Fig. 1).

Anders als der traditionelle setzt der moderne landwirt-
schaftliche Sektor qualifizierte Arbeitskräfte voraus,
die gerade in einem Entwicklungsland wie dem Sudan fehlen. Zur Ausbildung von Fachkräften sind daher in allen
mechanisierten Projekten Lehr- und Reparaturwerkstätten
eingerichtet worden, was zunächst zu einer Zuwanderung
von vor allem Grundschulabsolventen führte, die keinen
Zugang zur Höheren Schule hatten und die bis dahin eine
Reserve-Armee für die Entwicklung des traditionellen Sektors bildeten (siehe Kapitel 7).

Die Befragungen in einigen ausgewählten Herkunftsorten
von Traktorfahrern und Mechanikern haben gezeigt, daß
die Wahrscheinlichkeit der Abwanderung steigt, je stär-
ker ein Ort von der Mechanisierung betroffen ist, d. h.
je näher er bei Funktionsstandorten der Mechanisierung
gelegen ist bzw. je länger derartige Funktionsstandorte
existieren (Fig. 2). Diese Abwanderung ist insofern se-
lektiv, als vor allem aktive, junge, männliche Personen
abwandern (Tabellen 7.6 und 7.7). Das starke Ausmaß dieser Bevölkerungsmobilität hat dazu geführt, daß die Be-
völkerungsstruktur sowohl der Herkunfts- als auch der
Zielgebiete schon deformiert wurde, obwohl die Mechanisierung noch eine neue Erscheinung ist (Tabelle 7.5).

Die Untersuchungen haben ferner gezeigt, daß die Chancen,
am Wanderungszielort schnell eine Arbeitsstelle zu erhalten, umso größer ist, je höher die Qualifikation einer im
Zuge der Mechanisierung der Landwirtschaft ausgebildeten
Person ist. Das geringe Risiko der Arbeitslosigkeit am
Zielort erhöht die Bereitschaft zur Abwanderung. Untersuchungen unter den noch zu qualifizierenden Personen in
einigen ausgewählten Lehrwerkstätten deuteten darauf hin,
daß jeder nicht nur zur Abwanderung bereit, sondern dazu
sogar gezwungen ist, um eine seiner durch die Mechanisierung der Landwirtschaft erworbenen Qualifikation entsprechende Arbeitsstelle zu erhalten; denn für qualifizierte Arbeitskräfte existieren am Herkunftsort keine bzw.
nur begrenzte Beschäftigungsmöglichkeiten (Tabelle 7.8).
Informationsaustausch über das begrenzte Vorhandensein von
Arbeitsplätzen in anderen Gebieten ist bereits während
der Ausbildungszeit gegeben. Verwandte und Bekannte, die in
anderen Gebieten tätig sind, dienen nicht nur als Infor-
mationsquelle, sondern auch als Ablaufstellen für die, die
noch im Herkunftsort oder in anderen Gebieten sind. Die
Bereitschaft zur Abwanderung ist also nicht nur durch zu-
verlässige Informationsquellen, sondern auch durch die
Sicherung von Unterkunft und Unterhalt während der Suche
nach einem Arbeitsplatz motiviert (Kapitel 7). Entschei-
dend aber sind die Lohnunterschiede zwischen den verschiedenen Regionen. Es wurde bei den Untersuchungen in
drei Bewässerungsprojekten [1] festgestellt, daß die
Mobilitätsbereitschaft der Traktorfahrer und Mechaniker

---

1) Khashm el Girba am Atbarafluß etwa 400 km östlich von
der Hauptstadt Khartoum mit 200.000 ha und 21.000
Pächtern; El Rahad Projekt zwischen Rahadfluß und
Blauem Nil etwa 300 km südöstlich von Khartoum mit
einer geplanten Fläche von 328.000 ha und El Suki
Scheme am Blauen Nil südlich von Sennar mit 37.800 ha.
(Die Untersuchung fand im Zeitraum November 1979 -
März 1980 statt.)

außerordentlich hoch ist, so daß schon relativ geringe
Lohnunterschiede Anlaß zum Arbeitsplatzwechsel in erheb-
lichem Umfang sein können (siehe Kapitel 6). Die gesteigerte Nachfrage nach Traktorfahrern und Mechanikern
in neugeschaffenen mechanisierten Agrargebieten in jüng-
ster Zeit - wo entsprechend höhere Löhne angeboten wurden - hat mehrfach in den alten Agrarräumen dazu geführt,
daß die Zahl der dort beschäftigten Traktorfahrer und
Mechaniker sich so stark reduzierte, daß Fachkräfteman-
gel herrschte. Zum Ausgleich dieses Defizits wanderten
andere Bevölkerungsgruppen von ihren Herkunftsorten zu
(Fig. 1).

Den Höhepunkt solcher Bewegungen bildet die Abwanderung
der durch die Mechanisierung qualifizierten Arbeitskräfte
vom Agrarsektor in die Städte, vor allem in die Hauptstadt Khartoum und von dort ins Ausland, und somit
spiegelt sich die Fachkräftemobilität nicht nur räumlich,
sondern auch sektoral wieder (Fig. 1).

Qualifizierte Arbeitskräfte erstreben eher als unqualifi-
zierte einen höheren Lebensstandard. Da die sozial-ökono-
mischen Aufstiegsmöglichkeiten auf dem Land sehr begrenzt
sind, zeigen sich die durch die Mechanisierung der Landwirtschaft qualifizierten Arbeitskräfte zur Abwanderung
in die Städte und ins Ausland bereit. Bei meinen Untersuchungen in den drei ausgewählten Bewässerungsprojekten
wurde festgestellt, daß der überwiegende Teil (86.3 %)
der Traktorfahrer und Mechaniker beabsichtigt, in die
Hauptstadt Khartoum zu wandern, um dort eine Beschäftigung außerhalb des landwirtschaftlichen Sektors zu
suchen (Kapitel 5). Diese Feststellung wurde bestätigt
durch die Ergebnisse einer Befragung unter ausgewählten
Taxi- und Busfahrern in Khartoum, wonach der überwiegende

Teil (70.4 %) von ihnen bereits als Traktorfahrer und/
oder Mechaniker in mechanisierten landwirtschaftlichen
Gebieten gearbeitet hat (Tabelle 6.7). Als Hauptgrund
für ihre Abwanderung nach Khartoum sind u. a. die städti-
sche Attraktivität, erwartete Aufstiegschancen und nicht
zuletzt die Möglichkeit, ins Ausland abzuwandern, genannt
worden (Tabelle 6.8). Diejenigen, die Verwandte und Bekannte in Khartoum haben, sind unter den Befragten stark re-
präsentiert (Tabelle 6.12). Diese Feststellung ist sehr
wichtig, denn gerade in den Städten, im Gegensatz zu den
ländlichen Gebieten, sind die Beschäftigungsmöglichkeiten
für Traktorfahrer und Mechaniker sehr gering. Sie müssen
normalerweise mit langer Arbeitslosigkeit rechnen, bevor
sie eine ihrer Qualifikation entsprechende Beschäftigung
finden. In den meisten Fällen sind sie aber gezwungen, anderen Beschäftigungen nachzugehen, die mit ihrer Qualifikation gar nichts zu tun haben, in der Hoffnung, daß sie
im Laufe der Zeit ihre Ziele doch noch erreichen können.
Damit haben sie ihre bisherigen Tätigkeiten im Agrarsektor verlassen, und sie neigen nun dazu, ins Ausland abzuwandern.

Eine Beendigung derartiger Abwanderungsprozesse bzw. eine
Rückkehr zu ländlichen Gebieten ist noch nicht feststell-
bar. Eine Entscheidung darüber ist offenbar von den sozio-
ökonomischen Verhältnissen der verschiedenen Regionen des
Sudans abhängig; denn die sozio-ökonomischen Disparitäten,
die ursprünglich die bisherige Bevölkerungsmobilität verursachten, herrschen immer noch zwischen den verschiedenen
Regionen. Es scheint, daß diese Mobilität anhalten wird,
solange ein Lohngefälle zwischen den mechanisierten und
nicht-mechanisierten Regionen besteht und solange die
Qualifizierung von Arbeitskräften in Funktionsstandorten
der Mechanisierung möglich ist.

Die jetzigen Bestrebungen der Regierung, die mechanisierte
Anbaufläche auf Kosten der traditionellen Anbaugebiete
erheblich auszudehnen, werden mit Sicherheit die intra-
und interregionale Abwanderungstendenz sowie die ohnedies
gravierenden Land-Stadt-Abwanderungsprobleme weiter verstärken. Die Abwanderung ins Ausland wird dadurch begün-
stigt, daß qualifizierte Arbeitskräfte in den Ölländern
gefragt sind; dies zeigt die überragende Bedeutung der
Mechanisierung als Qualifikationsquelle.

F A Z I T
_____

Die Abwanderung der durch die Mechanisierung der Landwirtschaft qualifizierten Arbeitskräfte von den länd--
lichen Gebieten in die Städte und von dort ins Ausland
beschleunigt die bisherige Land-Stadt-Abwanderung und verstärkt somit den Druck auf die Ballungsgebiete. Diese
Entwicklung, die durch die Ausdehnung des modernen landwirtschaftlichen Sektors auf Kosten des traditionellen
Sektors hervorgerufen worden ist, hinterließ nur geringe
induktive Effekte auf die Entfaltung der übrigen Wirt-
schaftsbereiche. Das Endresultat ist eine verstärkte sektorale Disparität innerhalb der und zwischen den verschiedenen Regionen und verschiedenen Einkommensgruppen.

Diese Disparitäten werden dadurch weiter verstärkt, daß
die Importe von Inputs, die für die Entfaltung und Fort-
setzung des modernen Sektors, bei Fehlen einer Produk-
tionsmittelindustrie, notwendig sind, zu mehr Agrarexport-
gütern zwingen, auch bei sinkenden Erlösen, um dem Pro-
duktionsprozess die notwendigen Gelder zuführen zu können. Diese Tendenzen bewirken eine verstärkte Bevölke-
rungsabwanderung, die zu einer Beschränkung der Über-
schußproduktion im traditionellen Sektor führen kann.

Anders als die saisonale Abwanderung der unqualifizierten
Arbeitskräfte, die keinen nennenswerten Auflösungsprozeß
der traditionellen Formen der Produktion bewirkt, ist die
Abwanderung der durch die Mechanisierung der Landwirtschaft
qualifizierten Arbeitskräfte, sofern sie Verbindungen mit
ihren Herkunftsorten noch haben, als Ausgangspunkt der
Transformation der ländlichen Gebiete zu betrachten. Sie
sind tendenziell in den nationalen Produktionsprozeß einge-
bunden. Dennoch behindert dieser Teil der Arbeitskräfte,
aufgrund seiner höheren Mobilitätsrate und seiner
Neigung zur permanenten Ansiedlung in den Ballungsgebie-
ten, sowohl die Entwicklung des modernen landwirtschaftlichen Sektors als auch die Erzielung und Ausweitung eines Produktionsüberschusses in den traditionellen Sektoren.
Beide Arten von Behinderungen erschweren jede Art der Akku-
mulation, die für die Entwicklung des Landes notwendig
ist. Die dadurch verursachten verzerrten ökonomischen
Strukturen können nur durch die Beseitigung der fehlen-
den Integration in beiden Sektoren behoben werden. Einsei-
tige Versuche der Transformierung der Produktionsverhältnisse innerhalb eines Sektors sind unzureichend. Ich ver-
trete die These, daß die Konservierung der traditionellen
Produktionsstrukturen ein notwendiger Bestandteil des
Reproduktionsprozesses im Sudan ist, der überwiegend durch
den Ausbau des modernen landwirtschaftlichen Sektors ge-
kennzeichnet ist, der in seiner Entwicklung von der zeit-
weiligen Verfügbarkeit über Arbeitskräfte aus der traditionellen Landwirtschaft stark abhängig ist (TETZLAFF,
R., 1979). Jede Art von Maßnahmen, die zur Hebung der
Produktion im Substanzbereich beitragen kann, würde die
jetzige Abwanderungsintensität ohne Zweifel zunächst ver-
mindern, langfristig könnten aber überschüssige Arbeitskräfte freigesetzt werden, die dann produktiv in den anderen Produktionsbereichen eingesetzt werden könnten. Es

müssen aber im traditionellen Sektor Maßnahmen ergriffen werden, die über den eigenen Bedarf hinaus, zur Erhöhung der Exportproduktion und zur Substitution der Importe beitragen können. Nur dann werden sowohl die regionalen als auch die sektoralen Disparitäten vermindert, die die Ursache und Auswirkung von Bevölkerungsmobilität sind. Ein solcher Umwandlungsprozeß braucht aber eine bewußte, gezielte staatliche Intervention, die durch klare Prioritätensetzung innerhalb eines umfassenden Entwicklungsprogrammes charakterisiert ist.

LIST OF REFERENCES

ABD AL RAHIM, A. W., 1968:
  An enonomic history of the Gezira scheme
  1900 - 1956. (Unpublished Ph. D. Thesis,
  University of Manchester.)

ABDEL SALAM, M. M., 1976:
  Agriculture in the Sudan. In: An introduc-
  tion to the Sudan economy. (Ed.) A. M. El
  Hassan. Khartoum, pp. 38 - 75.

ABERCROMBIE, K. C., 1973:
  Agricultural mechanization and employment
  in Latin America. International Labour Review. July 1972, pp- 11 - 45.

ABU SIN, M. E., 1975:
  A survey and analysis of population mobility
  within northern and central Sudan. (Unpublished Ph. D. Thesis, Bedford College, England.)

AFRCAN DEVELOPMENT NEWSPAPER, 1975: No. 1

AGABAWI, K. A., 1968:
  Some development in the rain-fed agriculture
  in Central Sudan. Sudan Notes and Records.
  49 (1968), pp. 53 - 82, Khartoum.

AGOUBA, M., 1980:
  A functional literacy programme and its impact on agricultural development: an experi-
  mental project in Khashm el Girba. In:
  Non-formal education and development in the
  Sudan. (Ed.): Sadig RAHEED & Terry DANDELL.
  Khartoum; pp. 65 - 81. (University of Khartoum. Faculty of Economic and Social Studies and Research Centre.)

AHMED, B., 1972:
  Farm mechanization and agricultural develop-
  ment: A case study of the Pakistan Punjab.
  (Unpublished Ph. D. Diss., Michigan State
  University.)

BALDWIN, K. O. S., 1957:
          The Niger agricultural project: An experi-
          ment in African development. Oxford.

BARDELEBEN, M., 1968:
          Das Genossenschaftswesen im Sudan. Diss.
          Hamburg.

BARNETT, T., 1975:
          Production of cotton and the reproduction
          of underdevelopment. In: Beyond the socio-
          logy of development. Economy and society
          in Latin America and Africa, I. OXAAL,
          T. BARNETT and D. BOOTH (Eds.), London,
          pp. 75 - 93.

BARNETT, T., 1977:
          Gezira scheme. An illusion of development.
          London.

BART, Duff, 1975:
          Output, employment and mechanization in Philip-
          pine agriculture. Paper presented at the
          meeting of the FAO/OECD expert panel on the
          effects of farm mechanization, Rome, 4 - 7
          February, 1975. In: Employment, technolo-
          gy and development. Oxford, p. 70.

BASIC PROGRAMME:
          Arab Fund for Economic and Social Develop-
          ment. Basis programme for agricultural de-
          velopment in the Democratic Republic of
          the Sudan 1975 - 85. Summary and conclusions.
          kuwait, 1976.

BEALE; C. L., 1964:
          Rural depopulation in the United States:
          Some demographic consequences of agricultu-
          ral adjustment, Demography 1, pp. 264 - 272.

BELL, C., 1971:
          Landlords, landless and the distribution of
          income. Sussex. (University of Sussex. In-
          stitute of Development Studies.)

BERG, Eliot, 1961:
          Backward sloping supply functions in dual
          economies: The Africa case.
          Quarterly Lournal of Economics. 75 (1961);
          pp. 473 - 489.

BILLINGS, M. and S. ARJAN, 1970:
Mechanization and rural employment with some implications for rural income distribution. Economic and Political Weekly. Vol. 5, No. 26; pp. 21 - 64. Review of agriculture.

BILLINGS, M. and S. ARJAN, 1971:
The effect of technology on farm employment in two Indian states (Punjab and Maharashtra). In: Employment and unemployment problems of the Near East and South Asia. (Ed.): G. RONALD and H. LUBELL, New Delhi, Vol. 2; pp. 502 - 534.

BLANKENBURG, P. von and HUBERT, K., 1969:
The Khashm el Girba Settlement Scheme in the Sudan. An Appraisal for the World Food Programme, Rome, Institut für ausländische Landwirtschaft der Technischen Universität Berlin, in: Zeitschrift für ausländische Landwirtschaft, Vol. 8, pp. 328 - 364.

BLAUT, J. M., 1959:
"Micro-geographic sampling": A quantitative approach to regional agricultural geography. Economic geography. 35 (1959); pp. 79 - 88.

BOGUE, D. J., 1977:
A migrant's eye view of the costs and benefits of migration to a metropolis, in: BROWN, A. A. and NEUBERGER, E. (eds), Internal migration: A comparative perspective, pp. 167 - 182 (New York: Academic Press).

BOSE, S. R. and E. H. CLARK, 1969:
Some basic considerations on agricultural mechanization in West Pakistan. Pakistan Development Review, 9 (1969); pp. 273 - 308.

BREMER, F., 1977:
Endlose Voraussetzungen peripherer Entwicklungsprozesse an der Elfenbeinküste. Karlsruhe.

BROOKS, L., 1971:
Great civilizations of ancient Africa. New York.

BROWN, L. A. and MOORE, E. G., 1970:
The intra-urban migration Process: a perspective, Geografiska Annaler, 52B, pp. 1 - 13

CALDWELL, J. C., 1968:
Determinants of rural-urban migration in
Ghana, Population Studies, 22, pp. 361 - 377.

CALDWELL, J. C., 1969:
African rural-urban mogration: The movement
to Ghana's towns (Canberra: Australian
National U. P.).

CARR, M., 1973:
Tractors in a rural economy. Some social
and economic aspects of the introduction of
tractors into a rural economy: The case of
Ceylon (University of Edinburgh. Appopriate
Technology Conference. Paper No. RE/A-06).

CASTLE, B., 1966:
Growing up in East Africa. Oxford.

CAUFIELD, M., 1974:
Imperialism, the family and cultures of
resistance. Socialist Revolution. No. 20
pp. 67 - 85.

CLEASON, C. F., 1974:
Inter-regional population movement and cu-
mulative demographic disparity: an analysis
of census data in Tanzania, Geografiska
Annaler, 56B, pp. 105 - 120.

CLEASON, C. F. and EGERO, B., 1972a:
Migration in Tanzania. A review based on
the 1967 population census, Research No-
tes No. 11, University of Dar el Salam,
Bureau of Resource Assessment and Land
Use Planning.

CLEASON, C. F. and EGERO, B., 1972b:
Migration and the urban population - analysis
of population census data for Tanzania,
Geografiska Annaler, 54B, pp. 1 - 18.

CLARK, P,, 1972:
The migrant in Kentish towns, 1580 - 1640,
in: CLARK, P. and SLACK, P. (eds), Crisis and
Order in English Towns, pp. 117 - 163
(Londond: Routledge and Kegan, Paul).

CLARKE, J. I., 1965:
Sex ratios in Sierra Leone, Bulletin -
Journal of the Sierra Leone Geographical
Association, p, pp. 72 - 77.

CLAYTON, E. S., 1972:
          "Mechanization and Employment in East
          African Agriculture", in: International
          Labour Review, April 1972, pp. 309 - 334,
          Geneva.

CRIBIER, F., 1975:
          Retirement migration in France, in:
          Kosinski, L. A. and Prothero, R. M. (eds),
          People on the Move, pp. 361 - 373 (Lon-
          don: Methuen).

DAFALLA, H., 1975:
          The Nubian exodus, Khartoum.

DAK, O., 1968:
          A geographical analysis of the distribution
          of migrants in Uganda. Kampala, Makerere
          University. Department of Geography. Occa-
          sional Paper No. 11.

DALRYMPLE, D. G., 1969:
          Import and Planting of high-yielding varie-
          ties of wheat and rice in the less-developed
          nations. Washington (USDA Foreign Agricultural
          Service).

DAVIES, H. R. J., 1966:
          Nomadism in the Sudan. Aspects of the prob-
          lem and suggested lines for its solution
          (Tijdschrift v. Econ en soc. Geographie,
          57, pp. 193 - 202). Rotterdam.

DE GREGORI, T. R., 1969:
          Technology and the economic development of
          the tropical African Frontier. Cleveland,
          Ohio.

DEPARTMENT OF......
          see REPUBLIC OF THE SUDAN, DEPARTMENT OF ...

DESAI, R. 1963:
          Indian immigrants in Britain. Oxford.

DONALDSON, G. F. and MELNERNEY, J. P., 1973:
          Changing machine technology and agricultural
          adjustment. Paper presented to the joined
          conference of the American Agricultural Eco-
          nomics Society and the Canadian Agricultu-
          ral Economic Society, Edmonton, Canada,
          August 1973.

DUFFIELD, M., 1978a:
> Hausa and Fulani settlement and the develop-
> ment of capitalism in the Sudan. (Ph. D.,
> Centre of West African Studies, University
> of Birmingham).

DUFFIELD, M., 1978b:
> Peripheral capitalism and the social agricul-
> tural production in the village of Maiurno
> near Sennar. Khartoum.

DRUDY, P. J., 1978:
> Depopulation in a prosperous agricultural
> sub-region, Regional studies, 12, pp. 49 -
> 60.

EL BADRAWI, M., 1972:
> The transfer of Nubians to Khashm el Girba
> and its impact on the social life. (M. A.
> Thesis, submitted in Arabic to the Facul-
> ty of Arts, Cairo, Egypt.).

EL BAGIR, H., 1972:
> Nubians in their new homes. (Unpublished
> M. A. Thesis submitted in Arabic to the
> Faculty of Arts, Cairo, Egypt).

EL BUSHRA, E., 1976:
> An atlas of Khartoum conurbation, Khartoum.

EL HASSAN, A. M. (ed.), 1976:
> An introduction to the Sudan economy.
> Khartoum.

EL MANGOURI, H., 1978:
> Planning and development of irrigated settle-
> ment schemes in developing countries: Experi-
> ences from the Khashm el Girba scheme in the
> Democratic Republic of the Sudan. Diploma
> Thesis, Free University of Berlin, West
> Germany.

EL MANGOURI and HEINRITZ, G., 1981:
> Luftbild New Halfa - Projektgebiet (Republik
> Sudan).
> Die Erde. 112 (1981); pp. 1 - 10.

ELDRIDGE, H. T., 1965:
> Primary, secondary and return migration in
> the United States, 1955 - 1960.
> Demography. 2 (1965); pp. 444 - 455.

FAHIM, H. M., 1972:
          Nubian resettlement in the Sudan. Cairo.
          (American University in Cairo. Social
          Research Centre. Peprint Series. Nr. 13)

FAO PRODUCTION YEARBOOK 1977.
          Rome.

(The) Five Year Plan of economic and social development
          1970/71 - 1974/75. Khartoum 1970.
          (Republic of the Sudan. Ministry of Natio-
          nal Planning.)

FRIEDMANN, J., E. McCLYNN, B. STUCKEY & C. WU, 1973:
          Unbanization and national development: A
          comparative study in urbanization and
          national development. Los Angeles.

GAITSKELL, A., 1959:
          "Gezira": A story of development in the
          Sudan. London.

GALAL EL DIN, M. E., 1973:
          Internal migration in the Sudan since
          World War II, with special reference to
          migration to Greater Khartoum. (Ph. D.
          London.), London.

GALAL EL DIN, M. E., 1979:
          The Sudanese emigration. (Republic of
          the Sudan. National Research Council.)
          Khartoum. (In Arabic.)

GALTUNG, J., 1971:
          Members of two worlds: A development study
          of three villages in western Sicily. Oslo.

GETIS, A. & B. BOOTS, 1978:
          Models of spatial processes. Cambridge.

GIROURARD, Sir PERCY, 1913:
          In: East African Standard, February 8th,
          1913. Cited in: Raymond I. Buell: The
          native problem in Africa. 2nd pr. Vol. 1.
          London 1965.

GODDARD, A. D., W. T. S. GOULD & F. I. MASSER, 1975:
          Census data and migration analysis in
          tropical Africa.
          Geografiska Annaler. 57B (1975); pp. 26 - 41

GOTSCH, C. H., 1973:
Tractor mechanization and rural development in Pakistan. International Labour Review. February 1973; pp. 133 - 166.

GOUGH, K., 1978:
'The Green Revolution in South India and North Vietnam' in: Monthly Review, Vol. 29, No. 8; pp. 1 - 56.

GRANDSTAFF, P. J., 1975:
Recent Soviet experience and Western 'Laws' of population migration, International Migration Review, 9, pp. 479 - 497.

GREENWOOD, M. J., 1970:
'Large response in the decision to migrate', Journal of Regional Science, 10, pp. 375 - 384.

GRIFFIN, K., 1974:
The political economy of agrarian change. An essay on the Green Revolution. London.

GRIGG, D. B., 1977:
'E. G. Ravenstein and the "laws of migration" ', Journal of Historical Geography, 3, pp. 41 - 54.

GUGLER, J., 1968:
The impact of labour mogration on society and economy in sub-Saharan Africa. African Social Research. 6 (1968; pp. 463 - 486.

GUGLER, J., 1969:
On the theory of rural-urban migration. In: Jackson, J. A. (ed.): Migration. Cambridge; pp. 134 - 155.

HABASHI,W., 1966:
The development of agricultural production in the Sudan. (Lectures delivered at Extra-Mural Studies, University of Khartoum, in Arabic.) Khartoum.

HABERMEIER, K., 1977:
Bäuerliche Gemeinschaften, kapitalistische Exportwirtschaft und Wanderarbeit in West-Afrika. Karlsruhe.

HAEGERSTRAND, T., 1957:
Migration and Area, in Hannerberg, D. et al. (eds), Migration in Sweden, pp. 27 - 158, Lund Studies in Geography, 13 B (Lund: Gleerup).

HANCE, W. A., 1970:
Population, Migration and Urbanization in Africa (New York: Columbia U. P.).

HANNEN, D. F., 1969:
Migration motives and migrations differentials among Irish rural Youth, Sociologia Ruralis, 9, pp. 195 - 220.

HARRINGTON, R. E., 1972:
Changes in Employment of farm labour under the impact of increasing use of tractor in India, Japan, N. Korea, S. Korea and Taiwan, New York.

HARRIS, B., 1974:
The economic and spatial relations of tractorisation ind its implications for rural indebtedness in Hambantota district of Sri Lanka. Paper presented at the seminar on the project of agrarian change in rice-growing areas of Tamil Nadu and Sri Lanka, Centre of South Asian Studies, Cambridge University, December 1974.

HART, R. A., 1973:
Economic expectations and the decision to migrate: analysis by socio-economic group, Regional Studies, 7, pp. 271 - 285.

HASSAN ADAM, F. and M. KHIDIR, 1976:
Development of small-scale agriculture. In: Growth, employment and equity. A selection of papers presented to the ILO Conprehensive Employment Strategy Mission to the Sudan, 1974 - 75. (Ed.): A. M. EL HASSAN, Khartoum.

HAUSEN, K., 1970:
Deutsche Kolonialherrschaft in Afrika. Berlin.

HEINRITZ, G., 1977:
Die Entwicklung junger Bewässerungsprojekte unter dem Einfluß gruppenspezifischen Pächterverhaltens. Ein erster Bericht über sozialgeografische Untersuchungen im Khashm el Girba - Projektgebiet / Republik Sudan. Geographische Zeitschrift. 65 (1977); pp. 188 - 215.

HEINRITZ, G., 1978:
Social geographic problems in the Khashm
el Girba project, Sudan.
Land Reform. 1978, No. 2; pp. 25 - 35.

HEINRITZ, G., 1980:
Das Rahad Scheme. Ein neues Bewässerungs-
projekt in der Republik Sudan (MSKT).
München.

HEINRITZ, G., 1982:
The migration of Westerners in the New
Halfa and Rahad schemes, in: Heinritz, G.
(ed.): Problems of agricultural development in the Sudan, Selected Papers of a
seminar, Edition Herodot, Forum 2, Göttin-
gen, 1982, pp. 69 - 87.

HENIN, R. A., 1961:
Economic development and internal migration in the Sudan. Sudan Notes and Records. 44 (1961); pp. 100 - 119.

HERZOG, R., 1966:
Sudan, Bonn.

HILL, M. F., 1956:
Planter's progress. The story of coffee in
Kenya, Nairobi.

HILL, P., 1970:
Studies in rural capitalism in West Africa.
Cambridge University Press.

HIRST, M. A., 1975:
The distribution of migrants in Kampala.
East African Geographical Review. 13,
(1975); pp. 37 - 57.

HIRST, M. A., 1976:
A markovian analysis of interregional migration in Uganda, Geografiska Annaler, 58 B,
pp. 79 - 94.

HOPKINS, A. G., 1966:
The Lagos strike of 1897: an exploration
in Nigerian labour history. Past and Present: a journal of historical studies.
No. 35.

HOPKINS, A. G., 1968:
Economic imperialism in West Africa: Lagos
1880 - 1892. Economic History Review. 21 (1968).
pp. 73 - 92.

HOUGHTON, D. H., 1971:
Economic development, 1865 - 1965.
In: The Oxford history of South Africa. Vol. 2,
South Africa 1870 - 1966. Oxford.

HUNTER, J. M., 1965:
Regional patterns of population growth in
Ghana. In: Essays in geography for Austin
Miller. (Ed.): J. B. WHITTOW & P. D. WOOD,
Reading, pp. 272 - 290.

HUTTON, C., 1973:
Reluctant farmers? A study of unemployment
and planned rural development in Uganda.
Nairobi.

IFTIKHAR, A., 1975:
The Green Revolution. Mechanization and
employment. Geneva. (ILO mimeographed
World Employment Programme research working paper. For restricted distribution
only.)

IFTIKHAR, A., 1976:
The Green Revolution and tractorization;
their mutual relations and socio-economic
effects. Internation Labour Review. 114 (1976)

ILO (INTERNATIONAL LABOUR OFFICE)
African labour survey. Geneva, 1958.

ILO (INTERNATIONAL LABOUR OFFICE)
Employment, incomes and equality. A strategy
of increasing productive employment in Kenya.
Geneva, 1972.

ILO (INTERNATIONAL LABOUR OFFICE)
Growth, employment and equity. A comprehensive strategy for the Sudan. Geneva, 1976.

INGHAM, K., 1971:
Deutsch-Ostafrika: ein wirtschaftliches Ex-
periment in Afrika.
Afrika Verein. 3. (1961; pp. 1 - 27

INTERNATIONAL AFRICAN INSTITUTE AND UNESCO
Social implications of industrialization
and urbanization in Africa south of the
Sahara. London 1956.

ISZAEVICH, A., 1875:
Emigrants, spinsters and priests: the dynamics
of demography of Spanish Peasant Societies,
Journal of Peasant Studies. 2, pp. 292 - 312.

IZUMI, K. and RANATHUNGA, A. S., 1974:
          Employment and social constraints on paddy
          production under existing conditions. A
          case study of Hambantota District. Colombo.
          (Agrarian Research and Training Institute.
          Occasional Publication Series. 4).

JONES, H. R., 1965:
          A study of rural migration in central Wales,
          Transactions. Institute of British Geographers,
          37, pp. 31 - 45.

KAY, G., 1967:
          Social geography of Zambia. London.

KISS, J., 1977:
          Will the Sudan be an agricultural Power?
          Budapest.

KRAUTER, P. 1979:
          Die Entwicklung des non-formalen Bildungs-
          wesend in einem Land der Dritten Welt: Das
          Beispiel Kenya. München (U. P. Manuscript).

KULS, W., 1980:
          Bevölkerungsgeographie. Teubner Studien-
          bücher der Geographie, Stuttgart.

KUSUM, C., 1972:
          Mechanization of agriculture and labour de-
          velopment. New Dehli. (USAID Newsletter).

LAING, R. G., 1953:
          Mechanization of agriculture in the rainlands
          of the Anglo-Egyptian Sudan, 1948 - 51.
          Khartoum.

LAWTON, R. (ed), 1978:
          The census and social structure: An Inter-
          pretive Guide to Nineteenth Censuses for
          England and Wales (London: Cass).

LEE, E. S., 1966:
          'A theory of migration'. Demography, 3.
          pp. 47 - 57.

LEWIS, A., 1964:
          Thoughts on land settlement.
          In: Agriculture in economic development.
          (Ed.): E. EICHER & L. WITT, New York, Toronto,
          San Francisco, London.

LOWENTHAL, D. and COMITTAS, L., 1962:
        Emigration and depopulation: Some neglected
        aspects of population geography. Geographical
        Review, 52, pp. 195 - 210.

MALTHUS, T. R., 1798:
        An Essay on the Principles of Population,
        reprinted for the Royal Economic Society,
        1926 (London: Macmillan).

MARVIN, P. M., 1966:
        Maize in tropical Africa. Madison, Wisconsin.

MASSER, I. and GOULD, W. T. S., 1975:
        Inter-Regional Migration in Tropical Africa,
        Special Publication No. 8, Institute of
        British Geographers.

MATHER, D. B., 1956:
        Migration in the Sudan.
        In: Geographic essays on British Tropical
        Lands. (Ed.): R. W. STEEL & C. A. FISHER.
        Pp. 115 - 143. London.

McKELVEY, J., 1965:
        Agricultural research in the African world : A
        survey of social research. New York.

McLOUGHLIN, P., 1963:
        The Sudan's three towns: A demographic and
        economic profile of an African urban complex.
        Economic Development and Cultural Change. 13.
        (1963). Pp. 70 - 83.

MERLIN, P., 1971:
        L'Exode Rural, Cahier de l'I.N.E. D. No 59
        (Paris: P.U.F.)

METZGER, D., 1976:
        Reproduction and production: Unpaid and
        underpaid female labour force in the world
        economy. Starnberg (Unpublished manuscript.).

MICHAELSON; W., 1977:
        Environmental Choice, Human Behaviour and
        Residential Satisfaction (New York: Oxford
        U. P.).

MIDDLETON, J. F. M., 1960:
        'The Lugbara', in Richards, A. I. (ed.),
        East African Chiefs, pp. 326 - 343 (Lon-
        don: Faber).

MILLER, E., 1972:
> A note on the role of distance in migration: costs of mobility versus intervening opportunity, Journal of Regional Science, 12, pp. 475 - 478.

MINISTRY OF ...
> see REPUBLIC OF THE SUDAN, MINISTRY OF ...

MITCHELL, C., 1962:
> The causes of labour migration. In. Migrant labour in Africa south of the Sahara. Abidjan, (Interafrican Labour Institute. Commission for Technical Co-operation in Africa South of the Sahara.).

MITCHELL, J. C., 1961:
> Wage labour and African population movements in Central Africa.
> In: Essays on African population. London; pp. 193 - 248.

MOLOHAN, M. J. B., 1957:
> Detribalization. Das es Salaam.

MONSON, W. J., 1903:
> Report on slavery and free labour in the British East African Protectorate. In: Great Britain. Parliamentary Papers. Cd 1931. London.

NATIONAL COUNCIL OF APPLIED ECONOMIC RESEARCH,
> Techno-economic Survey of Maharashtra, New Delhi, July 1963.

NEWBURY, C. W., 1975:
> Historical Aspects of Manpower and Migration in Africa South of the Sahara, in: P. Duignan and L. H. Gann (eds.): Colonialism in Africa 1870 - 1960, Vol. 4, the Economics of colonialismn pp. 523 - 546. Cambridge University Press, Cambridge.

NEWBURY, C. W., 1961:
> The Western Slave Coast and its Rulers. Oxford, Clarendorn Press.

NEWBURY, C. W., 1965:
> British Policy towards W. Africa, Selected Documents 1786 - 1874. Oxford, Clarendon Press.

NEWBURY, G. E. and NEWBURY, C. W., 1969:
          'Annotated bibliography of Commonwealth
          migrations: the Tropical Territories:
          1 Africa (Oxford. Institute of Commonwealth
          Studies).

ÖSTERDIECKHOFF, P., 1980:
          Der Agrarsektor des Sudans.
          In: Tetzlaff, R. & K. Wohlmuth (Ed.):
          Der Sudan. Probleme und Perspektiven der
          Entwicklung eines weltmarktabhängigen Agrar-
          staates. Frankfurt/M.; pp. 257 - 385.

OLIVER, R., 1972:
          The missionary factor in East Africa. London.

OMINDE, S. H., 1968:
          Land and population movements in Kenya. Lon-
          don.

OSMAN, D. H., 1958:
          "Some Aspects of Private Pump schemes", Sudan
          Notes and Records, Vol. 39; pp. 40 - 48.

OSMAN, M. S., 1966:
          The possibilities and problems of the mechani-
          zation of agricultural production in the Sudan.
          In: Agricultural development of the Sudan.
          (Ed.): D. J. Show. Khartoum, Vol. 2. pp.
          302 - 357.

PAUL, A., 1954:
          A history of the Beja tribes of the Sudan.
          London.

PETERS, G. L., 1976:
          The sex selectivity of out-migration: an
          Appalachian example, Yearbook, Association
          of Pacific Coast Geographers, 38, pp. 99 -
          109.

PETERSEN, W., 1958:
          A general typology of migration, American
          Sociological Review, 23, pp. 256 - 266.

PIAULT, M., 1962:
          The migration of workers in West Africa.
          In: Migrant labour in Africa south of the
          Sahara. Abidjan; pp. 323 - 338. (Inter-
          African Labour Institute. Commission for
          Technical Co-operation in Africa South of
          the Sahara).

PORTER; R., 1956:
> An approach to migration through its mechanism, Geografiska Annaler, 38, pp. 317 - 343.

PROTHERO, R. M., 1968:
> Migration in tropical Africa, in: Caldwell, J. C. and Okonjo, C. (eds.), The population of Tropical Africa, pp. 250 - 263 (London: Longman).

PROTHERO, R. M., 1964:
> Community and change in African population mobility, in: Steel, R. W. and Prothero, R. M. (eds.), Geographers and the Tropics: Liverpool Essays, pp. 189 - 214 (London: Longman).

PRYOR, R. J., 1969:
> Laws of Migration? - the experience of Malaysia and other countries. Geographica (Kuala Lumpur), 5, pp. 65 - 76.

RAVENSTEIN, E. G., 1885:
> The laws of migration, Journal, Statistical Society, 48, pp. 167 - 235.

REITER, R. R., 1972:
> Modernization in the South of France: the village and beyond. Anthropological Quarterly, 45, pp. 35 - 53.

REPUBLIC OF THE SUDAN; DEPARTMENT OF LABOUR:
> Employer and employed persons ordinance, 1948 amendment. Khartoum, 1973.

REPUBLIC OF THE SUDAN; DARPARTMENT OF STATISTICS:
> Population and housing survey, 1964/66. Khartoum, 1968.

REPUBLIC OF THE SUDAN; MINISTRY OF AGRICULTURE:
> Working party's report on mechanical crop production schemes. Khartoum, 1954.

REPUBLIC OF THE SUDAN; MINISTRY OF AGRICULTURE, FOOD AND NATURAL RESOURCES:
> Bulletin of Agricultural Statistics of the Sudan (Annual Report). 1974/75, p. 45.

REPUBLIC OF THE SUDAN; MINISTRY OF AGRICULTURE, FOOD AND NATURAL RESOURCES:
> Sudan: Annual Report, 1975.

MINISTRY OF AGRICULTURE, FOOD and NATURAL RESOURCES:
Sudan: Yearbook of Agricultural Statistics,
1977.

REPUBLIC OF THE SUDAN, MINISTRY OF AGRICULTURE, FOOD AND
NATURAL RESOURCES:
Food investment strategy 1977 - 1985.
Khartoum, 1977.

REPUBLIC OF THE SUDAN, MINISTRY OF AGRICULTURE:
A brief review of agricultural resources.
Khartoum, 1978.

REPUBLIC OF THE SUDAN, MINISTRY OF CULTURE AND INFORMATION:
Rahad Irrigation Project. Khartoum 1977.

REPUBLIC OF THE SUDAN, MINISTRY OF FINANCE AND NATIONAL
ECONOMY:
Economic survey 1976/77. Khartoum, 1977.

REPUBLIC OF THE SUDAN, MINISTRY OF IRRIGATION AND HYDRO-
ELECTRIV POWER:
Irrigation by gravity from River Atbara.
In: Sudan Pamphlets. 26 (1955).
(Quoted in: Neue Zürcher Zeitung, 25. 5. 1977),
p. 4.

REPUBLIC OF THE SUDAN, SUDAN GEZIRA BOARD:
The Gezira scheme from within. Barakat, 1963.

RICHARDS, A. I. (ed), 1954:
Economic Development and Tribal Change:
A study of Immigrant Labour in Buganda (Cam-
bridge: Heffer).

RIDDELL,J. B., 1970a:
On structuring a migration model, Geographical
Analysis, 2, pp. 403 - 409.

RIDDEL, J. B., 1970b:
The Spatial Dynamics of Modernization in
Sierra Leone: Sturcture, Diffusion and
Response (Evanston: Northwestern, U. P.).

RODNEY, W., 1972:
How Europe underdeveloped Africa. Dar es
Salaam.

ROGERS, B., 1978:
African women in agriculture.
Africa. No. 78, pp. 70 - 71.

ROSEMAN, C. C., 1971:
Migration as a spatial and temporal porcess.
Annals of the Association of American
Geographers. 61 (1971). pp. 589 - 598.

SAVILLE, J., 1957:
Rural Depopulation in England and Wales
1851 - 1951 (London: Routledge and Kegan
Paul).

SCHOFIELD, R. S., 1970:
Age-specific mobility in an eighteen century
rural English parish, Annales de Demographie
Historique, 6, pp. 261 - 274.

SCHWIND, P. J., 1971:
Migration and regional development in the
United States, 1950 - 1960. Chicago. (Uni-
versity of chicago. Department of Geography.
Research Paper No. 133).

SHAHAK, K. I., 1977:
Mechanization of agriculture in the clay plains
of the Sudan, with special reference to Gedarif region (Unoublished Ph. D., Khartoum
University.). Khartoum.

SHYROCK, H. S. and E. A. LARMON, 1965:
Some longitudinal data on internal migration.
Demography 2. (1965), Pp. 579 - 592.

(The) SIX YEAR P1AN of economic and social development
1977/78 - 1982/83. Khartoum 1977.
(Republic of the Sudan. Ministry of National
Planning.)

SKLAR, R. L., 1975:
Corporate power in an African state: The
political impact of miltinational mining
companies in Zambia. Berkeley.

SOUTHALL, A. W., 1961:
Population movements in East Africa, in:
Barbour, K. M. and Prothero, R. M. (eds)
Essays on African Population, pp. 157 - 192
(Oxford: oxford U. P.).

SOUTHALL, A. W. (ed), 1971:
Social Change in Modern Africa (Oxford:
Oxford U. P.)

STATISTISCHES BUNDESAMT:
Länderbericht: Sudan. Stuttgart u. Mainz, 1976.

STATISTISCHES BUNDESAMT:
Länderbericht: Sudan. Stuttgart und Mainz, 1978.

STUCKEY, B. & M. F. FAY, 1980:
Strukturveränderung in der kapitalistischen
Weltwirtschaft. In. Starnberger Studien 4.
Frankfurt/M., pp. 90 - 168.

SUDAN COTTON GROWERS ASSOCIATION:
>Private Cotton Estates in the Republic
>of the Sudan. Khartoum, February, 1964.

SWAR EL DAHAB, A. M. S., 1978:
>Labour force in the manufacturing industry
>of N. Khartoum. A case study in demgraphic
>and socio-economic characteristics of
>industrial labour force in the Sudan.
>(unpublished M. A. Thesis, University of
>Khartoum.)

TAEUBER, K. E., 1961:
>Duration of residence analysis of internal
>migration in the United States. Milbank
>Fund Quarterly, 34, pp. 116 - 131.

TAEUBER, K. E., 1966:
>Cohort migration, Demography, 3, pp. 416 - 422.

TANNOUS, A. I., 1942:
>Emigration, a force of social change in an
>Arab willage, Rural Sociology, 7, pp. 62 - 74.

(The) TEN YEAR PLAN of economic and social development
>1961/62 - 1970/71. Khartoum 1960. (Re-
>public of the Sudan. Ministry of Finance and
>Economy. The Economic Planning Secretariat.)

TETZLAFF, R., 1979:
>Die "Durchkapitalisierung" der Landwirtschaft
>im Sudan und ihre Auswirkung auf den "traditio-
>nellen" Sektor. Eine Strategie zur Überwin-
>dung ländlicher Armut? In: Agrarreform in
>der Dritten Welt. Hrsg.: H. Elsenhans,
>Frankfurt/m. und New York, pp. 339 - 363.

TETZLAFF, R. und K. WOHLMUTH (Ed.), 1980:
>Der Sudan. Probleme und Perspektiven der
>Entwicklung eines weltmarktabhängigen
>Agrarstaates. Frankfurt/M.

THORNTON, D. S., 1964:
>The organization of production in the irri-
>gated areas of the Sudan. Journal of Agri-
>cultural Economics. 16 (1964).

TOTHILL, J. D., 1940:
>Agriculture in Uganda. Oxford, London.

UN (UNITED NATIONS)
>Structure and growth of selected African
>economies. New York. 1958.

WARD, W. E. F., 1952:
>A history of the Gold Coast, London.

WEBER, E., 1977:
    Peasants into Frenchman: The Moderniza-
    tion of Rural France, 1870 - 1914 (London:
    Chatto and Windus).

WHITE, P. and WOODS, R., 1980:
    The geographical impact of migration.
    London and New York.

WILKES, G., 1977:
    The world's crop plant germplasm - an endan-
    gered resource. Bulletin of Atomic Scien-
    tists. February 1977; pp. 8 - 16

WILSON, F., 1972:
    Labour in the South African gold mines,
    1911 - 1969. London.

WÖRTZ, J. G. F., 1966:
    Genossenschaftliche und partnerschaftliche
    Produktionsförderung in der sudanesischen
    Landwirtschaft. Frankfurt/M..

WOODS, R. I., 1979:
    Population Analysis in Geography (London:
    Longman).

WOLPERT, J., 1965:
    Behavioral aspects of the decision to
    migrate, Papers and proceedings,
    Regional Science Association, 15,
    pp. 159 - 169.

WOLPERT, J., 1966:
    Migration as an adjustment to environmental
    stress, Journal of Social Issues, 22, pp. 92 -
    102.

WORLD BANK:
    Sudan: Appraisal of the Savanah Development
    Project; Eastern Africa Region; Agriculture,
    credit and livestock. 1977. For official use
    only.

WYNN, R. F., 1971:
    The Sudan's Ten Year Plan of economic develop-
    ment, 1961/62 - 70/71: An analysis of achieve-
    ment to 1967/68.
    The Journal of Developing Areas. 5. (1971).

YUDELMAN, M., 1975:
> Imperialism and the transfer of agricultural techniques. In: Colonialism in Africa, 1870 - 1960. (Ed.): P. Duignan & L. H. Gann. Cambridge. Vol. 4, pp. 329 - 360.

ZELINSKY, W., 1971:
> The hypothesis of the mobility transition. Geographical Review. 61 (1971), pp. 219 - 249.

A P P E N D I X

Fig. 1: **Circulation of skilled labour force in the Democratic Republic of the Sudan as caused by agricultural mechanization**

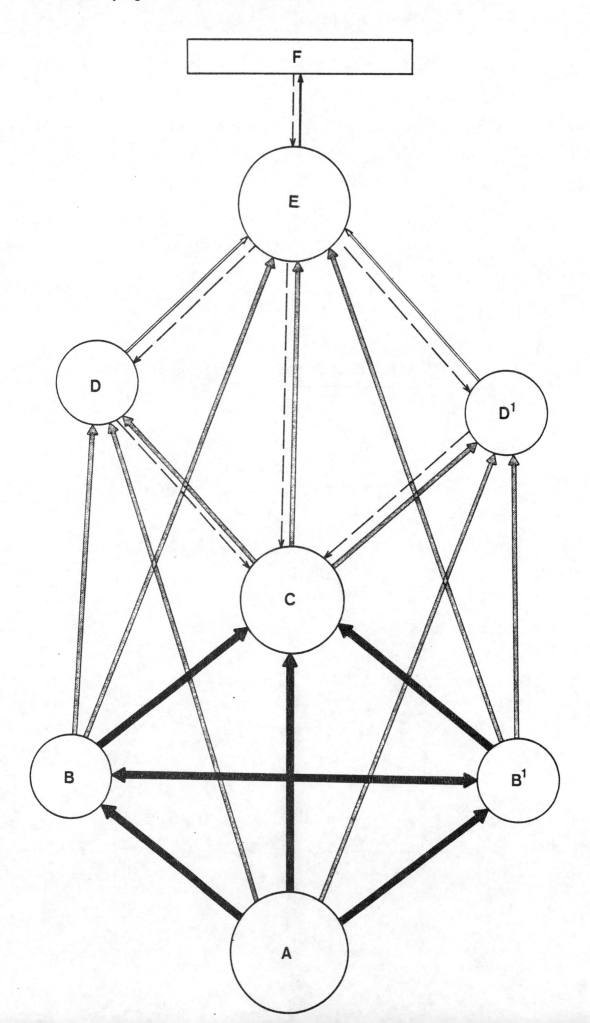

Key for Fig. 1:

A: Unmechanized areas as origin of unskilled labour force

B-B¹: Old mechanized irrigated and rain-fed agricultural schemes as training centres for rural youth

C: Recently implemented mechanized schemes as centres of attraction for qualified persons

D-D¹: Urban centres within and outside mechanized regions as alternative working places for qualified persons

E: Capital Khartoum as main target for qualified persons

F: Oil-rich Arab Countries as main preferences for high-qualified persons

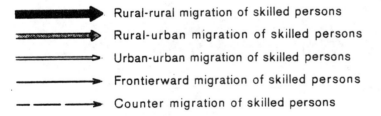

Rural-rural migration of skilled persons

Rural-urban migration of skilled persons

Urban-urban migration of skilled persons

Frontierward migration of skilled persons

Counter migration of skilled persons

Compiled by Hassan El Mangouri, 1982

Fig. 2   - 286 -

Qualifying effect of agricultural mechanization as a function of distance between place of origin and functional location (Workshop) as shown by a concrete example: El Masara Workshop in El Suki District

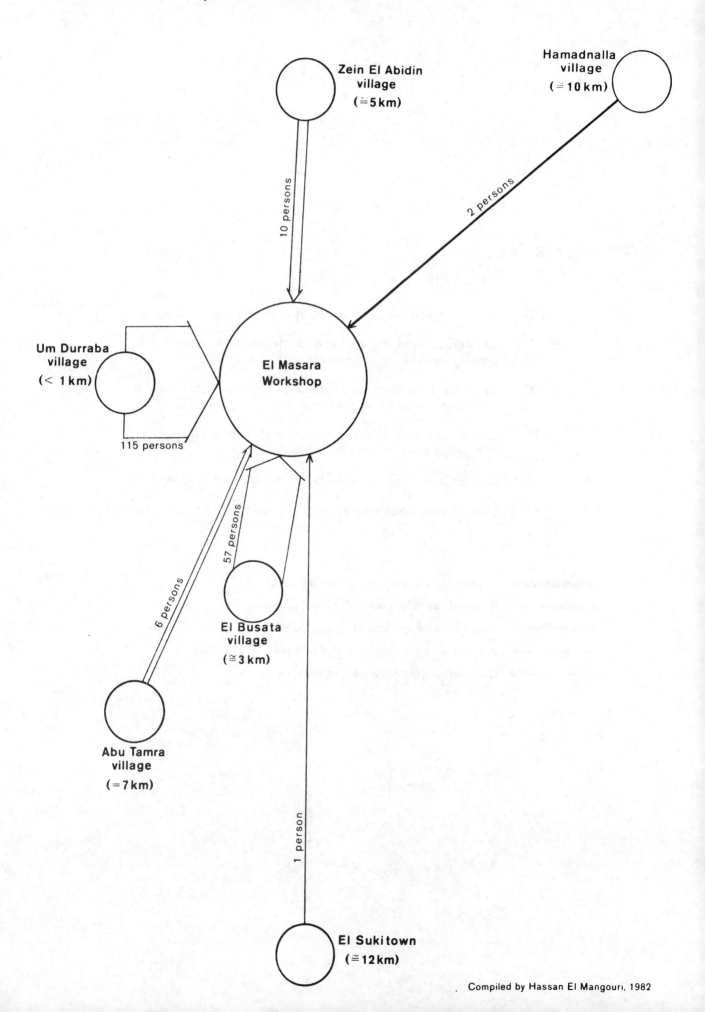

Compiled by Hassan El Mangouri, 1982

Map. 1:

The Democratic Republik of the Sudan
Regional Concentration of mechanized agriculture

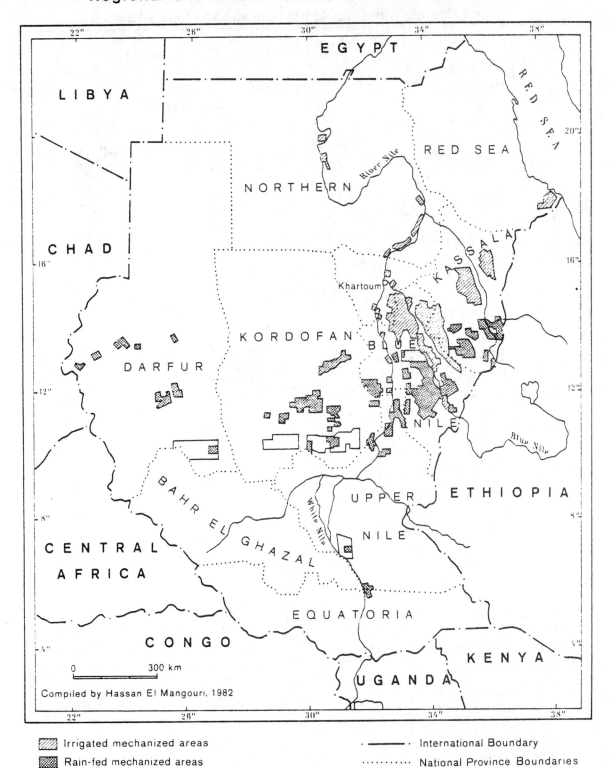

Compiled by Hassan El Mangouri, 1982

▨ Irrigated mechanized areas	·——— International Boundary
▨ Rain-fed mechanized areas	········· National Province Boundaries
▢ Planned mechanized areas	~◯ River/Lake/Sea

Map 2

CASE STUDY AREAS : The three selected irrigation settlement schemes
(Khashm el Girba, El Rahad and El Suki). Khartoum Conurbation and El Suki District
with El Masara Workshop, El Kurmuta and Abu Gara villages

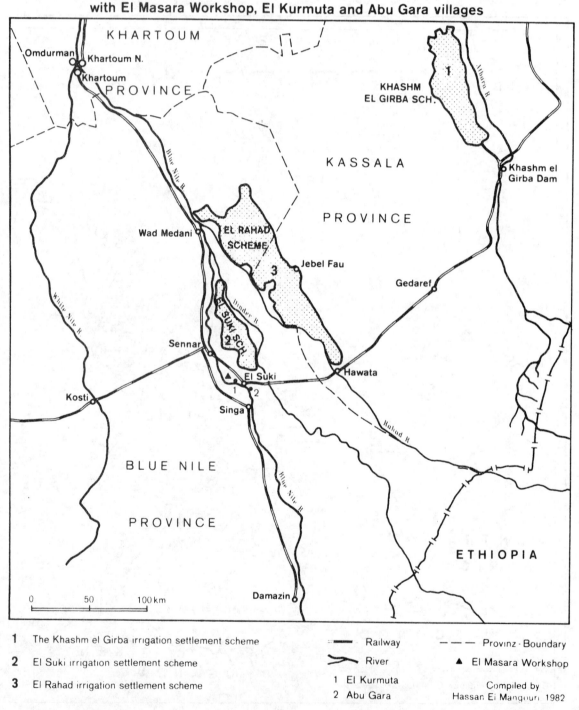

1 The Khashm el Girba irrigation settlement scheme	▬▬ Railway	─ ─ ─ Provinz-Boundary
2 El Suki irrigation settlement scheme	∿ River	▲ El Masara Workshop
3 El Rahad irrigation settlement scheme	1 El Kurmuta 2 Abu Gara	Compiled by Hassan El Mangouri 1982

ABHANDLUNGEN DES GEOGRAPHISCHEN INSTITUTS DER FREIEN UNIVERSITÄT BERLIN

Band 1: K. Schröder, Die Stauanlagen der mittleren Vereinigten Staaten. Ein Beitrag zur Wirtschafts- und Kulturgeographie der USA. 1953. 96 S. mit 4 Karten, DM 12,--

Band 2: O. Quelle, Portugiesische Manuskriptatlanten. 1953. 12 S. mit 25 Tafeln und 1 Kartenskizze. Vergriffen!

Band 3: G. Jensch, Das ländliche Jahr in deutschen Agrarlandschaften. 1957. 115 S. mit 13 Figuren und Diagrammen, DM 19,50

Band 4: H. Valentin, Glazialmorphologische Untersuchungen in Ostengland. Ein Beitrag zum Problem der letzten Vereisung im Nordseeraum. 1957. 86 S. mit Bildern und Karten,

Band 5: Geomorphologische Abhandlungen. Otto Maull zum 70. Geburtstag gewidmet. Besorgt von E. Fels, H. Overbeck und J.H. Schultze. 1957. 72 S. mit Abbildungen und Karten, DM 16,--

Band 6: K.-A. Boesler, Die städtischen Funktionen. Ein Beitrag zur allgemeinen Stadtgeographie aufgrund empirischer Untersuchungen in Thüringen. 1960. 80 S. mit Tabellen und Karten. Vergriffen!

Seit 1963 wird die Reihe fortgesetzt unter dem Titel

ABHANDLUNGEN DES 1. GEOGRAPHISCHEN INSTITUTS DER FREIEN UNIVERSITÄT BERLIN

Band 7: J.H. Schultze, Der Ost-Sudan. Entwicklungsland zwischen Wüste und Regenwald. 1963. 173 S. mit Figuren, Karten und Abbildungen. Vergriffen!

Band 8: H. Hecklau, Die Gliederung der Kulturlandschaft im Gebiet von Schriesheim/ Bergstraße. Ein Beitrag zur Methodik der Kulturlandschaftsordnung. 1964. 152 S. mit 16 Abbildungen und 1 Karte, DM 30,--

Band 9: E. Müller, Berlin-Zehlendorf. Versuch einer Kulturlandschaftsgliederung. 1968. 144 S. mit 8 Abbildungen und 3 Karten, DM 30,--

Band 10: C. Werner, Zur Geometrie von Verkehrsnetzen. Die Beziehung zwischen räumlicher Netzgestaltung und Wirtschaftlichkeit. 1966. 136 S. mit 44 Figuren. English summary. Vergriffen!

Band 11: K.D. Wiek, Kurfürstendamm und Champs-Elysées. Geographischer Vergleich zweier Weltstraßen-Gebiete. 1967. 134 S. mit 9 Fotos, 8 Kartenbeilagen, DM 30,--

Band 12: K.-A. Boesler, Kulturlandschaftswandel durch raumwirksame Staatstätigkeit. 1969. 245 Seiten mit 10 Fotos, zahlreichen Darstellungen und 3 Beilagen, DM 60,--

Band 13: Aktuelle Probleme geographischer Forschung. Festschrift anläßlich des 65. Geburtstages von Joachim Heinrich Schultze. Herausgegeben von K.-A. Boesler und A. Kühn. 1970. 549 S. mit 43 Fotos und 66 Figuren, davon 4 auf 2 Beilagen, DM 60,--

Band 14: D. Richter, Geographische Strukturwandlungen in der Weltstadt Berlin. Untersucht am Profilband Potsdamer Platz - Innsbrucker Platz. 1969. 229 S. mit 26 Bildern und 4 Karten, DM 19,--

Band 15: F. Vetter, Netztheoretische Studien zum niedersächsischen Eisenbahnnetz. Ein Beitrag zur angewandten Verkehrsgeographie. 1970. 150 S. mit 14 Tabellen und 40 Figuren, DM 19,--

Band 16: B. Aust, Stadtgeographie ausgewählter Sekundärzentren in Berlin (West). 1970. IX und 151 S. mit 32 Bildern, 13 Figuren, 20 Tabellen und 7 Karten, DM 19,--

Band 17: K.-H. Hasselmann, Untersuchungen zur Struktur der Kulturlandschaft von Busoga (Uganda). 1976. IX und 294 S. mit 32 Bildern, 83 Figuren und 76 Tabellen, DM 39,50

Band 18: J.-H. Mielke, Die kulturlandschaftliche Entwicklung des Grunewaldgebietes. 1971. 348 S. mit 32 Bildern, 18 Abbildungen und 9 Tabellen, DM 30,--

Band 19: D. Herold, Die weltweite Vergroßstädterung. Ihre Ursachen und Folgen aus der Sicht der Politischen Geographie. 1972. IV und 368 S. mit 14 Tabellen und 5 Abbildungen, DM 19,--

Band 20: Festschrift für Georg Jensch aus Anlaß seines 65. Geburtstages. 1974. XXVIII und 437 Seiten mit Abbildungen und Karten, DM 32,--

Band 21: V. Fichtner, Die anthropogen bedingte Umwandlung des Reliefs durch Trümmeraufschüttungen in Berlin (West) seit 1945. 1977. VII und 169 S., DM 22,--

Band 22: W.-D. Zach, Zum Problem synthetischer und komplexer Karten. Ein Beitrag zur Methodik der thematischen Kartographie. 1975. VI und 121 S., DM 19,--

Die Reihe wird fortgesetzt unter dem Titel:

ABHANDLUNGEN DES GEOGRAPHISCHEN INSTITUTS - ANTHROPOGEOGRAPHIE

Band 23: Ch. Becker, Die strukturelle Eignung des Landes Hessen für den Erholungsreiseverkehr. Ein Modell zur Bewertung von Räumen für die Erholung. 1976. 153 S., DM 29,50

Band 24: Arbeiten zur Angewandten Geographie und Raumplanung. Arthur Kühn gewidmet. 1976. 167 S., DM 22,--

Band 25: R. Vollmar: Regionalplanung in den USA. Das Appalachian Regional Development Program am Beispiel von Ost-Kentucky. 1976. X und 196 S., DM 18,--

Band 26: H. Jenz, Der Friedhof als stadtgeographisches Problem der Millionenstadt Berlin - dargestellt unter Berücksichtigung der Friedhofsgründungen nach dem 2. Weltkrieg. 1977. VII und 182 S., DM 18,--

Band 27: H. Tank, Die Entwicklung der Wirtschaftsstruktur einer traditionellen Sozialgruppe. Das Beispiel Old Order Amish in Ohio, Indiana und Pennsylvania, USA. 1970. 170 S., DM 20,--

Band 28: G. Wapler, Die zentralörtliche Funktion der Stadt Perugia. 1979. 132 S., DM 20,--

Band 29: H.-D. Schultz, Die deutschsprachige Geographie von 1800 bis 1970. Ein Beitrag zur Geschichte ihrer Methodologie. 1980. 488 S., DM 32,--

Band 30: M. Grupp, Entwicklung und sozio-ökonomische Bedeutung der holzverarbeitenden Industrien im Südosten der Vereinigten Staaten von Amerika. 1981. XII und 188 S. mit Anhang, DM 28,--

Band 31: G. Ramakers, Géographie physique des plantes, géographie physique des animaux und géographie physique de l'homme et de la femme bei Jean-Louis Soulavie. Ein Beitrag zur Problem- und Ideengeschichte der Geographie im achtzehnten Jahrhundert. 1981. II und 205 S. mit 8 Abbildungen, DM 28,--

Band 32: H. Asche, Mobile Lebensformgruppen Südost-Arabiens im Wandel. Die Küstenprovinz Al Bātinah im erdölfördernden Sultanat Oman. 1981. XII und 344 S. mit 20 Tabellen, 36 Karten und 20 Fotos, DM 36,--

Band 33: F. Scholz/J. Janzen (Hrsg.), Nomadismus - ein Entwicklungsproblem? Beiträge zu einem Nomadismus-Symposium, veranstaltet in der Gesellschaft für Erdkunde zu Berlin. 1982. VIII und 250 S. mit 6 Bildern und 25 Karten und Diagrammen, DM 22,--

Band 34: D. Voll, Von der Wohnlaube zum Hochhaus. Eine geographische Untersuchung über die Entstehung und die Struktur des Märkischen Viertels in Berlin (West) bis 1976. 1983. XII und 237 S. mit 76 Abbildungen, DM 32,--

Band 35: Hassan A. El Mangouri, The Mechanization of Agriculture as a Factor Influencing Population Mobility in the Developing Countries: Experiences in the Democratic Republic of the Sudan (Auswirkungen der Mechanisierung der Landwirtschaft auf die Bevölkerungsmobilität in Entwicklungsländern: Fallbeispiel - die Republik Sudan). 1983. VI und 288 S. mit 8 Abbildungen, 2 Karten und 49 Tabellen, DM 34,--